The Resourceful Mother's
Secrets to
Emotional Health

Also by the Author

*The Resourceful Mother's
Secrets to Healthy Kids*

The Resourceful Mother's *Secrets to* Emotional Health

Understand Yourself, Understand Your Child

Meredith Deasley, BA, RNCP, RHN
Kid's Life Coach

ISBN 978-0-9865163-1-3

Printed in Canada

18 17 16 15 14   1 2 3 4 5

Medical Disclaimer

The health information in this book is based on the training, experience and research of the author. Because each person and situation is unique, the reader should check with a qualified health professional before beginning a health program. Therefore, the author/publisher specifically disclaims any liability, loss, or risk, personal or otherwise, which is incurred as a consequence, directly or indirectly, of the use and application of the contents of this book.

Cover and book designed and produced with maximum efficiency and beauty by Heidy Lawrance, Cynthia Cake, and Beth Crane of www.WeMakeBooks.ca in Willowdale, Ontario.

Edited with wisdom and precision by Heather Ebbs of Editor's Ink www.editorsink.net.

Photograph of Meredith Deasley on Back Cover taken by AnnaLena Seemann. See www. photographybyannalena.com for more information and to view her incredible ability for capturing the essence of each individual.

How to Order:

Copies may be ordered online at **www.theresourcefulmother.com**.

Quantity discounts are also available for bookstores, health food stores, etc. For more information, please inquire at **meredith@theresourcefulmother.com**.

Visit us online at **www.theresourcefulmother.com**.

Dedication

I dedicate this book to my brother, Jay. You left this earth too soon but your suffering was not in vain. Thank you for encouraging me to finally tell our story, so that together we can help others heal. Thank you for being the first to love me fully and unconditionally, so that I might help others live from the purest place in their hearts.

Table of Contents

Chapter Five: Parenting Ourselves by Coming to Love Ourselves — 130

Acknowledgments

My girls, my biggest teachers, Taylor and Paige: Thank you for the honour of parenting you. It is an absolute privilege to know you and to learn from you each and every day. Your wisdom is behind all of my writing. The relationship we share is my greatest source of pride and joy.

My major teachers, my parents, stepmom, nanny, ex-husband and in-laws: I am grateful to each of you for the love you have given me and for the infinitely valuable lessons you have taught me. I always saw your greatness, even when you couldn't. Without meaning to, you contributed to the healing of thousands of people. I love you from the bottom of my heart.

My siblings, Jordan and Danielle: When our lives were filled with fear and chaos, the two of you entered our world and became our greatest healing forces. On behalf of Jay and me, thank you from the deepest part of our souls.

Pat and George Ashby: For forty years, my soul craved the love, respect, support, patience, thoughtfulness and generosity you continually bestow upon me. The girls and I cherish every moment we spend with you.

Jade Altavilla: Although you have left this earth, your wonderful example of living from your heart lives on in my mind. The name you gave yourself was entirely appropriate for you; when researching for this book, I learned that Jade represents the "goddess of compassion". I will be eternally grateful for the vast distance you and polarity therapy took me on my path to emotional wellness.

Grandma Ruby and her identical twin, Aunt Ruth: I am filled with gratitude for your love and for showing me how to love others, no matter what 'mistakes' they make. And thank you for showing me how to embrace life all the way into my nineties. I miss you both very much.

Aunt Sue: You have undergone and witnessed countless tragedies, yet you continue to open your heart so widely to everyone who crosses your path. You have always held the torch and blazed the trail of love and integrity within our family. Thank you.

Jacquie Foran: You have remained my best friend for over twenty-five years. You have listened to me, understood me, not judged me and shared your amazing perceptions with me time and time again. I am overflowing with gratitude for you and for our friendship.

Amal Tintinalli, Susan Howson and Michelle Leroy: I am filled with appreciation to you for guiding and teaching me how to transform the lives of children through kid's coaching. Susan, your methodology is the best I have seen, and I am honoured to have been taught by you.

I am deeply thankful to:

* All of my amazing friends, who listened to me and supported me throughout the years, in just the way I needed, particularly Heather Athanasiou, Cindy Bentley, Niki Brinton, Colin Carrigan, Sarah Clarke, Dawn Comeau, Bea Cowan, Joe Didiano, Ingrid Davis, Nicole Fisher, Kim Hewitt, Jill Hewlett, Kari Horn, Deb Kallitsis, Jodi Labelle, Nancy Morency, Christine Muscat, Krystal Pollock, Anne Rose, Kellie Stajer and Susan Surtees. Some of you have unknowingly contributed stories to this book to help others.

* My newest friends—Debbie Corrick, Carrie Demay, Judy Gouveia, "The Vixster" Hollingsworth and Heather Scher—for our nights out, adventures, laughs and unconditional love!

* The friends and alternative practitioners who have helped hundreds through your work and wisdom and who wrote sections of Chapter Ten, explaining how alternative therapies assist others: Karen Armstrong (Biophoton light therapist), Colin Carrigan (massage therapist), Nicole Fisher and Dave Huff (Bodytalk practitioner and master), Lesley Malchovich (writer and president of The Biography Centre), Nicholas Mazzoli (classical homeopath) and Laurie Stewart (flower essence consultant). Your extensive knowledge and passion for your profession astound me and warm my heart every time I speak to you.

* The friends and experts who read this book before it was published to ensure I covered every aspect of healing in the best way possible: Karen Armstrong, Pat Ashby (who also wrote alongside me one day a week for over two years while George Ashby catered to our every need), Colin Carrigan, Jacquie Foran, Nancy Morency and Susan Surtees. Your honesty, insight and quest for just the right words were just what I needed.

* All of the authors whose wisdom guided me on my personal journey to emotional well-being; I am forever indebted to you.

* The holistic practitioners who work tirelessly to help so many heal from their past. Your perspective was integral to my healing and, now, to the healing of others. Thank you for devoting your lives to improving the physical and emotional well-being of humankind.

* The children and their parents who have allowed me to help them turn their challenges into lessons. You fill my heart with joy.

* The spirits, guides, angels and God who showed me the way and continue to do so.

Introduction

This book is for everyone who *believes* it's possible to live our lives fully and happily, regardless of our past or present circumstances. This book is for everyone who *wants* to live their lives fully and happily but doesn't know how to accomplish this seemingly monumental task.

Society, as a whole, does not support or teach emotional health. The proof is that most of us don't even know what emotional health is. We become emotional healthy when we come to love ourselves, and we do this by speaking our truth and living with authenticity. Unfortunately, most us are taught that coming to love and cherish ourselves is selfish. We are taught to meet the needs of others, as opposed to our own. We are taught from the day we are born to operate more from our left brain (the thinking and logical side) than our right brain (the feeling and intuitive side). We are taught the concepts of right and wrong based on societal norms. We are taught to acquire happiness from external sources, as opposed to finding happiness internally. We are taught that certain feelings are good and certain feelings are bad, as opposed to using our feelings to meet our needs. We are taught that the world is a dangerous place and that others are our competitors and judges and that we are intrinsically weak and at peril. When this is what we are taught, healthy emotional development is extremely difficult.

We are the only species in the world that has a choice about how we direct our lives, yet the majority of us are at a complete loss about how to do it. *If we were taught to operate from our right brain, as well as our left, we would learn to sense and feel what is going on in our lives and move naturally to the people and circumstances that bring us joy.* We would naturally move away from the people and circumstances that bring us pain.

What we are taught determines the course of our lives. It also determines how we parent our own children. We are all aware that history often repeats itself. If we don't understand the inaccuracies of what we have been taught, how our childhood experiences affected us and who we really are, we are likely to recreate the damage to our children that was done to us in our childhood. We each have the opportunity to heal the unhealthy patterns from our past, rather than passing them onto our children. We each have the opportunity to come to love ourselves and parent our children differently from the way we were parented and our parents were parented.

This book is not just for the parents who want to raise the happiest children possible; it is for all adults who want to parent themselves the way they always wished they had been parented. The motivation for this book is to help you and those you know attain emotional health. My wish for you is that your perspective on everything that has happened to you in your life expands.

A new way of seeing is one of the most powerful things in the universe. I hope that you will learn to see every person and circumstance in your life through the lens of your heart.

This Book

In this book, you will learn why our parents raised us the way they did, what happened to us, including the unhealthy patterns we adopted, and how our childhoods affected us as adults (Chapter One). You will read about various sources of emotional education; our physical bodies, specifically our health challenges and cravings, are road maps pointing us in the exact direction we need to go to understand where we need to heal emotionally (Chapter Two). You will gain an understanding of why we remain victims and how to reframe your childhood story, no matter what has happened to you, and take responsibility for yourself. You will learn to identify, understand, feel and express your emotions and convert your negative, self-defeating beliefs into positive, self-affirming beliefs that improve every aspect of your life (Chapter Three). You will be provided with all the tools that you need to release your pain and heal within. You will gain the most comprehensive understanding of what forgiveness is and learn every nuance of what is involved in forgiving others, as well as yourself (Chapter Four).

The longest chapter of the book tells you exactly what you need to know about parenting yourself by coming to know and love yourself. It also explains how to know when you don't love yourself, what it's like when you are coming to love yourself and what it means to truly love yourself. I can assure you that the joy of self-discovery will be one of your greatest (Chapter Five).

Relationships are our biggest catalyst for emotional healing. Learn how to improve every relationship you have by reading the ten lengthy explanations for understanding and transcending the differences that exist between ourselves and others (Chapter Six). Discover how to prevent yourself from passing your negative patterns onto your children and understand your children like never before, as well as the lessons you can learn from them (Chapter Seven). Also, discover how to understand and support them best so that they handle challenges with ease and reach their maximum potential on this earth (Chapter Eight). Most importantly, you will find out how to help them come to love themselves (Chapter Nine). And don't think that you need to do all of this alone! There are all sorts of practitioners who want to help you heal. Read about how various therapies will assist you in your healing (Chapter Ten).

By reading the material within these pages, you will have the tools to improve your emotional health and happiness for life *and* be fully equipped to do the same for your children. I can hardly wait for you to start reading!

My Story

I tell you my story not so that you hear yet another sob story because it is a sad story.

I tell you my story not so that you feel sorry for me because you will, at least initially.

I tell you my story certainly not to hurt those who raised me, for I love each of them to this very day.

I tell you my story from my perspective only – a perspective that has grown in leaps and bounds over many years.

I tell you my story so that you know what is possible, for yourself and for others.

I was a much anticipated baby. My mother had five miscarriages before becoming pregnant with me. In order to carry me to full term, she was directed by her doctor to go on bed rest and consume a vodka and orange juice each day, in order to stay relaxed. Hmmm.

Two and a half years later, my brother, Jay, my best friend of all time, was born. Before he even hit two years old, our mother left our home. It was a dramatic time in our lives, rife with pain. Each time my father received proof of yet another affair my mother had participated in, he became more and more certain that her character would be understood in the court setting. My mother was diagnosed as mentally unstable by more than one psychologist. My father was one of the first fathers in the Town of Oakville to gain custody of his children.

My father, well established in the corporate world, hired a live-in nanny to help in the raising of Jay and me. She lived with us five days a week for about five years. Having been abused, in all senses of the word, by her mother, family members and others in her life, she was not the warm, motherly type. But my father, not knowing of those aspects of her life or how they had manifested in her, hired her for her intelligence, her vast experience and her strict ways when caring for children. He had been told that in a broken home, structure is key in keeping everyone centered.

Our nanny, filled with fear and insecurities, yelled at Jay and me regularly, was unreasonably strict, and hit us. Occasionally, she pushed us up against the kitchen wall and beat us. She forced us to eat foods we didn't like and always washed our hair with water that was far too hot. Her nickname for me was "Daddy's little girl"; I think because she was jealous of the love my father had for me. When Dad called home from his rare out-of-town business trips, she often felt I took up too much time talking to him, not allowing her enough time with him, and she would later wash my mouth out with soap, yelling and berating me the whole time. Jay and I lived in fear every single day that we spent with her.

I now know that our nanny did love us to the degree to which she was capable. When I had recurring nightmares, she covered a bristol board with pictures of gardens, found a light to shine on it in the darkness and had me look at it each night before falling asleep or when I awoke from a nightmare. She bought me a Mrs. Beasley doll and wrote in red marker on her back how much she loved me. She took us to the park often and to some nice restaurants and hotels. And each time I hugged her or massaged her back, I would feel her soften and momentarily accept my love.

While I resided with my dad and nanny, my mother's unhappiness with herself and her life pervaded her soul. My mother's mother had been extremely unhappy and felt abandoned in her marriage to an alcoholic. My grandfather couldn't hold down a job and moved his family from one city to another in search of a new start. My mother's mother disliked her own child. My mother was put to work at a young age, raising her twin brothers and a younger brother. She was given absolutely no nurturing or freedom to do what she wanted in life. As a result of that start in life, my mother did not even like, never mind love, herself. For most of my childhood, she told me that her mother was dead, even though she was alive and well. After she and my father divorced, my mother, following in her father's footsteps, became an alcoholic and moved to various homes in Oakville, then to various cities and countries, seeking the happiness she so desperately craved. She lived in Toronto, Florida, New York, Portugal and England, eventually settling in Vancouver. My brother and I had to visit her in each of these places.

For many years, my brother and I dreaded our visits with our mother. She wanted to spend time with us, but some women simply do not have the parenting instinct—my mother was one of those women. Undoubtedly, she had not been set a good example. When she still lived in Oakville, she would usually show up one or even two hours late to pick us up. I would hide in my dad's home so that she could not take me away with her. I remember her getting down on her hands and knees and pleading with me, pouring on the tears, to go with her.

Many times, my mother kept us longer than the law allowed her or would pick me up along the road on my way home from school when I was staying with my dad. I still remember her shutting out the lights and telling my brother and me to play hide and seek on a night that we were supposed to go back to our dad. I watched the red light of the police cruiser circle the walls and, at one point, I looked out the window and saw my dad in the back seat of the cruiser, eagerly awaiting our return. When our mother moved to Florida, Jay (four years old) and I (six years old) had to fly unaccompanied to visit her there. We threw up, side by side, almost every flight, fearing what would transpire with our mother. Over the years, we spent many nights literally trembling in our beds, listening to her alcoholic rages and often to the sound of glass breaking as she smashed mirrors, glasses or crystal dishes. She lied to us about every important aspect of her life, later explaining that she always felt that what she made up about her life was better than her real life. She was with many different men and would tell us that she was married to them when she was not, even changing her name a number of times. She lied to us about her education and careers. When I was ten years old, she moved to New York in order to live with an orthodox Jewish man she was dating, and she lied to us about her religion and told us we were Jewish. She taught us many aspects of the religion and made us wear symbolic jewelry of the Jewish faith when we were with her. Meanwhile, I was being confirmed Anglican at the private girls' school I attended, where many of my classes were taught by nuns. My mother shoplifted right in front of us and once asked for our help in covering up her acts. She told us to say that we wanted to spend more time with her and would tape-record her manipulated conversations with us and have us meet with her lawyer or attend court in hope that she would get more time with us. Yet when we visited with her, we were on our own for much of the time. I later learned that she simply wanted the money that she would receive, the more time she spent with us.

Like my nanny, my mother did love us to the degree to which she was capable. She believed in us and helped us believe in ourselves. She always made us aware of our talents and positive traits. She helped us manage other challenges in our lives. She wanted us to experience the world. We travelled to most of the United States, numerous European countries, South Africa and several islands. She bought us beautiful clothes and educational toys and books to exercise our minds.

Although I struggled with the women in my life, my relationship with my dad was far better. Having had a good childhood himself, he spent quality time with us on lunch hours, evenings, weekends and holidays; helped us sort out the lies from the truth; taught us the difference between right and wrong; had deep and meaningful conversations with us while we hiked, skied, camped, canoed and biked; went to fun places and just lived in the present moment. I still remember having a string of nightmares one week (my dreams usually involved being kidnapped by my mother) and my Dad picking me up out of bed in my nightie one night and taking me to the end of the driveway, where he set up a fire so that I could roast marshmallows and forget about my troubles.

After five years, my father dismissed our nanny and, a year later, married for the second time. We wanted a mother badly and were very excited about their wedding. Shortly after their marriage, when I was ten years old, the four of us moved to Port Credit in Mississauga. When I was twelve, my parents announced that they were expecting a baby. My little brother was born and two years later, my little sister. They became the light in my life and in Jay's.

It was in the early years of my dad's marriage to my stepmother that my dad moved up the corporate ladder to great heights and started working more than ever because he finally felt it was safe to do so. I would love to brag about his roles in the corporate world but he, always a modest man, would not want that discussed. Soon after my little brother and sister were born, we moved to Calgary for my Dad's work, and he started travelling copious amounts. His frequent and long absences created challenges for all of us at home, leaving us feeling abandoned by him. My stepmom's childhood had resulted in her being obsessed with perfection and order. How, may I ask, does a perfectionist with buried pain move to a new city, away from her seven siblings and her parents, and raise four children predominantly on her own? Talk about hell on earth for my stepmom.

I knew my stepmom needed help with all the housework and with my half brother and sister but I had hours and hours of housework that was scrupulously inspected and assigned to me when I least expected, often just when my friends wanted me to do something with them. My friends called me Cinderella. The four consecutive hours of weeding that I regularly performed throughout the summer months put me off gardening for years. If I missed a weed, she would point it out and ensure I removed it. Then there was the way in which I needed to help prepare food and clean up in the kitchen; every task had to be performed at a certain time and in a specific way, using certain utensils and dishes, vegetables cut to a specified shape and size, and the area I worked in had to be kept spotless. Having to do everything the way someone else wants you to do it and when they want you to do it only serves to teach you that your way is wrong and that you and your needs don't matter. People wonder how I can be a nutritionist who doesn't love to spend hours in the kitchen.

I could never be caught relaxing. My stepmom told me that if she couldn't relax, I couldn't relax. I have rarely seen her relax; she has always been an extremely hard worker. It took me years to retrain myself and learn that I deserved to relax and then come to know how to do it. And if my stepmom was awake, we needed to be awake. One time, she got Jay out of bed by pouring a bucket of cold water on him.

I think even more troublesome for us than her perfectionism and her inability to relax was the obvious love that my stepmom had for her children that she did not have for Jay and I. When I arrived home from school one day with a cold, my stepmom said, "You'd better not give that to my kids." I had thought I was her kid too. There were certain foods in the kitchen cupboards that were for her kids that we could not eat. There were pictures all over our home of my little brother and sister. Jay and I loved our younger siblings to bits, so we did not mind that they received the excellent treatment that they did, but we were certainly angry at our parents for the contrasting ways in which they treated their children.

Still more troublesome than her perfectionism, workaholism and the love bestowed upon my half siblings was the emotional abuse we underwent with our stepmom. The moodiness, anger and punishment to which Jay and I were subjected was non-stop. Yes, we were hit, as well. She refused to speak to me for up to a week at a time. Sometimes I did not even know for what I was being punished. One time I was grounded for a week because I came home twenty minutes late; meanwhile, my stepmom had no idea how much trouble it was for my friends to drive me home well before any of them had to be home. Each time I was grounded, I would not be allowed to speak to my biological mother, see my friends, spend time with the rest of my family or leave the house, except for school. My family would eat dinner without me, and I would come out of my room later, only to find a pot on the table that contained my dinner. Too often, I was left feeling as though I was an intruder in my own home.

One not-so-good day, my stepmom told me that I would likely spend the rest of my life in the office of a psychiatrist. On another not-so-good day, my stepmom told me that she had wanted many children, but raising my brother and me had ended that dream. I just couldn't understand what we were doing all the time that was so horribly wrong. I later learned that the challenges she had with my brother, trying to motivate him from a childhood of so little nurturing, came close to killing her. I also learned that my mother continually harassed my stepmom, trying to destroy her relationship with us every chance she got. My mother was devoted to driving a wedge between us, hoping that we would love her more. I remember my stepmom trying to plan a nice surprise for me and my mother planning something in the same time frame, so that it became impossible for my stepmom's plan to come to fruition. I imagine it would have been very difficult for my stepmom not to take her frustration out on the two of us.

Like my nanny and my mother, my stepmom loved us to the degree that she was capable. In our earlier years together, she sewed me wonderful clothes, tucked loving notes into my lunch kit and took us on fun day trips and vacations all over Canada. I enjoyed and continue to enjoy many great conversations with my stepmom and benefit from her advice. Once I had my own family, my stepmom spent hours and hours making delicious, healthy meals and coordinating fun activities for us when we visited. She handcrafted beautiful decorations for our home and spoiled her grandchildren with gifts. She, my dad, my girls and I continue to spend a few days a year together and communicate regularly.

As a child though, on every birthday that I could remember, whenever I blew out the candles, I wished for happiness. I now know that none of the people who raised us *wanted* to hurt us, that each had their own deep-seated pain that they wrestled with day in and day out. At the time, though, I resolved to get revenge against every person who raised me. The revenge I sought was to become a successful person, despite them all. And I wasn't talking financially.

It is important for you to know that despite the challenges I underwent as a child, I was always a positive thinker, lively and seemingly very happy. In those early years, I had lots of friends and was very healthy physically, other than having allergies and my tonsils removed.

At the age of seventeen, I finished high school and moved from Alberta back to Ontario to attend university, completely unprepared to enter the world at large. With me at university, my mother living across the world in Portugal and my dad travelling the majority of time with his work, Jay, only fifteen years old, started doing drugs, marijuana at first and then much worse.

Entering university, two years younger than most of my classmates and having had the childhood that I did, meant that university would be an even bigger culture shock for me than it would normally be. Many kids rebel when they leave home and acquire more control over their own lives. For me, that rebellion was tenfold and would last for years. I desperately wanted to be loved. I gobbled down sugar, particularly candy, the 'food' that injected feelings of love directly into my bloodstream, as fast as possible. Chocolate became another obsession. I drank alcohol at parties like it was going out of style and would spend the whole next day throwing up, mainly stomach acid. I started smoking without an ounce of peer pressure. I sought male attention and love more than would be seen as acceptable. I slept as much as I wanted because I could. I started a shopping obsession of inexpensive items that lasted until I finally came to love myself and was loved in return. (For more on my resulting unhealthy patterns, please see Chapter Two.)

When I was nineteen years old, my mother seemed to be making real headway on her healing journey. This resulted in many years of closeness between us. Soon after she began reading self-help books and taking courses, I started doing the same. I have read and learned from those books for over twenty-five years now. One of the books, in particular, had a huge influence on my healing and growth; it stated that our souls choose our parents in order to learn certain lessons. I had no idea if this was true but I told my roommate at the time that I was going to believe that I had chosen my parents; that way I could stop seeing myself as a victim. I proceeded to write down all of the lessons I had learned from the people who raised me. I began to move forward in my life with a whole new perspective. I later learned that changing our perspective is *the* most important factor in our healing.

Also, at the age of nineteen I met my future husband, which was most exciting. On our first night together, I told him that I could see myself marrying him. I also told him that having children with him would be the most important thing I would ever do, and it sure was. In the same year, I contacted the nanny who had left my life a decade prior, in hopes of learning more about my childhood. She had just come out of the hospital and was in severe pain. She told me I was her angel, calling her at the time that I did. We reunited in person and she apologized to me for how she had treated me as a child without me even raising the subject—a very rare occurrence. To this day, she continues to apologize to me for her ways, and our understanding of one another has deepened to such an extent that I have referred to my nanny as one of my closest friends for many years now.

Two months after turning twenty years old, I completed university with a BA in Sociology—no surprise at that choice of major. I entered the corporate world, wanting desperately to prove myself. I became one of the youngest managers at two well-known insurance companies. I worked very hard and for long hours, giving little time to myself, and eventually I spent the better part of a year in a full-on depression. I was saved when a top brokerage asked me to be their first female commercial broker, a job that I thoroughly enjoyed until the company went through a merger. In the end, I spent just over a decade in the corporate world.

I chose my future husband because he loved to laugh, party and break the rules—all of the underdeveloped areas of my life. He was hardworking and ambitious, like I was. Also like me, he had had a difficult childhood and had not even started to heal from it at the time we met. As a result, he was not a loving, nurturing kind of man. He didn't support me or encourage my dreams of owning my own business or authoring books. But it made me feel good inside to help him manage his challenges. It took me seven years to agree to marry the man I loved, because of my fear of making a mistake in choosing a partner and potentially ending in a divorce. In those years, I lived in Toronto with roommates until we purchased a home in Aurora. It took me five years after we were married to feel ready to bring a child into this world. Fear was a big part of my psyche. I knew that I wanted to be the mother to my children that I had never had.

Giving birth to my two girls, at the ages of thirty and thirty-two, brought me the greatest amount of happiness and growth that I had ever experienced. I raised my girls the way I had wanted to be raised. Some of you may have read my first book, *The Resourceful Mother's Secrets to Healthy Kids*, wherein I described the large health challenges we faced with our eldest and how we overcame them with optimal nutrition and alternative healing. When we had our second child, Paige, who also suffered from adverse food reactions, I registered and started my business, The Resourceful Mother, helping other parents heal their children on a physical level. At the age of thirty-two, I had finally found my calling. Later, I attended and graduated from nutrition school, gaining the highest mark in my class; this was one of the biggest but most wonderful shocks of my life.

On my husband's birthday, eight months after our second daughter was born, the police arrived at our doorstep to tell us that my brother, Jay, had passed away in Thailand, where he had been living for the past few months. A couple of weeks later, his autopsy showed that he had died of a drug overdose. Losing Jay was the greatest tragedy of my life. He was the one person who I knew loved me and whom I loved, regardless of what went on in our lives. He was the one person in my immediate family, the one constant, who had never hurt me and who had only made my life better.

Although Jay had an exceedingly high IQ, he had struggled with school the whole way through. As a result, he had even more challenges with my step-mom than I did, because she spent hours and hours trying to help him learn. A year after I left home, Jay was sent off to boarding school. Drugs and alcohol rapidly became a big part of his life. He told me that he kept hearing my stepmom's voice over and over in his head, even after he no longer lived at home, and all he wanted to do was drown it out. I, of course, knew all the other emotionally destructive aspects of our lives that had contributed to his need to 'escape.'

Once Jay finished school, he headed off to Lake Louise, where he remained for about a decade. There, he found another way to escape from the world. He became an excellent chef and created his own family with the kids there. They were also escaping from their lives and, together, they partied large. He was well loved but his love for himself never grew. When cocaine arrived in Lake Louise, Jay became one of its first customers.

Just after my youngest was born, Jay reached rock bottom with his drug use. Luckily, he didn't have enough money to support his habit for long. A few weeks after he had been off the drug, my mother arranged to get him to my home. My father had hired a drug addiction counsellor who helped us prepare for an intervention. We seemed to reach Jay; he told us that he was done with cocaine for good. At the end of the session, my mother, knowing how much Jay had wanted to go to Thailand to "find happiness", announced that she had purchased him a ticket to go there. I was shocked; Thailand was known as a major player in drug production and trafficking. I told my dad about our meeting with Jay and my mother's "gift", and asked, "Aren't we sending him to his death?" Dad talked to the drug counsellor, who told him that Jay, being around thirty years old, was an adult and we could not prevent him from going to Thailand. Jay could not have afforded to go had our mother not purchased him the ticket; clearly, she was still trying to receive the love that she could not give herself.

A few months after Jay arrived in Thailand, he died of a drug overdose. I do believe that he would have died at a young age, even if he had not gone to Thailand, but the trip probably hastened his death. Some of the last words he wrote in his journal in Thailand were "Come to me, inspire me, bring me back to myself! I don't want to be just a crazy drunk!" and "Please let me become a soaring, wise butterfly, who effortlessly helps everyone I meet, in one way or another." His final written words were "I'd like something pure and good to happen to me. Anything, as long as it is pure and good." My hope is that this book will help Jay accomplish his goal of effortlessly helping others, in one way or another. Ironically, a few years before Jay's death, at our grandmother's ninetieth birthday, Jay looked me in the eyes and said, "If you don't write our story, I will."

When Jay died, it was the first time that I needed my husband's help, but he didn't know how to help me. I always thought that if I needed him, he would be there for me. I then lost eight other family members and friends within three months of Jay's death. We spent the next five years watching my husband's father waste away and then die from cancer. And then over the next two years, we watched his mother die from cancer but that was far more difficult, as she wanted her boys to be her major caregivers in her final days. Those were dark days for us—so many loved and deeply cherished ones left this earth at once. Raising my girls, spending time with my friends and helping others got me through it all.

A couple of years later, after I had really focused on coming to love myself more, I determined that I no longer wanted to feel alone in my marriage. I wanted to be loved deeply, emotionally supported and adored, and I wanted the same for my daughters. I finally knew that I deserved this love and support but was aware that my marriage had never been based on this. I will not get into the details of what transpired between us; after all, my ex remains the father of my girls. What I will say is that he and I did not grow, as individuals, in our love for ourselves at the same pace, and this prevented us from transforming our marriage into a healthy, happy one. At the age of forty-one, after twenty-two years with my husband, I became single again. I gave up time with my girls (my biggest and hardest sacrifice, but, luckily, I got more time with them later on), my friendships with *all* of my husband's family and friends, my two beautiful homes, all their furnishings and everything that was familiar to me. There is always a price to pay for any separation but, for me, it was a rite of passage. I remember my ex-husband asking me, once I was in my new home, "Why do you want to be a victim?" And I remember the shock I felt upon hearing that question. My response was "Victim? I am not a victim; I am triumphant!" My love for myself grew like never before. Ironically, if my love for myself had not grown to the degree it had, I never would have wanted to leave my husband.

Soon after my marriage ended, I was driving home from a party where I had met a prince and princess of India and dined with some of the top polo players in the world. I stopped at a light and looked into the vehicle next to me. It was a police car with a prisoner in the backseat; his head was leaning on the cage wall in front of him in resignation. As I looked over at him, my mind was overcome with new perspective. I knew that this man probably had had an unhappy childhood and had not recovered from it. My heart went out to him; I knew there was another way, but he had not yet learned that. Emotional healing can be harder for males. Jay wasn't able to break free from his prison either. I vowed never to return to the prison that had been my life. I vowed that I would live my life to the fullest until the day I died. I also vowed to help others break free of their prisons, now that I was free.

Soon after that, a mother came to me, asking for help for her nineteen-year-old son, who had suffered from depression for the past five years. He had not completed high school or obtained his driver's licence. He was on three different antidepressants. I had no formal training in emotional healing, but it was at this time that I felt I had finally completed my own (I am told that we are never done healing, but I knew I had made huge strides). Within a few months of our first meeting and with the help of a homeopath I had recommended, this boy was well on his way with his own emotional healing and had entered college to learn how to help other children overcome depression. It was helping him that inspired me to acquire a designation in kid's life coaching. I had found my second calling. Ever since, I have been helping children, as well as some adults, with emotional healing, in addition to the physical healing work I do. Because of the life I have lived, there is no greater calling for me than helping others heal from their past and experience bliss.

Single again, I watched with interest as I attracted different men into my life. As my love for myself continued to grow, I became more and more selective in choosing a man with whom to enter a relationship. One night, I went dancing with some friends. Many men and women watched me with awe, as I danced for almost four hours. Unbeknownst to them, they were not just watching me dance. One cannot dance with the freedom and joy that I was dancing with unless one has transcended from pain. One needs to have experienced the contrasts in life in order to truly embrace living in joy. On that all-important night, my forty-three years on earth flashed before my eyes and I saw with great clarity the distance I had come. I was filled with pride that I had become the successful person I had set out to be so many years earlier. Am I perfect? No. No one is perfect, but I see my life as having been perfect for it led me to who I am today. And I am happy—really happy.

This is my story, written for you. This book is my gift to you. It is your guide to healing. And it is your guide to doing things differently with the child you bring into this world. All you need to do is follow the steps that I took to bring yourself back to your true essence, where happiness and joy abound.

One

The Most Important Relationship

Just as we have such a hard time understanding the overwhelming impact of what we eat on how we feel, we have difficulty seeing the tremendous influence that our childhood has on our adult lives. The relationship we have with our parents is the *most important* relationship we will ever have. It is our very *first* relationship and one in which the majority of us remain every day, year after year, for many years. It is a relationship that begins with us as helpless, completely vulnerable babies at the absolute mercy of older, more experienced and, hopefully, more capable adults. For many years after our birth, we live similarly to how we did inside the womb: in our parents' environment, cut off from the rest of the world.

The parent–child relationship forms our basic beliefs about ourselves and the world we live in. As a direct result of that relationship, we feel either loved or not loved or somewhere in between. Many of us suffer from a damaged sense of self-worth because we did not receive the love we needed in our relationship with our parents. Maybe our parents abandoned us, criticized us, hit us, were emotionally unavailable to us, regularly made us feel guilty, sexually abused us, controlled our every move, gave us too many responsibilities, didn't believe in us or our dreams, desperately overprotected us or simply provided us with poor examples of how to live happily. When any of these negative patterns of behaviour are consistent and dominant in our childhood, real harm is inflicted upon us, and we end up not fully understanding our value as individuals. And the more difficult our childhood, the wider the separation from our true selves becomes.

We are not responsible for what was done to us as helpless children. We are responsible for how we think about the past and choose to live our lives as adults.

If we did not receive the love we needed from our relationship with our parents as children, it becomes our responsibility, as adults, to give ourselves that love. In other words, if we were not parented in the way we needed, it becomes our responsibility to parent ourselves.

The Most Important Aspect
of the Parent-Child Relationship

 "The single most dramatic difference between healthy and toxic family systems is the amount of freedom that exists for family members to express themselves as individuals" (Forward 1989, 165).

We feel good about ourselves to the degree to which we feel we can express ourselves and have control of our lives. A baby or a child has little control over any aspect of their lives. This is something many of us adults don't spend much time thinking about; children have to go where their parents want them to go, when their parents want them to. They are cared for or spend time with people with whom they have not chosen to spend time. They are forced to wear clothes they might not have chosen. They need to go to school every day and spend time with teachers and students who may or may not see their greatness. And most importantly, a child has little control over what happens in their relationship with their parent. Without that control, it is absolutely impossible for an individual to have the freedom to come to know themselves, be themselves and love themselves.

The word "control", like many words, has been given a bad rap. When I say we each need control, I mean that we need personal power to be able to express ourselves in order for our needs to be met. I do not mean that we need to be able to control another person and get them to do what we want them to do—a very important distinction.

So what is the number one way that we can help our child, besides loving them? We need to come to understand them and their emotional needs, just as we must understand our child's body and respond to physical symptoms before they multiply and turn into health problems. To understand our child's emotional needs, we must allow our child to express themselves and we must give them some control. Am I suggesting we give them free rein? Absolutely not. We give a young child control by giving them choices. We lay out three outfits for them to choose from for a particular occasion. We ask them if they want to go to the grocery store with us before or after we play a game. We keep a range of healthy food choices in our kitchens and let them choose what they would like to eat and how much of it they eat. What are we teaching a child with these examples? We are teaching appropriate ways to dress for certain occasions; we are ensuring that nutrition is always paramount in our lives; and most importantly, we are ensuring that both their needs and ours are being met, knowing that those of a child are as important as those of an adult.

The more control we give our child, the more they come to know themselves, be themselves and love themselves and the happier they become. It is that important. If we squash their growing strength with our rules and demands, we weaken them. We need to let our child struggle against the elements of life, so that they can develop their strengths. Healthy families encourage individuality, personal responsibility and independence. Do you think that when our child has been raised with the themes of self-responsibility and independence, they will be able to make better choices when they leave home? Undoubtedly.

When we are young children, we operate primarily from the right brain (the feeling and intuitive side of the brain) because we have not yet developed our left brain (the thinking and logical side of the brain). Therefore, as young children, we are heavily influenced by the feelings and attitudes of others. In unhealthy families, individuality is discouraged and children must conform to the feelings, thoughts and actions of their parents. These children learn to define themselves in terms of their parents' feelings, instead of their own. If a mother tells her son he is good, he believes he is good. If she tells him he is bad, he believes he is bad. Young children have no reference point other than their parents.

If a child cannot express themselves without judgment or being told they are wrong, they are forced to deny the truthfulness and importance of their own feelings and perceptions. Many children end up lying about what they are thinking or feeling and guilt is often an accompaniment. And then when a child's every move is controlled, they rebel by misbehaving, crying often, having tantrums, running away, becoming verbally or physically aggressive, turning to drugs or alcohol to deaden their pain and fill their emptiness, or any number of other ways, none of which is to our liking. Or our children capitulate and do exactly as we say, resulting in their becoming desperate for approval or perfection, overly shy, clingy, fearful, quiet or depressed, just to give a few examples. These children have great difficulty in adulthood defining their own identity.

Because their own needs, feelings and thoughts were never encouraged, these children truly have no idea who they are, never mind love themselves or understand what constitutes a loving relationship.

Unhealthy Parent–Child Relationships
What Controlling or Authoritarian Parenting Does to a Child

Technically, all unhealthy parent–child relationships involve a strong element of control on the part of the parent. The controlling or authoritarian parenting style is still very much alive and well in the raising of today's children, which makes sense given that so many of us were raised by parents who adopted this approach.

Many parents believe that they are allowed to control their children simply because they gave them life. When parents control their children, they use intimidation or guilt to get their children to do what they want. They humiliate them, often ruling them with ultimatums. The feelings, opinions and needs of these children are unimportant and worthless, and the children know it. Many of these children perceive themselves to be weak and powerless. If children are told what to do without explanation and are forced to be obedient, they usually end up doing what others tell them to do without thinking if it is truly the right decision for them. The children who are taught to look outside themselves for answers eventually cannot look within for the answers.

Parents who have not healed from their past tend to view differences between individuals as a personal attack, instead of appreciating and encouraging their child's uniqueness. They want their children to be like them, to have their interests, and maybe even to depend on them, often with the belief that they are acting in their child's best interest.

Controlling parents use manipulation to get what they want, without ever having to ask for it, without ever allowing themselves to be vulnerable or risking rejection by stating what their needs are. Because controlling or manipulative parents are so skilled at hiding their true motives, their children live in a constant state of bewilderment; they know something is not right but they can't figure out what it is. When these parents impose their will over their child's, when they punish their child and tell them what to do "or else", they seem to win each power struggle, but, really, no one wins; all that happens is that the child is robbed of their integrity and ends up living in fear.

Living in fear is the bottom-line result of authoritarian parenting. Children parented in this way feel under attack. They put up defences around the parts of themselves that their parents don't approve of and try to protect their vulnerable inner selves by displaying tough outer selves. They keep themselves "safe", but at what cost? Repression prevents the growth and development of the whole person. **When parents reject or try to stifle a natural part of who their children truly are, we see the birth of self-dislike and sometimes even self-hatred in those children**. They will hate the parts of themselves that put their parents' love for them at risk. To children, rejection is the same as abandonment, and abandonment is the same as death. When children live in fear of being who they truly are and don't love themselves, they cannot experience true happiness nor can they spread love or fulfill their purpose in this world.

 "Children who are not encouraged to do, to try, to explore, to master, and to risk failure, often feel helpless and inadequate. Over-controlled by anxious, fearful parents, these children often become anxious and fearful themselves" (Forward 1989, 48).

Most controlling parents feel threatened by their children's happiness, instead of seeing it as representative of their parenting skills. Their children's interests are not important to them. Often when children of a controlling parent grow up and move out, their controlling parent feels deceived and deserted. Many of these parents deal with this by appearing to be loving and caring to their adult children. By "helping", they can keep tabs on their children and create situations to make themselves needed in their children's lives. But the controlled children rarely ask for this "help". Often when these children work up the courage to express their frustration to their controlling parent, they end up feeling guilty because their mother, the martyr, was simply "helping" them out. In fact, whenever the controlled child or adult tries to gain some control over their own life, they pay the price in guilt, frustration, anger and feelings of being disloyal to their parents. Adult children who continue to allow their parent to control them are reinforcing their parent's negative behaviour and enabling the victim, the parent.

When these adult children enter partnerships or have their own children, many become under-involved, because there is no way they want to dominate others the way they were dominated.

Why Do Individuals Become Controllers?

Individuals who become controllers still feel the familiar powerlessness and helplessness that they felt as children. Subconsciously or consciously, they have remained victims and live in fear. Unfortunately, by denying that it exists, control increases their fear. Rather than addressing their feelings, coming to peace with them and gaining personal power, these people try to create a world around them that is predictable and controllable; they don't like change. They exert control over others and their surroundings, trying to obtain the power they did not have as children and trying to cover up their own weaknesses and emptiness. Unfortunately, inside most bullies is a child who has been bullied or belittled. If controllers show emotion, they believe they are no longer in control because, to them, showing emotion is a sign of weakness. They believe that controlling others is a sign of strength, when, in fact, it is a sign of weakness. Controllers also have a very hard time empathizing with others and see empathy as another sign of weakness.

Once we heal the pain within us that creates our need to control others, we are no longer interested in controlling or winning. We become interested in learning about ourselves. We find that the more we are in control of our own selves and our lives, the more personal power we truly possess. When we have personal power, we win the hearts of others, effortlessly enlisting them on our team; we wouldn't even think of angrily controlling another.

"Control is an aspect of fear showing that we do not have confidence. It is an attempt on our part to keep ourselves safe and, for the most part, to keep others safe – our way. Having been hurt, we make up the rules for ourselves and for others about how not to be hurt" (Spezzano 2002, 68).

There are many other parenting styles, most of them involving a form of control on the part of the parent. The following is a brief explanation of some of them.

What Perfectionist Parenting Does to a Child

Parents who try to act perfect, end up making rules, making judgments and then, making pain. Perfectionists expect their children to be perfect. They expect them to be perfectly quiet, dressed, clean, polite, academically strong and the list goes on. Their hope is that if their child is seen as perfect, their family will be seen as perfect. If their child messes up, their child gets saddled with the blame, the shame and a host of other negative feelings that actually belong to the parents.

As children of perfectionist parents grow up, they either do everything possible to obtain their parents' approval or they rebel to such a degree that they acquire a fear of success.

There are many adults who were mistreated as children who believe they were raised by *perfect* parents. When these adults put their parents up on pedestals, they are agreeing to live by their parents' version of reality. This results in the adult children accepting painful feelings as a part of their life, not knowing that it is possible to transform those feelings into more positive ones. It is only when these adults take their parents down from their pedestals and find the strength to look at them realistically that they can begin to equalize the power in their relationship.

Why Do Individuals Become Perfectionists?

"Perfectionism is the continual judgment of yourself and others as deficient. The more you judge, the more deficiencies you see" (Zukav and Francis 2001, 169).

These individuals do not focus on the present moment easily but instead focus on their external environment, such as their personal appearance or compulsive cleaning and organizing, which prevents them from feeling their painful emotions and, subsequently, coming to know and love themselves. Their extreme need for external order disguises their internal chaos. When perfectionists become parents, they wield their unreasonable demands on their children. When the children fall short of those demands, the parents blame their children, instead of looking at themselves more closely.

These individuals do not love themselves for who they are, imperfections and all, so therefore they cannot love others and their imperfections. These individuals insist that their preferences are the best for others, instead of honouring the preferences of others. If you look at people and circumstances through the lens of your heart, as you will learn to do throughout this book, you will see that every person and circumstance in your life is there for a reason and therefore everything *is* perfect. (For more on perfectionists, please see Chapter Two.)

What Alcoholic or Drug-Addicted Parents Do to a Child

A child of an alcoholic or drug addict experiences their parent as emotionally unavailable and therefore learns to believe that the people they love will betray or hurt them. Subsequently, they end up petrified of true intimacy. **Jealousy, possessiveness and distrust run rampant in the relationships of many of these adult children.**

Many alcoholic or drug-addicted parents justify their own inadequacies or control their children by criticizing them. The child is left feeling that if they were not always doing or saying the wrong thing, their parents wouldn't be driven to drink. The family scapegoat is a common role for children in these families. Some try to match their negative self-image by resorting to self-destructive or delinquent behaviour. Others find ways to punish themselves subconsciously. Invariably, these individuals end up with low self-worth, much repressed anger and a high tolerance for mistreatment.

Not surprisingly, many of these children grow up trying to anticipate and fix the problems their parents are unable to fix; it is their way of trying to feel good about themselves. It is typical for adult children of alcoholics or drug addicts to have the need to rescue their parent. They often feel responsible for everyone else's feelings, just as they took responsibility for their father's and mother's feelings when they were young. They grow up believing that their job is to take care of everyone else and not expect anything for themselves. They go to incredible lengths to avoid confrontations with their parents and others because they don't want to be responsible for causing anyone pain and certainly cannot take on any more pain themselves.

Why Do Individuals Become Alcoholics or Drug Addicts?

Individuals become alcoholics or drug addicts because they are insecure, defeated or frustrated or because they have inner hostility. They have negative and destructive thinking. They become addicted to alcohol or drugs because they are in severe emotional pain stemming from childhood. They usually start out using alcohol or drugs because they have had negative experiences and want to escape from them. The more pain, stress, anxiety, insecurity and fears they experience, the more they want to anesthetize their repressed emotions and the more dependent they become on alcohol or drugs. The more painful their life experiences, the greater their dependence. These individuals want a fast route to happiness; they use stimulants or external sources of energy to feel free because they usually don't know how to heal from the inside out or, in some cases, don't want to do the work. Certainly there is no way that one can take control of their life when they are controlled by an addiction.

"We find a way to cope—not flourish, not soar, not enjoy and embrace, just flat out cope. Most of us turn to some form of dissociative practice, whether it's avoidance of the trouble, distraction from the trouble or addiction to a substance that separates us from the trouble. Avoidance, distraction and addiction are absolutely commonplace in our culture because imbalance is absolutely commonplace in our psyches. ... We distract ourselves from moving into wholeness, most likely because we haven't been taught that wholeness is real and attainable" (McLaren 2010, 77-78).

What Emotionally Abusive Parents Do to a Child

There are many types of abuse, but only emotional abuse, which includes verbal abuse, will be discussed here, as many people are unclear about what emotional abuse entails.

Emotional Fitness (Berger 2000) provides this explanation of emotional abuse: "Emotional abuse includes minor to major neglect; expecting perfection; controlling everything a child does including thinking and believing; verbal put-downs; screaming; attacking; criticizing; expecting our child to look after us emotionally; indifference to our child's well-being; discouraging independence; demanding loyalty, appreciation and gratitude; expecting our child to be responsible for things we are responsible for; undermining; threatening; trivializing; patronizing; withholding; using scare tactics; denying our child's feelings; abusing things our child values, such as their possessions or pets; isolating our child; harassing; not protecting our children from those who harm them; teasing; scapegoating and using punishment to control" (p 141).

When parents occasionally say something disparaging to their child, it is not verbal abuse. It *is* abusive to be constantly and cruelly insulting a child's looks, intelligence, ability or worth. Remember I mentioned that children believe what their parents say about them? It is vicious and damaging for a parent to speak to a defenceless child in this way.

These parents are taking their frustrations out on their child. Usually, they find something to criticize, even if their child is being good. As with the alcoholic or drug-addicted parent, they use criticism to control their children, saying things such as, "You're so lazy. Get off the couch and clean up this kitchen immediately!"

Many of these parents rationalize their behaviour by saying they are providing their children with necessary guidance. They say they are trying to teach them to be better people or that they need to toughen them up because it's a cutthroat world out there.

Children often justify abusive experiences by thinking that they caused them to happen or were in some way to blame. **Children of emotionally abusive parents end up overly sensitive, shy and untrusting of others in order to prevent themselves from being hurt further.** They grow up not knowing themselves and seek constant external approval because they don't love and approve of themselves. They also tend to pressure and penalize themselves with far more intensity than their parents ever did.

"Many children who come from an abusive background seem to always want to make things *right* for everyone. Their inner core has been so painfully violated that they want *peace at all costs*. They walk around in fear and trembling, hoping they will never be the focal point of anyone's verbal or physical disapproval" (Truman 2003, 123).

When these children become adults, they often become involved with abusive people. When those relationships don't work out, they often feel responsible for those failures, as well.

Why Do Individuals Become Emotionally Abusive?

No one can emotionally abuse another without having been emotionally abused themselves. What is the root cause of the behaviour? When individuals don't like themselves, they subconsciously don't want or feel they deserve intimacy with others. Abusing others keeps others away from them. These individuals project their guilt and discomfort with themselves onto those they abuse. And abusing others is another way to control people when they don't feel in control of themselves or their lives.

 "The more powerless we were as children, the more likely we will be a victim or an abuser as an adult" (Berger 2000, 137).

What Competitive Parents Do to a Child

Winning a competition fills us with feelings of competency. But this external means of feeling better about ourselves is only temporary and is no match for developing more permanent internal feelings of competency. (Please see Chapter Five for ways to accomplish this.) Unfortunately, it is common for children to be taught that they need to prove themselves or strive to be better than others. When the parent of that child witnesses their child winning a competition, they temporarily feel better about themselves. Healthy parents simply experience happiness for their children when they do well in competitions. Whether they come first, somewhere in the middle or last is really of no concern to them. They know that if their child comes last in a sport or activity, it is clearly not their talent.

Why Do Individuals Become Competitive?

Competitive individuals usually grow up with deprivation; they were deprived of food, possessions or love. No matter how much they have, they remain anxious or fearful of not having enough. And many of these individuals come from competitive environments themselves. When we become comfortable enough with ourselves, we have no need to prove anything or make ourselves appear better than another.

What Abandonment by a Parent Does to a Child

I would like to explain what happens to an abandoned child by sharing an example with you.

When a girl is abandoned by her father—perhaps he moves away (physical abandonment) or becomes a workaholic (emotional abandonment) or is emotionally distant—she is bound to feel unloved and angry (fearful). That anger can find an outlet in any number of ways. A common outlet in her adult life might be her relationships with other men. Most likely, she will crave relationships with men because of her lack of a relationship with her father. Her adult relationships may start out well, but each time she gets closer to a man, her fear of abandonment takes hold. The fear might then turn into hostility. She might find that men eventually leave her each time. The woman might believe that her hostility is justified because the men always leave her in the end anyway. She might not see that it was her fear and hostility that pushed them away.

Without being aware of it, she might also be blaming herself for her father's abandonment and subconsciously choose men who treat her badly or disappoint her. As long as she can let go of her anger at men in general, she doesn't have to feel angry with her father. If this woman came to see that she was transferring her displaced anger and mistrust from her father to other men, she might put an end to this pattern and veer from her lonely path.

Why Do Parents Abandon Their Children?

Some parents move away from their children because they consciously or subconsciously don't believe they are good parents. They believe that their children would be better off without them. Others move away because they need to meet their own needs after not having their needs met for many years prior. Others become workaholics or emotionally absent because they are burying or avoiding feeling their pain. They cannot focus on their feelings if they are focused on attaining their goals.

The Emotionally Unhealthy Parent

"Our imperfect parents had imperfect parents of their own. Fears, insecurities and desires get passed along for generations. Parents want to see their offspring make it in ways that are important to them. Or they want their children to be special, which in our competitive culture means more intelligent, accomplished and attractive than other people. They see their children through filters of fear (they might not get into a good college and be successful) and filters of desire (will they reflect well on us?)" (Brach 2003, 13–14).

The parents I have described (and other emotionally unhealthy parents I have not described) are not the monsters many think they are. ***These individuals are desperately needing and wanting love, acceptance and recognition, but their life experience has left them incapable of receiving these gifts.*** If their needs had been met by their parents and their life experience, they could, in turn, meet the needs of their child. Instead, the children of emotionally unhealthy parents end up inheriting their parents' pain and lack of love for themselves.

The coping strategy for most of these parents is to put their own needs first, instead of meeting the needs of their child. They are often described as selfish. Selfishness comes about when we don't love ourselves. Becoming an emotionally healthy parent often means balancing our own needs and survival instincts with the needs of our child.

Naturally, there are times when a parent's need is more important than that of the child's. A parent may need to work late one night and therefore might not be home when their child needs them. But if the less important needs of the parent are continually put first and the parent is continuously out late socializing or playing sports, their child ends up feeling unloved and unappreciated. A child under the age of five or six will feel sad, angry or confused any time their parent puts their needs before their own, because they simply don't have the ego development yet to comprehend that their parent has their own needs.

I once helped a mother and her ten-year-old son who had struggled to get along for years. The child had clearly communicated his needs to his mother many times but to no avail. I finally asked his mother why she didn't meet her child's needs, which included wanting to be picked up from school and activities on time and being allowed to spend some time with his friends outside of school. His mother responded by telling me that she didn't feel that these needs were important. She proceeded to explain that she worked hard all day and did the best she could to pick her son up from school on time. She was too tired to make arrangements with her son's friends' parents, drive him here and there, visit with the parents and so on.

The emotionally unhealthy or "selfish" parent turns on their child who is whining or misbehaving and angrily says, "Can't you understand I have things to do?" or "What is your problem?" The "selfish" parent has a hard time putting themselves in the shoes of another. This parent feels that that their children are preventing them from living the lives they want to live.

 "It is our unconscious and unmet needs that blinds us to our children's present needs" (Berger 2000, 66).

The only reason why a parent is blinded to the needs of their child or finds their child's needs to be less important than their own is that the parent's own needs are not being met and usually haven't been met over a long period of time. It usually starts in their childhood. Ironically, if these parents were to embrace their relationship with their child, their own needs would be met by meeting the needs of their child; both the parent's and the child's need for love would be met. In this way, the parent and child become one another's antidote, an opportunity that is available to both in many different circumstances.

I remember well the number of times one or the other of my girls wanted me to play. I had so much to do that I didn't feel I could spare the time. Whenever this happened, the disappointment my daughter experienced would weigh on me. Sometimes she would whine or misbehave because her needs were not being met, and that made my work even more challenging to complete. When I finally sat down and played, all of the stress in our home dissipated. Eventually, I realized that if I played with my girls immediately after school, it put us all in good moods and I was then free to do my work afterward, without the meltdowns.

Sometimes, it is by being selfless with our children that our needs are met. If you don't believe that children have the capacity to teach us to be selfless, think of a newborn baby. They need everything done for them; they ask that we drop everything to tend to their needs. If we rise to the challenge by feeding them often, keeping them dry and letting them sleep, they reward us with a first smile. Then more challenges are added: we need to feed them solids, play with them and help them sit up, crawl and walk, and we delight in watching them accomplish each of these milestones. Around the time they turn one, we need to continue to meet their survival needs while beginning to take on emotional challenges; it's time to start disciplining them and teaching them lessons on living safely and well. As they get older, the emotional challenges increase for both parent and child. All of this parenting takes hours and hours of time, energy and research; all of it takes selflessness on the part of the parent. And what are our rewards for learning selflessness? The love and respect we gain from our children—a love that can supersede all other forms of love. More importantly, we gain a healthy and happy child who grows up knowing and loving themselves, making this whole world a better place.

Being selfless does not mean never saying no or never setting limits with our children. It means putting our children first at important times and when possible. I was recently reminded of how I used to respond each time my eldest daughter, Taylor, who was hypoglycemic, wanted a snack. She would yell (yes, yell!) out of the blue, "I want a snack," and I would drop whatever I was doing and rush to her aid. Is it any wonder that my body and mind became exhausted and my thyroid became underactive? (You can learn more about that in Chapter Two.) In later years, when Paige came along, I calmly told Taylor that she needed to wait five minutes each time she asked for food. Eventually, I created her own snack cupboard within her reach, which really came in handy when I wasn't available to prepare something fresh.

We can't let our children run our lives; it is not good for them or us. *If we don't ensure that our needs are met regularly, we teach our children that our needs are not important.* In order to truly care for someone else, we have to know how to care for ourselves. (See Chapter Five to learn how to accomplish this.) We can't give away what we don't have. A mother can always do more for her family. She has to learn that being herself is enough. She has to learn when she has done enough for now.

So how does one find the right balance between being selfless and meeting one's own needs? A child needs to know of their importance in their parent's eyes. They need to know that they are on a team with us, their parents. A child needs to know that sometimes the needs of another come before their needs. A parent needs to know the same. If there is mutual respect for one another's needs and each is adept at putting themselves into the shoes of the other, we will know that we have achieved balance in this area.

What Emotionally Unhealthy Parents Do to a Child

 "When I don't feel connected—I will seek undue attention/
When I don't feel capable—I will seek power over others. /
When I don't feel I count—I will seek revenge. /
When I don't feel courageous—I will seek to avoid"
(Schafer 2009, 41).

When we focus on our own physical and emotional survival and would be described by others as selfish or when we are suffering so much within that we cannot meet the needs of our children, we are sending them a powerful message. The message is that our children's feelings are not important or acceptable, which they internalize as "I am not important" or "I am unacceptable" or "I am not loved or appreciated." This results in what the authors of *Giving the Love That Heals* (Hendrix and Hunt 1997) describe as "the wounded child." This book describes wounding as unintentionally stunting a child's impulse for wholeness in order to make them more acceptable to their parent. It explains that the wounded child splits into four different selves as a defence against the wounding. All four of these fragmented selves result in subconscious self-hatred.

The presentational self: This child turns into an actor in order to conceal the parts of themselves that they feel are not liked and display the parts of themselves that better serve their purpose. Often the presentational self is a parent's pride and joy—positive, charming and seemingly successful.

The lost self: This child lacks belief in their ability to think because their parents devalue their thoughts. They lose the ability to be empathetic because their feelings are being ignored. They "freeze" because their parents tell them to stop running or be quiet. The overweight child is hiding and is an example of the lost self.

The disowned self: This child doesn't act or hide. They disown parts of themselves and refuse to see their value, despite others seeing it. They spend their childhood trying to prove themselves to others and to themselves.

The denied self: This child denies parts of themselves and often doesn't even know it. They replace "unacceptable" parts of themselves with more satisfactory ones. Some children refuse to give their parents the satisfaction of crying or showing any emotion. This child becomes stoic and stores their anger and frustration.

Most emotionally unhealthy parents respond to their emotional challenges with denial, secrecy and, worst of all, blame. And the blame always targets the children. Each time a parent rejects or tries to stifle a natural impulse or function in their child, we see the birth of self-hatred. Each time a parent tells their child that they are wrong or bad or selfish or too loud or too sensitive or too anything, the child is shamed for displaying these qualities and the child's perception of themselves is altered. Really, what is going on is that each time a child's behaviour is met with criticism or punishment, a child unconsciously separates from their true self, their joy, their passion and their creativity and from living in the moment. For a child, rejection equals abandonment, and abandonment equals death. A child believes they must do everything possible to survive and will go to great lengths to protect themselves from parental rejection. They will hate and shut down the parts of themselves that endanger their parents' love and cause them to be rejected. Then they will present an "acceptable" version of themselves that will belong, be loved and be accepted. In essence, children are forced to sacrifice themselves to cover up the dysfunction and unhealthy aspects of their family life. When children lose touch with their authentic selves, they stop trusting themselves and then begin to believe that others cannot be trusted. Our lack of belief in ourselves and others leads to a lack of belief in the possibilities that exist for ourselves in the world at large.

"Something made it necessary for him, when young, to learn performance as a survival skill. For whatever reason, he came to feel at a tragically early age that deceit rather than authenticity was a normal mode of being. Conscious connection to his own deeper truth was superseded by a need to find whatever words or behaviour would help him survive a traumatic moment. Life taught him to behave falsely—not how to present himself as he truly is, in touch with his honest feelings and deeper truth—but rather to display with lightning speed whatever behaviour gives him a short-term emotional advantage" (Williamson 2008, 104-105).

Belief Systems Generating Negative Patterns

Unhealthy parent–child relationships result in five primary traumas or negative patterns: abandonment, abuse, betrayal, denial and rejection. The majority of children experience at least one of these traumas, and as a result, their childhood becomes the learning ground for guilt, resentment, fear, anger, inferiority and negativity in general. These childhoods, in turn, usually generate the same unhealthy patterns in adulthood.

"One of the places where we all tend to hold the greatest amount of unhealed fear is in our relationships with our parents, and until that fear is downloaded from our psyches, we tend to carry it like baggage into our adult relationships" (Williamson 1999, 192).

We store our feelings, thoughts and everything that surrounds each event of our childhood. Years later, something triggers us and instantly we are experiencing the feelings we felt in the past. *Even when we are eighty years old, we can actually feel the fears and insecurities that we felt when we were four.* What is happening is that the unfinished mental and emotional memories get stored and then re-activated. Each time we struggle in life, it is only because of our inner fears and our patterns of behaviour that came about from events or interactions in our past, events that caused us to repress our feelings or cast off parts of ourselves. All of our habits come from past experiences that caused us to form certain interpretations of ourselves. From those interpretations, certain thoughts came into being. Those thoughts made us feel certain ways, usually negative. Our need to separate ourselves from those unwanted thoughts guides us to find ways to make ourselves feel better. This is where self-defeating or self-sabotaging behaviour patterns initiate.

I want to share two examples of self-defeating or self-sabotaging behaviour. First, we often duplicate past conflicts and adopt certain patterns of behaviour, no matter how dysfunctional or painful, hoping that this time the conflict will have a positive resolution. Repeating the same behaviours gives us structure and a false sense of security, because it is easier to repeat the same pattern than it is to forge a new path. This is why many of us act just like the parent we dislike so much. This is why playing the role of victim or rescuer in our family often translates into playing the same role in all of our relationships. Secondly, when those of us who are parented by emotionally unhealthy parents become adults, we often choose cruel, abusive or distant partners and try to encourage them to love us the way our parents never did. We usually choose partners who mirror our true feelings about ourselves. A healthy relationship (See Chapter Six for a thorough explanation of a healthy relationship), one where we receive nurturing and respect, would feel unnatural to us and not match our perception of ourselves. This is also why adult children of alcoholics frequently marry alcoholics. This is why if we felt trapped when we lived with our parents, we may want to fight or flee when entering a committed relationship.

What are some examples of incorrect thoughts that come about from unhealthy parent–child relationships and then turn into beliefs? If our parents fought a lot when we were growing up, we might believe that relationships are a struggle. If our mother cheated on our father or failed to keep her promises, we might believe that women can't be trusted. If our parents were not physically or emotionally affectionate with us, we might believe we are unlovable or that we can't get what we want.

The book *Toxic Parents* (Forward 1989) does an excellent job of explaining the belief systems and resulting patterns that children adopt as a result of unhealthy parenting. I will now provide you with a few more examples of how the patterns present themselves and give you with a brief explanation of how to overcome these patterns.

The pleaser: Many children, denied of adequate time and attention, begin to feel abandoned, as though they don't exist or are invisible. Often when a boy feels that he doesn't exist in his mother's eyes, he spends an inordinate amount of time trying to please her. When he leaves home, this man believes that he needs to continue pleasing others in order to be loved. It is likely that he finds a similarly needy and emotionally damaged woman to take care of. This pattern perpetuates the emotional loss he experienced as a child.

If the man in this example was able to confront his feelings of emotional abandonment and realize the importance of his own needs and feelings, he would learn to set limits or boundaries on how much he gave himself to others and become visible again. He would realize that he deserves to be loved, adored and cared for and thus attract healthy relationships into his life. Ironically, he would find that when we are happy with ourselves, we automatically and easily please many more people than when we *try* to please others.

The golden child: Many children, denied love, feel they need to prove their worth through external achievements, as they do not know how to build their own self-esteem. Their worth depends on receiving compliments, awards and high grades. When they become adults, they are the ones who buy the fanciest cars they can afford and live in the largest of mansions. They feel that if they become super-competent, they will subconsciously make up for their parents' lack of competency. Becoming the family hero offers a child a coping strategy, as well as the safety and structure that they have been lacking. These children don't relax easily and are exceedingly hard on themselves.

If the golden child were to determine what they truly love to do and spend more time doing the things that make them feel good inside, they would experience internal achievements and forgo the need for external achievements.

The controller: You know a lot about controllers from earlier in this chapter, but I want to demonstrate how the negative pattern develops. Many children respond to the helplessness they experienced as children by constantly needing to be in control. When these children become adults, many of them choose partners they can control and to whom they feel superior.

If a controller were to recognize the pattern they are perpetuating, they would see where it came from and resolve to end it. Their response to different situations would change and they would recognize that they are safe now and don't need to obtain control of others in order to feel in control.

Unmet Needs

The bottom-line result of emotionally unhealthy parenting or emotionally unhealthy relationships of any kind is a child with unmet needs. Our needs are universal; we each need healthy food, sleep, love, attention, time, understanding and physical touch from the people we love, as well as freedom, curiosity and to be accepted for who we are. Yet many of us learn, at an early age, that our needs are unacceptable. Sadly, most children don't know they have unmet needs, never mind knowing what their needs really are. This is how most of us grow distant from ourselves. Unmet needs leave us with a deep sense of worthlessness, which then becomes the driving force behind our disconnected, unhealthy behaviours. Some people stop themselves from wanting anything, literally shutting down their needs, in an attempt to prevent themselves from feeling disappointment when their needs are continually unmet.

There are all sorts of displaced expressions of unmet needs. Examples include being selfish (discussed earlier), being unable to learn in school, being obsessed with helping and pleasing others and playing the martyr, having unrealistic expectations of others in our adult relationships hoping they will make us feel loved, having unrealistic expectations of our children hoping they will meet our needs, and having any kind of addiction. (Please see Chapter Two for more examples.)

Many of us struggle to get others to meet our unmet needs from the past. When we ask others to make us okay with ourselves, we are actually putting our self-esteem in the hands of others. This results in obsessive relationships, perpetual desperation, dependence, divorce and general unhappiness. Even if we obtain what we need from others, we don't obtain the satisfaction we desire because we know it's not the real thing. No matter how hard we try, no one can be the parents we wish we'd had. Those we love cannot heal our pain but they can certainly support us as we heal ourselves. When we heal ourselves, we fulfill our own needs and don't need others to meet our needs.

Parenting Ourselves

We all have choices. One of the choices is how to direct our energy. We can focus our energy on being resentful of our parents or on the time wasted being unhappy in our childhood. Or we can use that energy to help us take responsibility for our adult selves and for generating happiness within our lives and within the lives of those we meet.

Parenting ourselves involves taking control of our lives and learning how to provide ourselves with the love that we never received as children. In order to do this, we need to understand that we can change ourselves but we cannot change our parents. We need to understand that our well-being is not dependent on our relationship with our parents. We need to understand that we can heal from our childhoods, no matter how bad they were; we just need to commit to doing the work.

If our parents never complimented us as children, we have two choices for dealing with that gap. We can feel sorry for ourselves for the rest of our lives, feel unworthy and remain victims. Or we can come to understand why we don't take compliments well when we receive them and why we have a hard time complimenting others. We can dismantle an unhealthy behaviour pattern from our past in just five minutes if we have the courage to look at ourselves honestly. All we need to do is become aware of our unmet needs that created the unhealthy pattern and the part of ourselves that we hid or denied (our wounded place that needs to be healed), feel the pain that resulted from this pattern and forgive ourselves and others for the pain we experienced. (Please see Chapters Three and Four for more information on each of these healing steps.) We can then adopt healthier patterns for ourselves going forward, continually meeting our own needs and coming to really love ourselves. *And the more we are able to acknowledge and meet our own needs, the easier it is to accept and love our parents for who they are and to forge healthier relationships with them and others.*

The process of healing from our childhood is a gradual one. Our goal is to convert our feelings of being worthless, unlovable or inadequate into loving ourselves, more and more every day of our lives. This process can be painful, shocking, lonely and mentally exhausting. But eventually, our true self that has been hiding all these years will be released. We will experience our unique, strong and loving selves and live the lives we want to live. Think of the unveiling of the prince in *Beauty and the Beast* after having lived most of his life as the beast. Like the prince, we each have the capacity to live the lives we want to live.

I believe it is our destiny to learn how to parent ourselves. I believe it is our destiny to recognize and heal our unhealthy belief systems so that we pass on predominantly healthy belief systems to our children, keeping in mind that we are human and can never be perfect. Fittingly, once we come to love ourselves, we see the perfection in ourselves, in others and in the world at large. And we learn that the *most* important relationship we will ever have is really with ourselves. Our relationship with ourselves is the *only* relationship that is eternal.

Two

Identifying the Need to Heal
Using Sources of Emotional Education

" The truth about our childhood is stored up in our body, and although we can repress it, we can never alter it. Our intellect can be deceived, our feelings manipulated, our perceptions confused and our body tricked with medication. But some day the body will present its bill, for it is as incorruptible as a child who, still whole in spirit, will accept no compromises or excuses, and it will not stop tormenting us until we stop evading the truth" (Alice Miller, as cited in Lincoln 2006, 5).

If we pay attention to the ways in which we would describe ourselves, our physical challenges or illnesses, the pain or injuries we have endured, our obsessive behaviours or interests and our cravings, we can learn about the wounded parts of ourselves and heal them. Each of these aspects of ourselves is a source of emotional education.

Ways We Would Describe Ourselves

Each of these ways of thinking or behaving is the result of having unmet needs resulting in destructive patterns. Every one of them indicates that we need to come to love ourselves. Do you recognize yourself in any of the following statements?

- I make excuses for why my life isn't working out the way I want it to, rather than taking responsibility.
- I hide my strengths and power by acting weak so that no one will notice me or give me a hard time.
- I don't believe in possibilities for myself or the future.
- I feel left out, unappreciated, used or taken for granted by others.
- I dread having to communicate with or visit my parents.
- I don't like to feel my deeper emotions.

- I am a perfectionist with my personal appearance or my surroundings or while performing projects.
- I blame myself for everything that doesn't go right.
- I blame others for everything that doesn't go right.
- I am a jealous person; I compare myself and compete with others.
- I lie.
- I don't want to forgive others.
- I feel that I am not good enough, that I don't matter or that there is something wrong with me.
- I can't trust others.
- People don't see me the way I really am.
- I frequently complain.
- I regularly regret my actions.
- I am filled with resentment.
- I often cry.
- I constantly and inappropriately apologize to others or make excuses for actions taken or words spoken.
- I have a hard time saying no.
- I give to others so that I can get something back.
- It is hard for me to receive help, compliments or love from others.
- I am afraid to speak my mind.
- I don't like to be alone.
- I am impatient.
- I feel superior to others.
- I cannot laugh aloud or often.
- I take things personally.
- I am defensive.
- I have an addiction (e.g., to food, alcohol, drugs, sex, work, shopping, gambling, computer use, shoplifting, working out, etc.).
- I have an obsession (e.g., with a musical group, movie star, television series, etc.).
- I am really shy.
- I talk incessantly.
- I am hard on myself or blame myself.
- I am unable to play; I have a hard time having fun.
- I often feel anxiety, fear or anger or experience these feelings easily.
- I don't feel happy.

- I have pain in my body.
- I have physical symptoms, conditions or disease.
- I am often sick or easily become sick.
- I have no energy.
- I attract unhappy people into my life.
- I am critical and judgmental of others.
- I don't know how to relax.
- There is something I want to do to improve about my life but I find myself unable to do it (e.g., exercise, eat more healthily, etc.).
- I feel like something is missing in my life.
- I am unkind to others.
- I dress in dark colours and have a hard time bringing myself to dress in bright colours.
- Things never go right in my life; e.g., I break things a lot, get lost, lose items, get in arguments with people, buy items that need to be returned or am always dealing with hassles.
- I have trouble sleeping or staying asleep.
- I hardly ever sing or dance and would be hard pressed to try.
- Others are not drawn to me.
- I am unhappy in my relationships.
- I feel the need to control others.
- I yell at or hit others.
- I am negative.
- I don't like looking at myself in the mirror or in pictures.
- I feel I have no choices.
- I always need to be right.
- I have extramarital affairs.
- I have many sexual fetishes.
- I am shy and inaudible.
- I harm myself physically.
- I have an eating disorder.
- I hate my job.
- I often feel that I have nothing to look forward to.
- I keep myself really busy.
- I feel the need to prove myself to others.
- It is hard for me to be open with others because I expect them to reject the "real" me.

- I get very angry or depressed when others criticize me.
- I am afraid of making mistakes so don't like to do new things.
- I am afraid to ask for things from others because if they were to refuse me, I would feel unworthy.
- I choose boyfriends or girlfriends who are unattractive because anyone who is attractive would not want to be with me.
- I give too much and sometimes let people use me because I can't imagine why anyone would want to be with me for me.
- Much of what I do seems wrong, stupid or incompetent.
- I feel unworthy.
- I don't feel safe.
- I don't keep my word and have a hard time keeping my promises.
- I spend a lot of time putting out fires.
- I gossip and watch soap operas.
- I have a lot of bad luck.
- I avoid people who admire me or love me because they obviously can't see me clearly or are worse off than I am.
- Solving another's problems or relieving their pain is the most important thing to me, no matter what the emotional cost to me.
- My good feelings depend on receiving approval from others.
- I will do anything to avoid making others angry with me.
- I hold back from expressing my affection and love for others.
- I pretend everything is fine in my life even though it isn't.
- I feel so unworthy that I am certain that things will never change or improve and I feel hopeless.
- I cannot express my feelings and therefore am explosive or aggressive with others.
- I blame everyone else for my problems.
- I am filled with self-doubt and self-blame.
- I feel guilty often.
- I need to be needed by others.
- I help others to the detriment of myself.
- I am frequently disappointed by my job, others or life.
- I am always trying to please others.
- I try to make others feel sorry for me.
- I hold back from expressing my emotions.
- I am afraid to speak my mind because I don't like conflict.

- I am always explaining and justifying my actions.
- I am uncomfortable with discussing my negative feelings.
- I poke fun at or make negative comments about those I love.
- I am scared of being abandoned.
- I am scared of being hurt.
- I always need to be right.
- I am always sarcastic.
- I can't be myself.
- I have no or little sense of humour.
- I feel I don't deserve to be loved.
- I have a hard time receiving compliments.
- I am self-absorbed or selfish.
- I sabotage myself in my relationships.
- I am not good at setting boundaries or limits with others who impose upon me.
- I easily lose my temper over small matters and say things I later regret.
- I am overweight or go on eating binges when I am upset.
- I continually have money challenges.
- I always want undue attention from the opposite sex or anyone.
- I am filled with regrets and resentments when it comes to my childhood.
- I am not good at nurturing myself.
- I am afraid of disapproval or rejection.
- I am afraid of commitment.
- I still compete with my siblings.
- I am bored and have no reverence for life.
- I don't want to live.

If you see yourself in any of the above statements, you are experiencing emotional pain. **Finding and healing the cause of our emotional pain is at the root of our growth as individuals.** We cannot reach our full potential as individuals without doing this work. The rest of this chapter is dedicated to helping you find the cause of your emotional pain.

Sources of Emotional Education

Emotions: The Link to Physical Illness

Our bodies let us know if we are not being our authentic selves. They let us know if there is something to address at an emotional level. Physical symptoms, conditions and disease express the feelings we are unconscious of and push into the shadows. Physical illness is the language our bodies use to speak to us. The shadows within us are where we put the feelings that are unacceptable to us.

The thoughts and emotions that lead to most sickness in our bodies are criticism, anger, resentment, guilt, shame, grief and fear. Here is a brief description of each and their resulting unhealthy physical manifestations. (For more information on these thoughts and emotions and their healthy expression, please see Chapters Three, Four and Five.)

Criticism comes about from a feeling of wanting to control everything. It arises when we have a childhood where control was crucial to our acceptance, quality of life and sometimes our physical or emotional survival. When we desperately want control of our lives, we end up with conditions such as arthritis.

Anger comes about when we have unmet needs. We experience obstacles that we can't overcome. Instead of taking responsibility for ourselves and determining how to overcome the obstacle, we often blame or attack other people. Anger creates conditions such as boils, burning, fevers, infections and inflammation.

Resentment arises when we feel victimized and powerless. It turns into tumours and cancer.

Guilt is anger at ourselves, usually for putting the perceived feelings of others before our own. It leads to pain and self-punishment. Emphysema and herpes are examples of illnesses that result from guilt.

Shame is rooted in guilt and low self-esteem. Listening to our inner voice prevents shame. Shame results in illness in the life support system such as the blood, the liver and the immune system.

Grief is how we react to loss and deprivation. It affects the respiratory system and the fluid treatment systems such as the kidneys and the bladder. Suppressed grief results in lung challenges, ear infections, sinus difficulties and heart problems.

Fear is worrying about future pain, it prevents us from making the changes we need to make in our lives. It affects the stomach, heart and throat and manifests in adrenal, digestive and intestinal disorders. Chronic fear results in kidney and bladder disorders.

Physical Challenge or Illness: The Link to Emotions

 "When energy leaves your energy system in fear and doubt, it can only bring pain. When energy leaves in love and trust, it creates health and gratitude" (Zukav and Francis 2001, 215).

Dr. Bernie Siegel was one of the first medical doctors to write extensively on the link between emotions and physical illness. In *Peace, Love and Healing* (1989), he states that few of us live up to our potential. He explains that illness can make us aware of the fact that we have stopped living our lives and describes illness as our greatest dreams trying to come true. He has witnessed illness putting many people on the path to self-realization; illness helps us remember who we are. **Siegel also reminds us that there are individuals who have permanently healed themselves from every type of cancer—every such case involved a change in the individual's feelings and thought patterns.**

Many people have a hard time understanding the connection between our emotions and our body parts. The best example I can give you involves the heart. Has anyone you really loved, died? Or has anyone you loved ever ended a relationship with you against your will? If so, do you remember how your heart felt? I remember when my brother died, my heart literally ached. I asked my dad if he was experiencing the same thing, and he was. If our emotions do not affect our body, why did my heart hurt? Why did my dad's heart hurt? Interestingly, as soon as the autopsy had been performed on my brother and I came to understand why he had died, my heart stopped hurting. Once I obtained the truth and stopped fearing what had happened to him, I was able to apply compassion and acceptance to my loss, and the pain in my heart stopped. I continued to mourn for years, but my suffering eased the more I understood. It is when we fight the truth that we suffer the most.

If we don't know what area of ourselves we need to heal on an emotional level, we can use our physical body as a road map. Each physical ailment or pain is connected to an unhealthy thought or belief pattern that needs healing. Here are few examples:

Acne: When we have acne, we dislike ourselves or we don't feel as though we are moving forward with our lives. We feel picked on and resent authority. We can suddenly erupt in anger. The acne can be a means of staying clear of others; we both desire and dread being with others.

Allergies: When we have allergies, we need to ask ourselves, "Who am I allergic to?" Allergies represent suppressed rage at another. Allergies mean that we are not aware of our own power or self-worth. We didn't get the love we needed as a child and are suffering from unresolved pain from our childhood.

Asthma: When we have asthma, we were either smothered by our mother's love or ignored. Asthma occurs when we are unable to breathe on our own. It is caused by feeling stifled and unable to take charge of our own life. Asthma is crying inside.

Bladder infection: The emotional causes behind bladder infections are worry, being afraid to let go, holding onto old ideas and being "pissed off" (pardon my language, but I felt it was important for you to know this). When we suffer from frequent bladder infections, there is usually a need to get rid of something toxic in our lives—things, situations or people. We might be thinking "I don't dare" or "I am deeply unhappy" or "I can't expect any better."

Bronchitis: When we have bronchitis, we feel unsettled, fearful or anxious. We have feelings of deep despair to get off our chest. When we regularly contract bronchitis, we grew up in an angry family and took on the chaotic environment within ourselves.

Common cold: When we catch a cold, too many things are happening at one time, resulting in chaos and confusion. We are crying within because we feel we are unable to do anything about the circumstances of our lives; the helplessness creates the congestion. There is some information that has been buried at a subconscious level for a long time; it has now come to the surface and needs to be acknowledged.

Ear infection, right ear: Challenges in the right ear represent the thought process of "I don't want to hear it!" We are extra sensitive to external voices, that is, what others are saying. We may be fearful of what we are hearing or we might be trying to shut out criticism or conflict around us.

Ear infection, left ear: Challenges in the left ear represent the thought process of "I don't want to listen to myself." We are extra sensitive to our inner voice, fearful or not wanting to hear it. We may be trying to avoid internal criticism or conflict.

Eczema: When we have eczema, we believe that it is not safe to be ourselves. We feel guilty and uncomfortable with being ourselves. We feel blocked from doing what we want and often feel powerless. We tend to hang onto the past. We are therefore super-sensitive to ourselves and our environment, deeply feeling any loss of love. For these reasons, we literally start to grow a second skin.

Female problems (e.g., menstrual problems, vaginitis): When we have these challenges regularly, we are rejecting femininity or not wanting to be a woman. We don't like ourselves. We could feel resentment at our father for not being there for us or feel betrayed by him.

Influenza: When we contract the flu, we are feeling overwhelmed by negative forces or beliefs and feel weak and helpless—"at their mercy". There is a fear that the worst is going to happen to us, and as a result, we are afraid of taking life in fully. We may feel unsupported or unprotected and may be undergoing great change at this time.

Headaches: When we have headaches, we are negating and criticizing ourselves. We can ask ourselves, "How have I just made myself wrong?" The goal is to forgive ourselves and let it go. Headaches can also be a symptom of repressed rage. We can ask ourselves "What am I angry about?" Sinus headaches are caused from being irritated by someone who is very close to us; often there is frustration about insufficient support and love from those to whom we are closest. Migraine headaches are caused by wanting to be perfect and putting a lot of pressure on ourselves. Migraines come about from not going with the flow of life and a dislike of being controlled by others.

Heart challenges: When we have any challenges with the heart, we have had long-term emotional pain and lack joy in our lives. We are blocking intimacy or love from our lives.

Immune system challenges: When we have a weakened immune system, we are unable to stand up for ourselves. We are often not conscious of our feelings and therefore are not setting the necessary boundaries.

Nail-biting: When we bite our nails, we are chewing away at ourselves. We are frustrated at not being able to take charge of our life and manifest our desires. We may have anger issues, particularly with our parents, and feel as though we are alone.

Overweight: When we are overweight, we are protecting ourselves with a layer of fat from the people or things that we fear, including ourselves. We may be having a hard time forgiving.

Skin problems (e.g., hives, rash): Skin problems result when we are thinking, "I hope I pass the audition." We have intense concerns about how we think others see us and often have deep insecurities and fears. We might be letting things or others "get under our skin." We have a strong desire for affection but are fearful of being hurt if we search for affection and do not receive it.

Stomach aches: When we have stomach aches, we are scared and unable to assimilate the current happenings in our lives. We have a great need to be loved. We are fearful of not receiving love and are angry to be in this position; we are trying to suppress these feelings. The stomach holds nourishment and digests life.

There are a number of publications where the links between emotional and physical well-being are described. I find the information to be utterly fascinating. Louise Hay's book *You Can Heal Your Life* is perhaps the most well-known source. *Messages from the Body* by Michael Lincoln (also known as Narayan-Singh Khalsa) is another excellent resource.

You can use the information from books like these and other sources to uncover clues about the emotional challenges you need to address when the time is right for you. Over the years, clients have come to me knowing that something is not right within themselves or within their lives but not knowing where to start. Often, I look at the physical manifestations in their bodies to determine what we need to look at from an emotional standpoint.

Let's walk through this process together. A client comes to me who has horrible periods each month. Each time she gets her period, she experiences bad cramping and spends at least one day throwing up. Vomiting occurs when we are disgusted and disturbed by aspects of our life; this is "revulsion-expulsion". The client's experience suggests to me that there is at least one woman in this client's life who is causing her to reject being a female or that there is an aspect of being female that is not sitting well with her. Remember, the woman in my client's life is not actually causing the reaction; rather, it is my client's reaction to the woman that is causing a physical manifestation. If my client were to later develop a cyst on her ovary, another female challenge, the cyst would be an indication that the issue had still not been resolved.

How might I help my client resolve her female health challenges? First, we would examine and heal her relationships with the women in her life. We would determine what boundaries needed to be set so she sees that these women do not need to rule her world or represent the type of woman that my client wants to be.

One teenage client who suffered from bad periods was afraid about the possibility of birthing her own children in the future, because she had heard horror stories about giving birth. She also didn't ever want to be responsible for a baby, although she thought she would be able to handle raising an older child if she had help. She said that she was angry that she even got a period because she was never going to use her reproductive system. She was scared that she would have to bear a child because of pressure from family members. We discussed the fact that she does not need to do anything she doesn't want to do and talked about all the repercussions of not following our own hearts. Women have many options available to them these days, and we don't need to give birth ourselves. I presented adoption as a likely option for her, and she then set an intention that she would have a very supportive partner to help her raise their child. We both recognized that at any time in the future, she might change her mind, but we did not discuss this because her fear was too great to air that possibility. *Interestingly, once the boundaries are set in our minds, our fear around different possibilities can dissipate, if not disappear, and our bodies can return to health once again.* This is exactly what happened with this client.

Challenges with Body Parts (Pain or Injury): The Link to Our Emotions

There are even links between emotions and each body part. Here are two examples:

Knee challenges: We are having troubles bending our knees and moving forward with our lives. These troubles arise from a fear of failure.

Shoulder challenges: "Everything always falls on my shoulders." We are shouldering too much responsibility. We feel we are carrying the weight of the world on our shoulders. We have a hard time carrying our responsibilities in a joyful way.

Challenges with the Left or Right Side of the Body: The Link to Our Emotions

Each side of the body has specific meaning. For most, the right side of our body represents the masculine aspect of our interactions and our ability to give to the universe. The left side of our body represents the feminine aspects and our ability to receive from the universe. For some people, the meaning of each side is reversed. Here's a quick test: Clap your hands at an angle. If your left hand automatically went on top of your right, then your sides are reversed; your right side is your feminine side and your left side is your masculine side.

When there are challenges with the masculine side of our body (pain or injury), we are having a hard time expressing our masculine qualities, such as independence and power. We are probably having issues with the men in our lives, and we may be having challenges with giving and letting go. When there are challenges with the feminine side of our body, we are having a hard time expressing our feminine side, such as intuition, creativity and emotions. We may have difficulty nurturing or feeling compassion for ourselves. We are probably having issues with the women in our lives, and we may be having challenges with receiving help from the universe.

For example, if we feel pain in the masculine side of our body, we are alerted to look at the males in our lives, particularly those to whom we are closest. Are we having problems in our relationship with our father, brother or partner? Or are we not standing up for ourselves and stepping into our power? We need to examine the relationships in our lives and what is holding us back from being the people we want to be.

I remember having pain in a number of areas of my body over many years. *Generally, pain represents self-punishment and it comes from being in relationships that hurt.* For many years, I felt guilty for who I was, what I needed, what I did and what happened within my family. I had deep feelings of separation from others and anger that my life was not unfolding the way I wanted it to. My belief system was exactly the belief system that lies behind chronic pain. People who experience pain are often those who have been taught to never express their anger, which, of course, perpetuates the pain.

I remember thinking, "Why does the body have to always communicate with me? Can't it let me get away with anything? Even for just a little while?" The body communicates with us at all times, whether we like it or not. The solution is to become aware, to decipher the messages the body is relaying and then to do the work to heal the belief system within ourselves that is manifesting in our bodies.

Obsessive Behaviours or Interests: The Link to Our Emotions

Commonly, our society labels and puts down people who have obsessive behaviours or addictions. In fact, these people are in pain and need healing and support. When we become aware that workaholism, perfectionism, pleasing others, boredom and drug or alcohol addiction, to give a few examples, are all techniques for avoiding our negative emotions, we can begin the process of adopting healthier patterns.

I am going to briefly explain a few of these techniques so that we can gain new perspective on what we are actually doing when we employ them. For more information on these avoidance techniques and others, I highly recommend *The Heart of the Soul: Emotional Awareness* (2001) by Gary Zukav and Linda Francis.

Workaholism

Those of us who become workaholics are running away from our painful emotions. Workaholics concentrate and complete projects with utmost precision. Often, we go from one project to another or one job to another with obsessiveness. The particular projects may have no value to us but they help us to avoid feeling.

Many workaholics seek approval. We work long hours and do an incredible job of each project in order to obtain accolades from others. We do not see our own value and want to be told of our value by others.

Perfectionism

 "Perfectionism is an attempt to inhabit an imaginary world in order to avoid experiencing the world in which you live" (Zukav and Francis 2001, 167).

When we try to avoid painful emotions, we focus on how our circumstances should be as opposed to how they are. By keeping busy and perfecting the world around us, we avoid feeling and healing our painful emotions. This can lead us to engage in compulsive cleaning, organizing and completing to-do lists. When we strive for perfection and spend an inordinate amount of time rearranging our external world, we are attempting to obtain external power. We are looking outside ourselves, instead of looking inward.

Perfectionism is the perpetual judgment of ourselves and others as lacking. No matter how hard we work at it, our clothing, appearance, home, projects and life never seem to meet our expectations. And the more we judge, the more lacking we find ourselves and others to be.

Pleasing others

When we constantly try to please others, we seek the love from others that we do not feel for ourselves. When this is our modus operandi, we are constantly anxious; we watch how we look, speak and act and we do everything we can to avoid rejection. When we are pleasers, we do not feel worthy to ask for what we need. And when others offer to help us, we do not accept their help; we cannot accept their love or caring because we feel we are not worthy. The unfortunate aspect of being a pleaser is that when we do not appreciate ourselves, others cannot appreciate us either.

People who need to please and people who are always angry seem to find each other; fear rules the thoughts of both these individuals. Pleasing is a method of masking our fear of losing love or never receiving it. Pleasing others becomes our technique for preventing the pain of feeling unworthy.

Food Cravings: The Link to Our Emotions

The body never fails us; it is we who fail to listen to its wisdom and trust its guidance. Our food cravings are a source of valuable education about our emotions (and sometimes, nutritional deficiencies). Individuals are drawn to certain textures, fat content, flavours and smells of various foods for a reason. Here are a few examples:

High-fat foods such as French fries, cheeseburgers and milkshakes represent fear. When we crave these foods, we are generally fearful of facing something in our lives. We might need to change something we don't like or stand up to someone. The fear feels like emptiness, and the fat fills the stomach like nothing else.

Nuts or nut butter are craved when we are looking for fun in our lives. Nuts are also crunchy, and crunchy foods are craved by highly stressed individuals.

Breads, rice and pasta are comforting and calming foods that are often craved by highly stressed individuals.

Cookies, cakes and pies are craved when we are hungry for hugs, pleasure and reassurance.

Candy is craved when we need energy, rewards and entertainment.

 "Here is the important bottom line: we crave foods and overeat in an attempt to regain equilibrium and peace of mind. Our cravings are always for foods that correspond to our ignored gut feeling. If your gut is telling you to have more fun, but you ignore your gut, you will crave a food that contains pyrozine, such as peanut better, cashews or walnuts. This is because pyrozine triggers the pleasure centre of your brain. The body always attempts to achieve homeostasis, and if you ignore your gut feelings, your appetite will seek to fulfill the body's needs through food cravings" (Virtue 1995, 228).

Doreen Virtue's book *Constant Craving* (1995) contains the incredibly thorough and accurate information on the subject of cravings. In it, she lists pages of drinks or foods that we crave, including brand names, with an explanation of why we crave that food and what affirmation we can adopt to overcome the craving. Examples include the following:

Beer is craved when we want to block feelings of anxiety. We desire more love, excitement and appreciation. Affirmation: I trust my inner strength to see me through the ups and downs. I allow myself time-outs to feel refreshed.

Chocolate-covered nuts are craved when we are frustrated because our love life is not going as desired. We are losing patience with our relationships. Affirmation: I have control over my life and take charge of meeting my needs.

Cheese is craved when we are always preparing for the worst and feeling exhausted. We desire comfort and love. We are feeling fearful and negative. Affirmation: My energy shines brightly within me. I replace my fearful thoughts with feelings of love.

Coffee is craved when we feel overburdened with unwanted responsibilities. We are trying to conjure up enthusiasm for projects that we really don't believe in. We often hold a job that doesn't match our natural talents or interests. We wake up each morning dreading the day ahead. The coffee consumption helps to get us through the day when our fears and self-doubt stand in the way. We also drink a lot of coffee when we are worried about our finances. Affirmation: I focus my thoughts on the real source of energy—the truth and guidance within myself.

When we are emotionally hungry, even if we have just had a full meal, we feel like we are starving. It's our heart and soul that are feeling hungry or empty. My purpose in writing all of this is to get you thinking the next time you have a physical challenge or illness, experience pain or injury, notice an obsessive behaviour or interest or have a craving. What aspect of your heart and soul do you need to feed? What are your unmet needs? From what relationship or incident in your past did it stem? If we each adopted an affirmation, how different would we feel? (For more on affirmations, please see Chapter Four.) If we each became aware of our underlying pain and negative patterns and addressed them, how different would our lives be? How different would our world be?

We can also tell a lot about a person's emotional state by looking at other sources of emotional education such as their appearance, body language, voice, commonly used expressions or words, the types of things that go wrong in their lives and their dreams. Entire books are devoted to each of the sources of emotional education.

One Individual's Presentation of Emotional Pain and Subsequent Healing: A Case Study

It would be helpful at this juncture to provide you with a case study of an individual so that you can see how a person's childhood and life experience manifest physically and emotionally. It makes sense to use myself as your case study, since you have already read My Story at the start of this book.

In this case study, I am going to describe my physical appearance, behaviours and health challenges before I started to heal and then explain the ways in which those aspects changed once I began healing. I share these personal details with you for a number of reasons. I speak later on in the book about the importance of allowing ourselves to be vulnerable: If I can't be open and vulnerable, how can I hope that you will be? I also want to encourage you to examine yourself differently from how you have before, determine if you need to heal and which aspects of yourself might need healing, and see the possibilities for yourself. I hope to provide you with insight into the ways we look, behave and feel based on where we are in the process of becoming whole again. There are some aspects of my life that I have not shared with you in the interest of protecting those I love, but I sometimes find myself sharing those details when I meet with people individually, when they are suffering from similar occurrences.

This is my description of myself then and now:

Appearance

After I left home, I wore beige, cream and white clothing so that I wouldn't be noticed. In later years, I wore a lot of black, brown and grey to mourn the death of my true self as I continued to live in my self-made prison. My clothes were also very conservative, and most of my skin was covered, at all times. In the years when I was very focused on healing, I wore a lot of green—the colour most representative of healing. For many years now, I have worn bright colours almost every day, even if it is just one bright item, and very few of my clothes are considered to be conservative.

I didn't used to wear jewellery or carry purses because, again, I didn't want to be noticed. I was also ashamed to be a woman; I couldn't even say the word "woman". Now, I love jewellery and I always have a small purse somewhere nearby, even if I am not carrying it. When I started to heal, I began wearing a one-carat diamond solitaire on a gold chain. As my love for myself grew, that solitaire also grew, until eventually I was wearing a diamond heart the size of a toonie (Canadian $2 coin) and I started wearing diamonds on my wrists and hands every day. They were imitation, of course, but I reached a point where I literally felt as though I was sparkling.

For many years, I wore too much makeup. It was another way for me to hide. I didn't want anyone to see me without it because I felt I was unattractive. When I finally came to love myself, I allowed people to see me without my makeup. Today, I wear much less. Some ask why I continue to wear makeup at all; I wear makeup and put effort into my appearance because it makes me feel good inside and to cover up my sun spots!

I used to keep my hair rigidly coiffed with Joico Ice hairspray holding every hair in place. I wanted to look perfect, so others would love me. I wore it up or pinned back every day, never loose and down. Now I hardly ever wear hairspray, and the messier my hair gets, the more I seem to like it. When I attend functions, I usually pin it back in some way, but for everyday living I wear it loose. I have to admit that I still have perfectionist tendencies, but I don't spend a lot of time being a perfectionist. For example, when I see myself on television with poor lighting and bad camera angles, I can still get a bit down, but the feeling quickly passes.

I used to check myself in the mirror numerous times a day, trying to ensure I looked perfect because I didn't love the person I was and I thought others wouldn't love me, unless I looked just right. Now I go hours without looking in the mirror —sometimes just when I get ready in the morning and that's it.

I didn't like my body and never stood naked in front of a mirror, never mind in front of anyone else, including my husband. I didn't like my body because I didn't like myself. I would not go for massages because I didn't want to risk being seen. At the gym, I had an intricate process for changing without anyone seeing me. It was when I became pregnant with my first daughter that I began enjoying looking at myself in the mirror naked; the pride and wonder of carrying a baby in my own body was overwhelming. Now, I like my body, even with the aging it has undergone. My clothes show more of my body now than they did when I was in my twenties. And I have gone for monthly massages for years now.

I used to slouch forward, protecting my heart. Now I stand and sit tall and sometimes feel my heart radiating out to others, particularly when giving seminars to rooms full of people.

Behaviour

I did not have an audible laugh until I was in my twenties. How could I? I had not been allowed to be my own person and therefore was not happy. Now people tell me they love to hear me laugh, and I love to laugh and do it often. It's a deep laugh, brimming with joy. Even my smile has changed over the years; there doesn't seem to be an ounce of holding back when I smile now.

I often did not know what I wanted, which made me seem as though I was a very easygoing person. I remember when my brother came to visit me when we were adults and neither of us knew what we wanted to spend our time doing; we stood there asking each other what we wanted to do, neither of us having an opinion or an idea. When I reflected on this later, I realized that it should have been a big red flag: both of us had been controlled to such a degree that neither of us knew ourselves enough to discern what we liked or did not like. Nowadays, I always have a preference for what I want to do and know of its crucial importance in coming to love ourselves.

I didn't like confrontation and would do anything to avoid it. I was afraid of others and of being hurt. I would accept the blame for all sorts of things that were not my fault. I remember the first time I stood up for myself and how well it was received, which made me want to do it more and more. Today, the people in my life thoroughly enjoy and count on me speaking my truth.

I wouldn't want to ask anyone to help me. I did not think I was worthy enough to put anyone out of their way. Now I am deeply grateful for the number of times others offer to help me and for the number of things they do for me. I feel that there is a good balance between what I give and what I receive.

Smoking and drinking are forms of self-destruction that attack our heart. I smoked and drank excessively in my late teens and twenties. It helped me escape from my pain. I was angry at my helplessness as a child and angry at the adults who had rejected me, and I enjoyed rebelling against them. I was proud of being able to drink men "under the table", sometimes having twelve rye and diet cokes in an evening but still managing to function. As you learned in My Story, my hangovers were so bad that I threw up the whole next day, mainly just stomach acid, and usually until seven p.m., only to do it all over again the next weekend. Now I go three months without having a drink and can't remember the last time I was drunk. I haven't smoked since the day I learned I was pregnant, nor have I craved a cigarette. I love these descriptions of what is really behind smoking:

"Smoking creates a smoke screen around the user—a seeming barrier against the world—but the false boundaries (and the physical deterioration that smoking causes) eventually break down the smokers' ability to set real boundaries. Smokers then become less able to deal with the world. Soon they must smoke on a schedule in order to anesthetize their jangled and unprotected psyches. But the pain isn't truly addressed, the emotions don't actually go away, the thoughts don't subside permanently, and the world doesn't stop turning" (McLaren 2010, 82).

"Heavy smoking masks a deep feeling of being totally unworthy of existing" (Hay 1999, 158).

I always kept myself busy and could not relax. I did not want to look inside and take responsibility for what was not going right in my life. And if I was always busy, I felt I must be doing worthwhile things as opposed to "doing nothing" and accomplishing nothing. This was all part of me trying to prove myself to others and to myself. (You will read in Chapter Four how I put an end to that pattern.)

I spent hours shopping—shopping for just the right clothes that would make me think I was beautiful and shopping for clothes and items for my girls. I shopped to distract myself from dealing with my challenges. I shopped to fill the void in my life; I didn't feel I was enough and therefore always wanted more. Shopping also gave me a sense of personal power, which I didn't feel I had. Thankfully, I had no interest in spending my money on expensive clothing. I still love to shop, but the obsession has ended.

I did nothing spontaneously. I didn't drop in on anyone, and it didn't go well when anyone dropped in on me. If I was asked to do something without a few days' notice, I did not participate. I needed everything planned and scripted, because I felt there had been too many years where I was not in control. Now, I love spontaneity and have recently had to curb my impulsive desire to have fun, so that I could write this book!

I invariably ended up telling people "my victim story" within a short time after meeting them. Now, there are many people in my life who know nothing or very little of my past. Many think I have never had a challenge in my life. How they think that is possible with anyone on this earth is beyond me!

I told people about myself and shared my thoughts but could never look them directly in the eye for long because I didn't want people to see that I still wasn't truly happy, despite many years of working on myself. Now, I can look people in the eye for long periods of time, knowing I have nothing to hide. I feel the opposite way now; I want them to see into my soul and see how truly happy I am.

My creativity was stifled for years because I did not know who I was, never mind allowing myself to relax long enough to be creative. Now my creativity ignites seemingly effortlessly.

I was a master at pleasing others and I spent most of my time proving myself, which worked wonders for me in the corporate world but was dreadfully detrimental to my soul. I was always "doing the right thing" and explaining that to others, just so they would love me. Now, I am a master at pleasing myself and have more to offer my children and others as a result.

I took everything personally because of my insecurities. Now, when someone doesn't act in a way I expect, I wonder what has happened in their lives to make them unhappy.

I judged and criticized others because I didn't like who I was. Now I love myself and know that when others are not kind to me, they simply don't love themselves.

I didn't want to abandon anyone because I had such a fear of being abandoned myself. Each person who helped raise me, in one way or another—even my mainstay, Jay—abandoned me in some way. Now healed and years later, I can abandon those who do not treat me the way I finally know I deserve to be treated.

I allowed myself to be controlled by others until I was over forty years old. Now, everyone in my life is clear that I will not be controlled. I will change my mind if another convinces me of something, but on my own accord.

I didn't know how to be affectionate, to hug or kiss or even to enjoy hugging or kissing because affection was not a part of my experience growing up. Now, I spontaneously hug and kiss others and enjoy it. I wouldn't describe myself as a huggy or kissy person, but I have learned that my love language is actually physical touch (more on that later).

Fear pulled me by the hand through the alleys and around the corners of life. I saw true love and freedom only in the movies and the numerous books I read. I didn't even know I was governed by fear; for many years, I lived in denial that I was unhappy.

I had never been nurtured, so I had no clue how to nurture myself. Others offered to help me from time to time, and I never accepted. Independence was all I knew and accepted for myself. Then a counsellor told me that it was time to have a love affair with myself. He thought I knew how to do that. Learning what that entailed began my conscious journey of coming to love myself.

Health Challenges

Bodies under stress either go into fight (attack others, i.e., outer-directed rage) or flight (run away, e.g., drugs, or physical or emotional self-isolation) or they freeze (attack ourselves, i.e., inner-directed rage) or they react in a combination of these ways. My body froze as my main response. I moved and walked with stiffness from my teens until I was around forty years old. I had excruciating neck pain in my thirties. Now I walk with my arms swinging with fluid movement, feeling so free, still noticing the contrast to how I used to move. The way I dance now is in complete contrast to the way I danced years ago; I dance with wild abandon, coming up with "moves" in the spur of the moment. Perfect strangers feel the need to talk to me and join me in fun on the dance floor–men and women alike.

I craved sugar and chocolate, wanting to feel loved and experience sweetness in my life. Today, I still love those foods, but they represent a small part of my diet. Friends have stopped remarking on what is in my fridge because they are now used to seeing lots of fruits, vegetables and other healthy foods line the shelves. I have learned how to meet my own needs so that food is rarely needed to fill the void.

As a teenager, I had horrible periods that put me in the sick room at school for at least one whole day each month with cramping and vomiting. In my twenties I had an ovarian cyst. In my thirties and the early part of my forties, my body was in actual pain and swollen due to stomach aches, Candida, bladder, kidney and sinus infections, major digestive issues and allergies. I also suffered from hypothyroidism. Some of the emotional connections to these health challenges were explained earlier in this chapter. Candida is caused by anger and frustration. The kidney is the partner organ; kidney challenges are caused by disappointment and challenges with our partner. Digestive issues come about when we are not digesting our lives well. Hypothyroidism comes about when we put the needs of others before our own and refrain from speaking our truth. Today, my body feels delicious and pain is a rare occurrence. I still have slight digestive challenges and hypothyroidism but both areas of my body become ever healthier as time goes on. Now in my forties, I feel younger than I did in my twenties.

Healing

Once I made the necessary changes in my life and forgave myself and others, all of my unhealthy patterns ended and my fears took a back seat in my life—actually just a small corner of a back seat. I replaced my fear with love for myself. I readily and frequently nurture myself by lying still on my bed doing nothing but breathing, spontaneously dancing like no one is watching and taking short naps in the middle of the day—it feels so good to me to afford myself these luxuries, as well as many others.

I wake up each day at peace, feeling completely healthy physically and emotionally. Life excites me; I see life as an adventure and wonder what fun I will get up to or who I am meant to run into or meet each time I leave my home. I always feel like something entirely wonderful is coming around the corner for me yet am completely happy if my life were to remain the way it is forever. I am the epitome of positive thinking and can help anyone turn the negatives in their lives into positives, if they so desire. I smile and laugh easily.

It is so easy for me to be vulnerable and admit my mistakes and the lessons I have learned. I am thrilled to share my experiences fully with others because the lessons I gleaned from each experience continually amaze me. I feel very connected to the universe, to others and to myself because I have finally come to love myself and, therefore, others. Do I still have a distance to go in coming to love myself? Yes, you will read further on that we spend our lives coming to love ourselves. (Please see a more complete description of what it means when we come to love ourselves in Chapter Five.)

 "All healing is related to the ability to give and accept unconditional love" (Truman 2003, 49).

Three

Understanding Ourselves with New Perspective

" Every human being is born with a healthy emotional system. We love and accept ourselves when we are born. We don't make judgments about which parts of ourselves are good and which parts are bad. We dwell in the fullness of our being, living in the moment, and expressing ourselves freely" (Ford 1998, 3).

Healing is a lifelong process of returning to the wholeness and well-being we experienced as very young children. The more we heal ourselves, the more we let go of our fear and our self-defeating patterns and release ourselves from our self-imposed prisons. But first, we need to come to understand ourselves and our lives in a new way.

Do We Need to Heal?

How do we know if we need to heal?

- Did you see yourself in one or more of the self-statements in Chapter Two that demonstrated the need for emotional healing?
- Did you experience abandonment, neglect, abuse (physical, emotional or sexual), denial, betrayal, guilt or fear-induced parenting or were you overly controlled?
- Are you hurting inside or seeing yourself as a victim, as a result of the wrongs that you feel were committed against you over the course of your life?

If your answer is yes to any of these questions, then you can begin the journey to emotional healing. The *first step* toward healing is acknowledging that there is something out of balance with our thought or behaviour patterns.

Do We Want to Heal?

The *second step* is wanting and deciding to become whole again. Do you want to heal?

The attendees at my nutrition seminars ask me if they need to improve their nutrition when they are experiencing only a few physical symptoms. My answer is always, "How badly are those symptoms bothering you? That will be your determinant." And now when we look at the need for emotional healing, I ask you, "How happy are you? How pleased are you with the way in which your life is going? How does your body feel? How much do you love and respect yourself?" Your answers to these questions will be your determinant. Any physical or emotional symptom or condition can be overcome if we want to open our eyes to the possibilities and move on.

Seeing Ourselves as Victims

Many of us see ourselves as victims. Feeling as though we are victims is a natural response. We may not feel like victims all the time; we may feel like victims only when we are with certain people or in certain circumstances.

What Keeps Us Seeing Ourselves as "Victims"?

There might be any number of reasons why we continue to see ourselves as victims, which in turn prevents us from healing from our past:

- We might be in survival mode, just trying to get through each day, raising our children.
- We are not taught how to respond to painful experiences in healthy ways.
- It is easier to choose one of the three coping mechanisms: fight, flight or freeze. It is easier to be angry and aggressive with others than to face the truth that we are hurting inside or that we are scared. It is easier to run from our pain by moving to a different country, getting lost in our addictions or staying busy. It is easier to live on the adrenaline rush that comes from running around all the time. It is easier to feel needed in many different places at once rather than looking within. It is easier to shut down and stop having intimate relationships with others when those we love hurt or leave us.

- We took responsibility for our parents' mistakes and carried that responsibility with us for decades and cannot possibly take on any more responsibility. It can be easier for a child to blame their parents' failures on themselves than to think that their parents are flawed. If our parents are alcoholics and we have carried the responsibility for their mistakes year after year, it is too exhausting for us to take on any further responsibility.

- It is easier to blame others for the challenges we have in our own lives. Some of us have experienced such pain in our lives that we believe that the only way we can cope with the pain is to blame others. Blaming others gives us an excuse for not having the strength to make the changes that we know, in our hearts or subconsciously, to be necessary. "Blaming others temporarily relieves us from the weight of failure" (Brach 2003, 17). When we blame others for being wrong, it allows us to feel right. The more inferior we feel, the more uncomfortable we are with admitting our faults. Blaming others is saying that they should be different from how they are, which can never be the case.

- We have always had things go wrong in our lives, and that is what we are used to; that is our comfort zone. I have seen people make chaos in their lives because they don't know what to do when there is none. When there is chaos or drama, we don't need to look at ourselves more closely, which is one of the hardest undertakings of all.

- We are in denial. We live our lives day to day, not lifting our heads up long enough to know that our lives could be better. Or we don't want to be honest with ourselves because that would hurt too much. We don't want to admit to ourselves that we are suffering. ***But we all suffer; it is part of the human condition. It is the overcoming of suffering that is rare and incredible.*** Alternatively, we think we are happy as a clam, believing that things "really aren't so bad." Or we are such positive thinkers that we don't even know we are unhappy or realize that we see ourselves as victims subconsciously. Living in denial allows us to cover our wounds and still function, but it also prevents us from accessing and healing our feelings and meeting our needs.

- We are afraid that if we were to change our ways, we might lose the love of one or more people who are important to us. Ironically, it is only the people who truly love us unconditionally who love us when we do what is right for ourselves; the rest really don't matter.

- Here's the big one: We might secretly enjoy being a victim. How might we gain something from being a victim? We like the admiration that comes our way when we tell our stories from the past. Imagine - we actually survived such atrocities! Remaining a victim keeps us from having to reach our potential. "Terrible things happened to me so I can't possibly achieve such and such." Sometimes it's safe to remain the victim; it is how we have always felt and we may be frightened of feeling any differently. Maybe we feel that things would become worse for ourselves if we left our comfort zone. Holding onto what we know is the biggest reason we remain victims.

- Some of us want to remain victims because we believe that if we made something of ourselves, our parents, the very people who hurt us, would take credit for our success or our happiness and we couldn't bear that. We subconsciously punish our parents by remaining victims.

Behind each of these possible reasons for remaining a victim is one big reason: fear. We are afraid that if we delve into our past, it will be too painful. We are afraid that if we try to improve our circumstances, we will be worse off than we are now. If we think that the pain of changing is greater than the pain of staying the same, we simply won't change. We are afraid that we will find that these awful circumstances occurred in our lives because we deserved them and that we are not good enough for better things to happen to us. This is simply not true.

I hate to tell you this, but feeling as though we are victims is actually the easy response. Right now, you might be mulling over your past, suffering over and over again as you recall each episode in your life that inflicted pain on your wonderful being. Maybe the memories literally bring you to your knees and cause you to ask, "How can you tell me that this is the *easy* response? I am dying inside. These memories eat away at me each and every day. They prevent me from ever feeling truly happy."

I am here to tell you that when we see ourselves as victims, we are putting ourselves through that suffering, day after day, year after year. What if I were to say that you don't need to do that anymore? What if I were to tell you that each of us is responsible for how we feel? Any number of horrific things can happen to us, but it is up to us how we respond to each occurrence; we choose to remain victims or become victors.

For example, by remembering how your mother used to hit you on a regular basis and continuing to hate yourself because you believe that she must have hated you to hit you, you are giving the power of how you feel over to her. By remembering how your father worked so many hours and was rarely home and continuing to feel as unimportant as he made you feel, you are giving the power of how you feel over to him. You are letting your mother make you feel hated and unworthy. You are letting your father make you feel unimportant and lonely.

Did your mother hate you? Or see you as unworthy? Did your father think you were unimportant? Both of these are unlikely. But if either of them *did* feel that way, it is only because of the level of unhappiness they were feeling in their own lives at the time.

The cost of letting our fear govern us can be seen in the unhealthy patterns in our lives. But the biggest cost of all is the love we cannot feel for ourselves. Each of us has the strength we need to run our lives differently and come to love ourselves. Our strength will appear as soon as our desire to improve our lives is stronger than our desire to stay in our current circumstances.

 "Our deepest fear is not that we are inadequate. Our deepest fear is that we are powerful beyond measure. It is our light, not our darkness that most frightens us. We ask ourselves 'Who am I to be brilliant, gorgeous, talented and fabulous?' Actually, who are you not to be? You are a child of God. Your playing small does not serve the world. There is nothing enlightening about shrinking so that other people won't feel insecure around you. We are all meant to shine as children do. We were born to manifest the glory of God that is within us. It is not just in some of us; it's in everyone. And when we let our light shine, we unconsciously give other people permission to do the same. As we are liberated from our own fear, our presence automatically liberates others" (Williamson 1992, 190–91).

Telling Our Stories

"Pain is inevitable, but suffering is optional" (Brach 2003, 106).

Each of us has stories. We have a story about our childhood and we have stories about every day we have lived since. We each need to tell our stories to others or journal them in order to relieve some of the pressure we feel from our challenges, as well as to learn and grow as individuals. Let's face it, hearing stories is interesting. Some of them motivate us; some of them make us grateful for what we have; some of them help us to learn lessons; and most of them are an excellent way to connect to one another.

It is when we allow our negative stories to define us and determine what is possible for ourselves that we stifle our growth as individuals. It is when we allow our stories to negatively control our feelings, thoughts and behaviours that we engage in unhealthy patterns and abusive behaviours. It is when we allow our stories to make us feel unlovable, unworthy and unimportant that we cause ourselves to suffer each and every day and remain victims. If we continually relay to others the aspects of our lives that have not worked out for us, the trouble we foresee for ourselves down the road, the negative ways others perceive us or how others fail to meet our needs, we cannot make things better for ourselves. You see, if we have not healed from the past, we are continually going over these incidents in our minds and using them as reference points to determine who we are, what we believe and what choices to make. This focus on the past makes it very difficult to live in the present or grow toward a better future.

"Living inside our stories guarantees us a life filled with fear and wanting. The fear tells us to watch out, to hide, and to play small so we won't be exposed. The wanting drives us to violate our souls, trying to grasp onto anything that might make us look or feel better. When we are wanting, when we are grasping, when we are judging ourselves or others, we can be sure we are in our stories. Outside our stories, there is no wanting. There is only the belief and inner knowing that everything is as it should be" (Ford 2002, 179).

Reframing Our Stories

"There is no reality in life, only perception" (Dr Phil McGraw).

When we reframe our stories, we look at what happened to us with new perspective. We put a new frame around a picture or an event to alter the way we look at it and change its meaning. One of the greatest aspects of being human is that we can make choices. Our interpretation of the painful events in our lives can either disempower us or empower us. We can look at our past through eyes of fear (our wounded self) or eyes of love (our healed self). The stories we choose to tell can change our inner emotions and thereby change the course of our lives.

Unfortunately, most of us are raised to believe that our painful or challenging experiences are bad. What if we were to look at those bad experiences in a different way? What if we were to see that every obstacle gives us opportunities to overcome it and to evolve?

- Our bad experiences can help us connect with who we are. The traumatic events in our lives, the experiences that wound us, help us heal and become all that we can be. My brother's death reinforced how unhappy our childhood had been. It made me grateful to be alive and proud of the person I had become, having taken the route of immersing myself in self-healing books.

- Our bad experiences can be opportunities. How I was treated as a child made me one of the most compassionate and loving people you could ever meet because I did not want others to be treated the way I had been treated.

- Our bad experiences can connect us to finding our purpose here on earth. My eldest daughter being so sick was my opportunity to heal her, which then led me to embrace the power of nutrition, find one of my callings and help others heal.

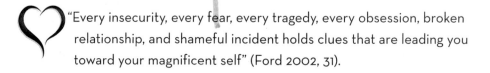

"Every insecurity, every fear, every tragedy, every obsession, broken relationship, and shameful incident holds clues that are leading you toward your magnificent self" (Ford 2002, 31).

Life has a way of throwing situations at us that help us go deeper and become more aware. No one can sail through life without being presented with obstacles and tests. Many people view their losses or mistakes as a wrong turn in their life's path, as opposed to integral parts of their growth. Carolyn Myss explains in *Anatomy of the Spirit* (1996) that once we set our sights on the lesson, as opposed to our wounding, we achieve the significant benefit of symbolic sight and can then see the truth being delivered to us through the challenge. *Every person in our lives and every interaction with another can be a tremendous opportunity for our inner healing and growth.* At every setback and heartbreak, we can ask ourselves, "What does this create the opportunity for?" or "What did I learn from this experience?" This is when we find our gifts.

Some of the lessons that we can learn from the events in our lives include compassion, kindness, opening up, patience, balance, self-discipline, honesty, giving without expectations, surrendering, forgiving, trusting, self-sufficiency and having the courage to build intimacy with others. And when we learn lessons, we attain greater wisdom, perspective and appreciation for our lives and ourselves.

Wayne Dyer clearly explains in *Manifest Your Destiny* (1997) the valuable lessons that seemingly negative behaviour patterns can teach us. Addiction can teach us the euphoria of purity. Anger can teach us the ecstasy of love. Ingratitude can teach us gratitude. Hoarding can teach us the enjoyment of giving. Our pain can teach us how to live in the moment and be more loving of ourselves and others. Dr. Judith Orliff, in her book *Emotional Freedom* (2009), explains other lessons. Depression can teach us to develop hope. Jealousy can build our self-esteem. Frustration can teach us patience. Loneliness can teach us connection to others. Anxiety can cultivate inner calm.

"What has happened until now was a set of lessons—often extraordinary, often painful. Yet all that was ever going on was that you were being given the chance to become the person you're capable of being. Some lessons you passed, and some you failed and will have to take again. Some you enjoyed, and some you resisted and might have hated. But they've left you—if you choose—a better person, a more humble person, a more available person, a more vulnerable person, a wiser person, a more noble person. And from that, all things are possible" (Williamson 2008, 61–62).

In order to tap into our courage and live the lives we want to live, it is necessary to revisit our past, reframe our stories and then embrace our past. Every one of us has been hurt and disappointed. None of us can forget the events that shook us to our very core and made us feel as though we were a victim. But when we assign meaning to every experience we undergo, the possibility of coming to a new understanding of these experiences and the lessons learned is ours for the taking. Then we are free to focus on the aspects of our childhood that did go well and our parents' strengths. We can come to love and cherish our stories for the ways in which they have contributed to who we are by looking closely at the events or people who hurt us, bringing new awareness to our experiences, taking responsibility and ending the struggles or unhealthy patterns in our lives. Every horror story has the potential to catapult us into reaching our maximum potential as human beings.

When we are young children, we need an adult to reframe things for us. A mother is irritable with her son. The son could think, "Mommy doesn't love me." Then the boy's father tells his son that Mommy is tired because she was up all night with the boy's baby sister. This reframes the situation and the little boy can see that his mom does love him—she is just not feeling rested at this time. *If an adult doesn't reframe things for us when we are children, we need to reframe our childhoods once we become adults.*

Taking Responsibility

"In my experience, the turning point in therapy occurs when we take responsibility and stop denying and minimizing both our real childhood experience and what we are doing in the present to keep ourselves from feeling" (Berger 2000, 23).

Our whole personality is built upon ways of thinking and behaving that help us avoid feeling pain. Emotional healing and real growth can begin only when we *decide* to face our pain. Pain resides within our hearts, and our hearts affect every aspect of how we live our lives. When we heal our hearts, we *decide* to no longer participate in the struggle with ourselves; we see that resisting is wasting our precious energy; we *decide* to take responsibility for ourselves. When we decide to take responsibility and begin doing so, we have taken the *third step* toward healing. This is when we start to see ourselves clearly. We align our personalities with who we really are and we can finally step into our power. When we take responsibility for ourselves, we agree to do what feels right for us as opposed to what feels right for others. We choose love rather than fear; we choose loving ourselves rather than fearing ourselves. Many of us can take responsibility for the good that exists in our lives but have a hard time taking responsibility for the bad. It is only when we can take responsibility for the bad that we become truly empowered and come to love all parts of ourselves.

"The pain you experienced when you were two, six, or eight is just beneath the surface of your consciousness. Until it's transformed, it's always there driving your life. Most of us never explore our core beliefs to see if we've consciously chosen them. I meet people every week who want to be artists or write books, but they are sure they can't fulfill their desires. When I ask them why, they tell me they're not talented or educated enough. They have confidence in their reasons, but not in their dreams" (Ford 1998, 114).

Taking Responsibility in Childhood

As children, we were totally dependent on the adults who raised us to have our needs met. Blaming ourselves and others was the only way we could protect ourselves from the pain we experienced when our needs weren't met. When we blamed ourselves, we kept the myth of a good family alive and gained a sense of control when we had none. We couldn't afford to see our parents as uncaring or inadequate, so it made more sense for us to see ourselves as worthless or inadequate.

Since blaming was our only form of defence for so many years, it is no wonder that it is so difficult to let go and stop blaming once we are adults. Most of us still believe that the responsibility for meeting our needs rests outside us. Some of us spend years waiting to be rescued by Prince Charming or a miracle. As long as we blame or wait to be rescued, we are not letting go of being a victim of life's circumstances and we are not taking responsibility.

What is the healthier alternative to blaming ourselves or others? The healthier alternative is to take responsibility for ourselves, that is, to parent ourselves. We now know that we are not responsible for what happened to us as innocent children, but we are responsible for recovering from the pain of our past. How do we do this?

Taking Responsibility in Adulthood

"All control begins with taking control of the feelings we hold in our heart, because these feelings determine the thoughts we hold in our conscious mind" (Truman 2003, 17).

As adults, we regain the control we lacked in our childhoods by taking responsibility for ourselves. We take responsibility by identifying and understanding our current feelings of inadequacy and linking them back to our childhood. We look truthfully at our childhood, our parents' childhood and our relationship with our parents. We honestly express our feelings to our parents, become separate individuals from them, change our negative behaviours or patterns and gradually come to love ourselves.

We take responsibility by looking at five things:

- Our feelings and emotions: We start taking responsibility for our relationships and aspects of our lives that are not going the way we want them to by identifying, understanding and expressing our feelings. What happens in our lives only mirrors our thoughts and, ultimately, our feelings.

- What happened to the adults who hurt us: You already learned that people treat each other badly only because they are in their own pain. An individual can mistreat us only if they were mistreated. An adult will hit us only if they were hit. An adult will yell at us only if they were yelled at. When we delve into our parents' past, we find out what made them the people they are.

- The negatives and positives that came from our relationship with our parents: We learn from both their negative examples and their positive examples.

- Ways to express and release our negative feelings in a more healthy way (Chapter Four is dedicated to this topic.): Acknowledging that we have negative feelings is the first step to turning those feelings around. ***If we are continually stuck and cannot find satisfaction in our lives, it means we are carrying resentment.*** Standing up to our parents or the people who hurt us is one example of a way in which to release those feelings. When we love ourselves enough to stand up, share our feelings with those who hurt us, let them know implicitly that our feelings matter and that we are hurting, we complete an integral step in healing ourselves.

- Ways to come to love ourselves and others: Read on for lots more information on this topic.

Here is an example of someone learning how to take responsibility for the first time. This example has nothing to do with parenting; it simply describes the concept of taking responsibility. A man ran a baseball team, and one of the players on that team was his brother. Both of them were heavily involved in and loved sports. The brother had a lot of anger that continually caused him to be suspended from the games or tournaments, and sometimes the whole team was disqualified because of his actions. Year after year, the team faced these repercussions. One day, the man who ran the team shared his anguish with me over the team's fate. I told him that he needed to take responsibility for these challenges. He looked at me in absolute shock and said that the challenges were his brother's fault! I reminded him that he ran the team and therefore it was his responsibility to choose appropriate players for that team. It took a long time for him to grasp the concept that *he* was causing these repercussions for the team and that he needed to decide when he was going to improve things. Some players questioned remaining on the team because of these constant challenges. A few left knowing that if they wanted to enjoy playing, it was up to them to take responsibility for themselves and find another team to join. Eventually, the man who ran the team told his brother he could not play on the team. Years later, the brother rejoined the team on the condition that he manage his anger and he complied.

What else does taking responsibility entail?

Taking responsibility means we need to allow ourselves to be vulnerable and truthful with ourselves. Only the truth will help us move forward. **When we admit to a weakness or to a mistake or to having a negative emotion, we pry our hearts wide open.** Until we can do this, we live in pride, which blocks our path to healing and coming to love ourselves. It is only by allowing ourselves to be vulnerable and viewing that vulnerability with a certain amount of love that we can begin to take responsibility and live the lives we want to live.

When we are vulnerable, we become aware of our truth, and when we speak that truth (to the right person), our whole world opens up. I was always a positive thinker, so it was easy for me to say I was happy all of the time when really I was not. The day I realized that I was not happy in my marriage (became aware of my vulnerability) and told my best friend (viewed my vulnerability with enough love to admit it) was the day that I began taking responsibility for trying to improve my marriage. The person we choose to speak our truth to can help us accept our vulnerability even more. I invite you to choose a trusted friend or family member to whom you are willing to admit a weakness or mistake that you made.

Taking responsibility means noticing our negative feelings so that we can convert them into more positive responses. For example, say that a woman is always criticizing her husband. She needs first to become aware that she is constantly criticizing and then to become aware of how her actions are making her feel inside. She might feel miserable, guilty, angry or sad and thus see her experience with her husband as negative. It is only by noticing how she is feeling that she can begin to improve her situation.

Taking responsibility means acknowledging that we are co-creators of the dramas we live as adults. ***Realizing that we have participated, often subconsciously, in the choices that have brought us the most pain is a hard pill to*** *swallow.* Taking responsibility means saying to ourselves, "I created this. I'm responsible for this. I can change this." We each have the power to do things differently; we simply need to harness that power. If we want to stop feeling stuck in our bad experiences and change our patterns (dysfunction, irresponsibility, entitlement, narcissism, fear, etc.), we need to see how we are participating in or contributing to those experiences.

The woman in the prior example was always criticizing her husband for his moodiness and bouts of anger, but she was doing nothing to try to help or change the situation. She was thus participating in her own unhappiness. If she were to take responsibility by learning to how to meet her own needs and love herself more, she might find she didn't have as much to complain about. Then if she started complimenting her husband for the things she feels that he does right, he might feel more loved by his partner and therefore manage his moods and anger more easily.

 "Our problems transform themselves into our medicine when we learn to face how we created them to begin with" (Williamson 2008, 52).

Taking responsibility means we need to ask ourselves some tough questions, such as "What is the message being relayed to me by these circumstances?" or "What is the gift this experience offers me?" Looking at this last example, this woman turned her "bad" experiences with her husband into loving and appreciating herself more and an improved marital relationship—talk about great gifts!

Taking responsibility means realizing that we are responsible for our reactions in any moment. When we understand this, other people and circumstances will have no control over us. I remember a time when the subway broke down, preventing my friend and me from getting home at the usual time. She was so angry! She carried on and on, letting her anger and disappointment overcome her. I reminded her that the breakdown was beyond our control and we had better just decide whether we wanted to make our own way home or wait for the subway to be operational again.

Similarly, we can turn things around with people who try to upset us. Let's pretend that my friend proceeded to be upset with me for not sharing in her anger at the inoperative subway and subsequent inconveniences. I could become upset with her in turn, or I could realize that she was lashing out at me because of the situation she was in. **When we come to understand the unmet needs of** *the other person, which have nothing to do with us, the other person's anger with us loses all power.* If my friend were then to focus on understanding herself, instead of being upset with me, her anger would also lose all power.

Sometimes, taking responsibility means deciding to have the courage to surrender. (For more on surrendering, please see Chapter Five.) Here is an example that incorporates all aspects of taking responsibility for ourselves as adults. A woman is married to a man who can never hold down a job. The two of them have four children to support. The situation goes on for years and the woman becomes tired of always being hounded by the creditors. She becomes filled with blame and anger toward her husband. When this woman came to me, I asked her how having a husband in these circumstances had served her. Allowing herself to be vulnerable and truthful, she admitted that as long as he was continually messing up and losing his job, she got to be in control. She got to always be "right" while he continually looked like the failure. I asked her if she would rather have control in another way. She said yes. After much discussion, she decided to have courage and finally surrender and she convinced her husband to do the same. She and her husband took a different kind of action. They sold their home, moved into a rental, filed for bankruptcy and he started his own business doing what he loved and excelled at. The pattern of anger and blaming ended. Taking responsibility also means forgiving ourselves and others. Forgiveness allowed this couple to move forward together with new, happier lives. (Please see Chapter Four for more about forgiveness.)

The gift of taking responsibility for the circumstances of our lives is being able to harness the incredible inner strength and power we each possess. When we do that, we see how much we have grown and our love for ourselves can only flourish. If we don't take responsibility, we give our power away to someone else; why would we want to do that?

Exercise

For the next 48 hours, become aware of the choices you are making in each moment. Your awareness of your choices will continue to increase until you can easily see that you, not others, are dictating what goes on around you. It might help you to say out loud, "I choose to _____" each time you go somewhere, do something or spend time with someone. This will help you become conscious of what you are doing and decide whether you truly want to do what you are about to do or be with whomever it is you plan to see.

Working With Our Feelings and Emotions: The Key to Transformation

Identifying, Understanding and Accepting Our Feelings and Emotions

 "What we feel forms the cornerstone of our perceptions, our dreams, our motivations, our reflections, and our values—who we are" (Jawar and Micozzi 2009, 38).

What do all emotionally unhealthy parents have in common? They avoid dealing with their painful feelings. Self-help author Iyanla Vanzant (1998) calls the state that we enter when we don't acknowledge our feelings "emotional dishonesty". The feelings that we are unaware of are behind every challenge, pain, trauma and sickness we experience. ***Taking responsibility for our feelings is the most important step we can take toward achieving emotional health.*** It is only by taking responsibility for our feelings that we come to understand and stay connected to our inner selves. Our feelings are behind every choice we make and every way in which we behave or react. Our feelings determine our thought patterns, our beliefs and our attitudes. Our feelings determine what happens in our lives. Honouring our feelings and trusting ourselves are the biggest steps that we can take in making the changes we need to make to live more peaceful and joyful lives. This is how we begin the process of gaining the control of our lives that many of us did not have as children.

Examples of feelings include pain, pleasure, relaxation and sleepiness. A feeling only becomes an emotion if it is expressed or moved. Even the word "emotion" comes from the Latin word "emotus", which means to move outward, that is, motion. Examples of emotions include anger, worry, fear, sadness, joy, relief, hope and pride. Emotions are the outward expression of our feelings. When I was younger, I was captivated by Gary Zukav's work. He has a name for the continual study of the changing emotions within us: "emotional awareness" (Zukav 1989; Zukav and Francis 2001).

We are always experiencing feelings and emotions, whether we are aware of them or not. Once we are in touch with our inner selves, we realize that our feelings and emotions are actually neutral. Our emotions change depending on what we are experiencing, and our feelings and emotions are good or bad only if we believe them to be good or bad. It is important that we not judge them.

Unfortunately, the majority of us have been taught about the rightness or wrongness of what we feel, which is probably the main cause of our emotional dishonesty. We tend to hold onto our emotional pain and disappointments because we have not been taught how to deal with them effectively and healthily.

"Keeping the emotional body clear is essential to good health. ... Undigested emotions, like undigested food, result in the accumulation of toxicity in our physiology" (Chopra, Simon and Abrams 2005, 169).

Each of our emotions carries a truth; trapped, repetitive or seemingly irrational emotions tell the truth about something. Each has its own wants, needs and purpose. These emotions help us come to know ourselves better. The simple act of paying attention to our feelings and emotions—our inner world— shows us the core meaning of our lives.

"Each emotion is a message from your soul. ... Your emotions are a song written only for you" (Zukav and Francis 2001, 42).

We experience both positive and negative emotions; we are human. If we allow our positive and negative emotions to flow, notice them, welcome them and allow ourselves to feel and express them from the heart, our personal growth, love for ourselves and relationships will flourish. Positive feelings are based on love. Negative feelings come from fear. Positive, joyful emotions make us aware that we are on the right track and keep us on the right track. Negative, painful emotions make us aware that there is a lesson to learn or that an area of ourselves needs emotional healing. Similarly, symptoms, conditions and disease notify us that our bodies need physical healing. Negative emotions will not go away unless we address them, and neither will symptoms, conditions or disease.

Each of us is made up of contrasts; we have generosity and greed, strength and weakness, conservatism and sexiness, and so on. Our job is to recognize all of our elements and embrace our wholeness. Our job is to recognize our negative emotions, such as anger, and thank them for pointing out that we can no longer live with certain circumstances or people in our lives.

What else do negative feelings do for us? Real joy and real happiness can exist only in relation to all of the emotions. If we had never experienced sadness or pain, it would not be possible to truly experience joy. Anger and shame help us set boundaries with others. Sadness offers rejuvenation; we all know how good it feels to have a good cry. Healthy and properly focused fear allows our intuition to kick in and protect us from danger.

We have to be aware of and truly feel our feelings in order to heal them. When we let ourselves experience our feelings of shame or sadness, for example, we can begin to see ourselves with compassion. Real change cannot begin until we allow ourselves to feel how bad things really are or were. We need to become conscious of the fact that we are not happy; that we don't feel right inside; that we are blaming or judging ourselves or others; and that we are defensive, upset, jealous, guilty, anxious, angry or sad when we are with certain people or in certain circumstances in our lives. The majority of our feelings are subconscious. It is when we become conscious of these feelings and name them that we stop the feelings from influencing us at a subconscious level. Awareness is actually how we become conscious, and once we have this awareness, real change can begin.

Animals don't hide or lie about their feelings; they love to be seen and understood. But as humans, we are taught certain feelings are okay to feel or express and others are not. If our feelings or needs are met with acceptance, then we usually feel it is okay to have those feelings and needs. When they are not met with acceptance, we ignore and repress our feelings and needs, see them as bad or feel humiliated for having them. Often, we find unhealthy ways to meet them. This unhealthy denial or repression of feelings usually begins in our younger years. It reminds me of when doctors discourage us from following our instincts by telling us it is normal for babies to be spitting up, contracting diaper rashes or experiencing colic, just because it is so common. This is not normal; these babies are experiencing symptoms, and the symptoms need to be addressed at a root level before they turn into conditions. That is the subject of my first book.

How many times have you heard someone say, "You shouldn't feel that way?" Many of us spend far too much of our time and energy doubting ourselves, pleasing others, trying to live up to the expectations of others and trying to be perfect. Many of us are afraid of losing control or looking foolish if we express our emotions. Many of us are filled with false ideas about our feelings, which cause us to disconnect from our innate intelligence, natural healing abilities and true selves. The suppression of feelings weakens us, and many of us end up emotionally underdeveloped, all so that other people can feel comfortable. What happens with those feelings that are denied or repressed?

 "Our emotionally deadening culture makes us believe that deep empathetic living is impossible, as if true feelings or brilliant visions would slow us down unnecessarily or prevent us from meeting the rent, raising the kids, or turning the thankless crank. That's not true, of course, but the overwhelming message in our culture tells us that we can't stop to feel or dream because we have to keep moving" (McLaren 2010, 195).

If we are not aware of our negative feelings, we cannot see our wounds, and therefore we cannot separate from them. They possess us. This causes us to snap or yell at another, withdraw into ourselves, develop addictions, be overcome with resentment or laugh uncontrollably. When we experience these behaviours, the circumstances of our lives may not be what we desire. When we hide our emotions, we lock them deeper into our bodies, where they can become even more powerful and eventually create sickness. It is only when our wounds are visible and truly felt that they can be worked on and healed. We need to stop resisting life and stop stifling ourselves to transform pain into emotional health.

"Our thinking occurs in the conscious part of us. Whereas, the feeling is in the subconscious part of us. The challenge is in getting to the subconscious" (Truman 2003, 65).

This does make the process of recognizing and accepting our feelings somewhat tricky. If we are trying to become conscious of our feelings, concerted effort makes it easier to spot them. *It is when we under-react or over-react to a situation or a person that we know it is time to address our feelings.* Our feelings are always correct but if a feeling seems too big, then we know that it is generated from our past, has probably been felt many times before, and needs to be identified and addressed.

"When we act as adults we subvert our healing power, keep ourselves frozen in unhealthy patterns, and diminish our lives in denial. As we observe ourselves we can become aware of our recurring problems. The driving force behind these is undoubtedly some unfelt feeling from the past. A person who can never find anything and who is constantly asking his wife 'Where's my shirt? Where are my new socks?' is probably acting out a desire to be looked after. A young person with purple hair and a safety pin in her left cheek is likely acting out a need to be seen or trying to make the inside pain visible. A man acting out by being sexually promiscuous probably needs to feel how much he wanted and needed his mother and father to hold him. The act-out may not be harmful or a problem; it could be just a love for long hot baths which may be an acting out of the need for warmth not received as a child" (Berger 2000, 22).

In her book *Emotional Freedom* (2009), Judith Orliff describes emotional freedom as the capacity to give and receive more love. She talks about the importance of learning to view ourselves and others through the lens of the heart and giving birth to our finest, freest selves. The more positive and loving feelings we experience, the better we feel about ourselves and the better our lives will go. It is impossible to hold onto negative feelings, such as anger, when we are operating from our hearts. It is learning how to have compassion for ourselves and others that helps us operate from our heart and transform negative emotions into positive ones. Then we are free to be our true selves, respecting every feeling and aspect of ourselves.

"Our experiences in life are actually our own state of mind being projected outward. When we have a state of mind that indicates inner peace, joy, love and well-being—then peace, joy, love and well-being is what we naturally project outward and, consequently, these positive states of mind bring us positive experiences. … And the negative also holds true" (Truman 2003, 4).

It's important that we discuss the meaning of our different emotions and what they are communicating at a deeper level.

Happiness

Happiness is an emotion that emerges when we understand, identify and express our various emotions. Happiness emerges when we take the steps to emotional healing and come to know and love ourselves. You might be surprised to learn that those who have learned to be happy are often the ones who have suffered the most. Happiness is an emotion that can come about only when we decide we want to be happy. It comes when we decide to focus on what is going right in our lives as opposed to what is wrong. When we are happy, we attain our greatest wisdom. When we smile a genuine smile, we are bringing our happiness forward and sharing it with others.

Fear and anger

"All painful emotions are expressions of fear" (Zukav and Francis 2001, 116).

Gary Zukav and Linda Francis state that underneath anger lies pain and underneath pain lies fear. They explain that anger is the fear of believing that we are not capable or worthy of being understood. In other words, at the core of anger is lack of self-worth and the belief that we won't be alright, that our needs won't be met, that we will experience future pain. In fact, lack of self-worth is at the root of all emotional pain. We are afraid that others will not understand us or love us; we are afraid of commitment; we are afraid of attaining success; we are afraid that we are going to age badly or be sick; we are afraid that we won't have enough money, just to give a few examples.

"All judgment, hatred, jealousy, and fear stem from people not realizing their true greatness. Lacking awareness of our perfection keeps us feeling small and insignificant, and this goes against the natural flow of life-force energy—that which we really are. We go against ourselves" (Moorjani 2012, 140).

The only fears we are born with are a fear of falling and a fear of noises. All other fears are given to us by the adults who raise or influence us. *Our fears emerge when we are not nourished by our relationships. The way to lessen our fears is to experience the love and understanding we missed out on as children.* The more connected we become to ourselves and others, the more we feel we belong and the safer we feel. When we feel safe, fear doesn't arise.

"Newborn infants, because they have no past, lack all defenses; a baby is completely vulnerable to any intruder or harmful influence, utterly dependent upon outside protection to survive. Yet, paradoxically, no one is more invulnerable than a newborn child, because it has no fear" (Chopra 1997, 110).

When fear is expressed unhealthily, we recognize it as rage, abuse, violence, selfishness, corruption, addiction or obsession. When fear is repressed, we recognize it as resentment, apathy, depression or illness. When fear is misdirected, we recognize it as judgment or criticism against others. When fear is diverted, we recognize it as suffering or martyrdom. When we think of angry people, we would never imagine that they are actually scared, but it is certainly easier to be angry than to allow ourselves to appear scared. The more hostile a person is, the more scared they really are inside. And when we create enemies, we have a false sense of control, which makes us feel as though we are doing something about a problem, which in turn makes us feel superior and as if we are right when, really, we are only temporarily reducing our fears.

Anger can only arise when we are responding to people or situations that are important to us. Our anger arises because we are being protective or defensive. We only protect or defend the things that are important to us. It is vital for us to pay attention to those people or situations that trigger us because they point to the aspects of our lives where healing is needed.

Therefore, people who are angry "are actually deeply caring people, because anger always runs in direct proportion to concern. ... They are feeling too much of the world for their comfort and their boundaries are in tatters. Their hearts are usually in pain because they don't know how to address their profound concerns in healthier ways" (McLaren 2010, 180).

"Feeling our sadness and fear is actually more difficult than exploding in anger, yet it's essential. … We must see with total clarity that what is not love is fear. And we must understand that every negative emotion therefore derives from fear. When we allow ourselves to feel the fear and sadness that lie behind our anger, our judgments undergo an extraordinary transformation, and our fury turns into compassion. This is an important issue if we really want to change the world" (Williamson 2002, 93–94).

Anger and fear are only problems when we do not identify, understand or express them, when we express them inappropriately or when we don't take responsibility for them. For example, when we hold in our anger, it can find an outlet in depression. When we don't explore our fear, it can result in anxiety. Unresolved anger can result in irritability. When we become aware of our underlying fear, we know that our thoughts are racing, that our body feels tight and agitated and that we feel compelled to run away. Often the first emotions that arise when we begin healing from our distractions, addictions or avoidance behaviours are anger and fear. When we can express our negative emotions healthily, we know true healing has begun.

There is, of course, a positive aspect of anger: Anger arises because we are defending our personal integrity when we are not being treated the way we want to be treated. It also arises when we feel misunderstood or when our needs are not being met. Anger always means that something in our lives needs to change. When we stand up for ourselves, we are honouring our anger, which helps us meet our needs and rediscover our individuality and strength. Assertiveness is the healthy expression of anger. When we hold onto our anger, we don't know how to defend ourselves and can end up being mistreated by others.

The positive aspect of fear is that when used properly, fear makes us instinctual, focused and able to respond effectively to our environment. Fear is the intelligence that takes over our bodies, minds and emotions when we're driving slowly in a snowstorm, checking our mirrors, easing out of the way of struggling cars, fully concentrating on the road and remaining safe. There is another important positive aspect of fear: Whatever we are most afraid of doing but think of regularly is what we need to be doing; that is how we extinguish our greatest fears. (For more on facing our fears, please see Chapter Five.) Have you heard it said that if you are not scared of the dreams you have for yourself, they are not big enough? A minor example of this is being afraid that someone is going to call us and that we are not going to like what they have to say. It is when we face our fear and call them that we can say goodbye to our fear of the unknown.

Because fear and anger are the most commonly felt and are usually behind all other "negative emotions", I placed a lot of emphasis on explaining them. Now I will briefly explain the meaning behind other "negative" emotions.

Apathy

Apathy prevents us from moving through our emotions because it is the attitude of "I don't care." Many teenagers adopt this emotion because they are close to being ready to live their own lives yet they remain controlled by parents and schools. All they can do is get through each day until time sets them free. This is one of the reasons why so many teens are bored and end up watching too much television or spending too much time on the computer. Apathy often masks the anger within.

To end apathy, our true emotions need to be identified or expressed. Are we angry, tired or depressed? What are we trying to avoid? What are we truly feeling?

Sadness

Sadness stems from unmet needs. Unexpressed sadness or anger can result in depression. Sadness helps us determine what we need to release in order to relax and let go of things that don't serve us. If we honour the loss of a friendship, for example, by feeling it fully and then recognizing some of the positives that stem from the loss of that relationship, we can move forward with ease. If we fight the loss or refuse to let go of a friendship that no longer makes us happy, we cannot move forward with ease.

Shame

Shame is the emotion that arises when we are disappointed with ourselves or feel unworthy. Shame can help us start listening to our inner voice and restore our boundaries when we have broken them. When we are ashamed about lying to someone, we can beat ourselves up for doing it or we can determine why we felt the need to lie and change things so that we don't lie to that person again or feel the shame for doing so. Did we think that the person we lied to would judge or dislike us? If so, do we need to set boundaries or limits with that person so that we can be ourselves with them? Do we need to become more accepting of ourselves so that we no longer feel the need to lie about ourselves? (Please see Chapter Five to learn more about setting boundaries.)

Confusion

Confusion occurs when we are not following our instincts or when we are succumbing to our fears. If we set intentions and goals, all confusion ends. If we stay in a relationship that doesn't work for us, we often find ourselves behaving in ways that are not congruent with our real selves, and confusion ensues. We can set a goal of working on coming to loving ourselves and set a date for say, six months from now, to re-evaluate whether our relationship is meeting our needs by then. We should find that our confusion ends.

Grief

We grieve the loss of relationships whether they end because of time, distance, inner growth or death. We grieve the loss of a job, a home, a way of life and all sorts of things. We need to grieve our losses. When we do not allow ourselves to feel the pain and loss, we become traumatized by death or loss each and every time we witness it. The greatest grief is for the parenting we wanted and didn't receive. (Please see Chapter Four for more on grieving.)

Guilt

"[W]hen we're inspired, we're totally engaged in the now. ... All guilt and regret simply serve as ways to avoid being here in the only moment we have, which is now" (Dyer 2006, 32).

Guilt comes about when we feel we have disappointed others. We can feel this way when we don't listen to our inner voice of wisdom. Guilt is a *bad* thing when we are regretting our past or thinking about what we should have done or said. When we feel guilty, we expect punishment. This will cause us to attract people and situations that validate our unresolved guilt. To overcome guilt, we need to take responsibility. Guilt is a *good* thing when it ends our procrastination. Guilt is a *good* thing when we look back to times in which we were misguided and change the way we handle things in future.

"If you don't feel the guilt, how will you ever reach your motivation to make amends? If you don't feel the self-loathing, how will you ever reach the motivation to act more responsibly next time? If you avoid the pain, you'll miss the gain. Just suppressing the monsters only makes them larger. Allowing them out—and facing them—is the only way to make sure that they will ever go away" (Williamson 2008, 57).

The bottom line is this: If we are not happy with how we feel physically or emotionally or we are not happy with any aspect of our lives, it is our feelings and our resulting thoughts and beliefs that need to be addressed. We cannot listen to others telling us how to feel or how to be.

Exercise

Goodbye Mother, Hello Woman (Boynton, Boynton and Dell 1995) provides an excellent exercise for helping you come to understand your feelings and where they came from. Simply respond to the following statements and questions:

- I feel sad when …
- I feel guilty when …
- I feel angry when …
- I feel pleasure when …
- I feel happy when …
- I can trust when …
- I feel pain when …

Reflecting

Think back to your childhood. Recall what feelings were discouraged in your family.

- What feelings were allowed?
- What was the most pervasive feeling coming from your mother (or father)?
- What was the most pervasive feeling felt by you as a young (child)?
- What feelings are you allowed today?
- What feelings would you like to change?
- What feelings would you like to feel? (p 70)

Feeling Our Feelings and Emotions

It is important that we witness our feelings and emotions. Emotions are thoughts that we feel in our physical bodies. Our negative thoughts tend to trigger uncomfortable bodily sensations such as pain or tightness in our chest, neck, stomach or other area. If we allow ourselves to feel the sensation, we find that the charge of our emotion slowly dissipates.

Expressing Our Feelings and Emotions When We Are Alone

Ideally, emotions pass through us naturally. We will have times of bliss and times of sadness or anger. The idea is for us to encourage our emotions by letting them flow and nurture them by recognizing and expressing them. When we express our emotions, we release them from our bodies. And sometimes, expressing our feelings helps us accept them more fully.

When we are young children, we release our emotions naturally and immediately. We cry, yell, state our feelings, stamp our feet, hit something or someone or have a tantrum, to give some examples. (By the way, hitting someone is the only unhealthy example here of how a child might express emotions.) When we get a bit older, we are often taught to keep our emotions under control. When we are teenagers, we feel more intensely than at any other time in our lives and selfhood is a major theme. It is no coincidence that many teenagers choose this time to express themselves. Certainly, when teens blame their parents for everything that has gone wrong in their lives, it is a healthy stage of their development, because their anger separates them from their parents and helps them find their own identities. ***Wouldn't it be wonderful if teens were taught to honour their negative feelings for the healing forces that they are and encouraged to express themselves in a healthy manner?*** Then, teens could convert their blame into taking responsibility for themselves.

How do we feel and express our emotions in a healthy manner? When we feel a negative emotion, such as sadness, the idea is to recognize that we are feeling sadness, welcome it with patience and curiosity, feel it overtake our body and let our tears fall for as long as we want. We don't need to do anything else with our sadness until we are ready; we simply need to stay in the moment. No one can tell us when we will be ready to take the next step. We now know that if we distract ourselves from feeling the sadness or push the feeling away, it will not really go away. Each time we have a full emotional release, our minds and bodies are cleansed. Most of us have felt the relief that comes when we finally say something we have wanted to say for a long time. When we feel that we have fully felt all the sadness and our tears no longer fall, the next step is to determine why the feeling came to visit us and what wisdom it has to share with us. What is behind our sadness? Is it a recent unmet need or one from our distant past? What can we do to meet that need? If we determine the answer to that and then take an action step toward meeting that need, we start to view our sadness differently. This is how we work through each painful experience. Our sadness remains a negative emotion only if we can't turn it into a positive, but each of us has the possibility of turning sadness into happiness; some of us just need to be reminded of that. (For a more detailed explanation of healing from each experience, please see Chapter Four.)

Remember, every emotion is essential to our well-being, and emotions need to be in motion for there to be health and healing. When *we* honour our feelings, others honour our feelings. Many of us are taught that expressing our emotions is a sign of weakness, but I hope you are seeing that it is, in fact, a sign of strength.

Expressing Our Feelings and Emotions to Others

"The most difficult language to communicate is the language of feelings. One of our greatest challenges as human beings is to effectively communicate with other people what we truly feel. Perhaps the most significant and consequential challenge we face, however, is acquiring the ability to communicate congruently with ourselves" (Truman 2003, 1).

We need to express our feelings and emotions to those who can help us and we need to express ourselves to those who hurt us. Obviously, it is far easier to express our emotions when what we are saying is being well received. If someone we trust is asking us about our feelings and is interested in discussing our feelings with us, we can uncover our conscious and subconscious feelings with them. This person could be a friend, family member, therapist, counsellor or life coach. A professional is usually well educated in helping us express ourselves truthfully and congruently with the person we are deep inside. Some professionals have specific techniques for uncovering our subconscious feelings.

When we are expressing ourselves to those who hurt us, it is important that we wait until we feel centred. It is also important to choose the right time to express our emotions; we cannot express our emotions to someone who is exhausted, stressed out or experiencing acute pain themselves and expect that our feelings will be well received. If our conversation doesn't go well, we want to know that it wasn't because of bad timing, which is something that is within our control. (For more information on expressing ourselves to those who hurt us, please see Chapters Four and Six.)

 "A conscious person is a feeling person, one who is aware of what is going on outside and inside. The more congruent we are, the more our inside matches our outside, the more real and emotionally fit we are" (Berger 2000, 16).

The more we trust our own healing capacity, the more we notice it helping us and the more often we find ourselves making wiser choices. ***It takes courage to***

tell the truth about how we feel and to expose our hurt and fear because we don't know how it will be received, but when we do, we give permission to others to do the same. And when both parties are authentic, compassion and intimacy enter our relationships, and we are deeply rewarded.

(Please see Chapter Four to learn of the many ways to express and release our negative emotions in a healthy manner.)

Changing Our Thoughts, Changes Our Beliefs and Behaviour Patterns

To paraphrase James Allen (1902), all that you achieve and all that you fail to achieve is the direct result of your own thoughts.

If we hold a thought long enough and repeat it often enough, that thought becomes a belief. Many of the thoughts or beliefs that guide us are not even true; they are illusions of the mind. Most beliefs and rules are formed in response to needs; they are generated by parental, cultural and peer expectations and by our need to feel loved, to belong, to feel safe and to feel good about ourselves. You read earlier how beliefs and belief patterns get started in our childhoods, when our perspective is extremely limited, to say the least. One incorrect perception can lead to another and another until our perceptions of ourselves are completely off base. We feel inferior to everyone else because we have been taught to think and feel that way. When we are constantly corrected as children, we begin to think that we are always wrong and that everyone is superior to us. Here are some other incorrect beliefs: Life is too hard. No one can be trusted. I need to be perfect. I shouldn't disappoint anyone. I am not good enough.

When we experience emotional pain, it is often because we are looking at something incorrectly or we are being told that we made a mistake. When we desire to improve the way we feel or certain aspects of our lives, we need to become the master of our thoughts and feelings, instead of allowing them to control us. Every undesirable feeling can be converted into a desirable one. ***There is always one viewpoint in any situation that brings us true peace.*** When we find that new viewpoint, our confidence is restored and we can move forward to a whole new level of success.

Our beliefs determine our reality. To begin the process of inner healing, as adults, we start by changing some of our thoughts or beliefs. By changing our thoughts or beliefs, we change our feelings and our experience of life. We each suffer according to the amount and severity of negative beliefs that we hold for ourselves. We can choose to believe in anything, and that includes believing in ourselves. Until we do this, our pain will endure.

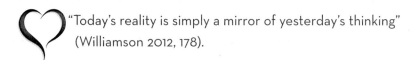 "Today's reality is simply a mirror of yesterday's thinking" (Williamson 2012, 178).

Sometimes though, our negative feelings are so strong that we will not allow new thoughts to come to mind. That is when we need to resolve our feelings. We change both our thoughts and feelings by learning different perspectives from others. We can also learn about those perspectives from self-help books, by meditating, by taking the right homeopathic or flower remedy or essential oil (See Chapter Ten for more information) or by raising our own children. Changing our thoughts and feelings can happen instantly or can take time.

Let me give you two examples of changing our thoughts and, subsequently, our response or behaviour. When my daughter Paige was eleven years old, she played baseball for the fourth year in a row with her dad as her coach. She was one of two girls on the team and one of the few girls in the league. I could count on one hand the number of games her team had lost in the four years. It was the final inning of the final weekend's tournament game. Paige decided to try to steal third base. A player on the opposing team just missed tagging her, but nonetheless announced that she was out. The umpire called the out and the game ended. Her team had lost by five runs. Tears fell down Paige's face as she walked off the field. In her face, I could read her utter disappointment in the unfairness of it all and the fact that her team had lost on the final weekend. I felt her question her skill and her ability to discern what was fair and what was not. Once she was back at the bench, I walked over and told her that we all knew it was an unfair call. She nodded but said nothing. A short while later I watched as her dad awarded each team member their trophy for being the league champions, reminding the kids that this was simply an end-of-season tournament. I watched Paige start goofing around with her teammates, making jokes and eating watermelon.

Within half an hour or so, I was astonished to see that Paige was just fine. As we walked home, I asked her what she had done to turn her feelings around from pure devastation and sadness to feelings of contentment. She seemed surprised by my question. She thought for a moment and then said, "I remembered how well I had played all game and all season and felt proud of the job I had done." That's it. She could have taken her negative feelings about what happened and turned them into a belief that she wasn't a good ball player, that she should have made it to third base faster, that her opponent didn't tell the truth, that the world was not fair. But no, this girl's self-esteem was healthy. This girl wasn't going to let circumstances change who she was. Paige perfectly demonstrated how to turn negative feelings into positive thought patterns and peace within.

Serendipitously, a few minute later we walked past a girl in a soccer uniform crying. I looked at Paige and said, "I guess she just needs a new way to look at things."

Paige happily responded, "Yup!"

Now I will give you an example of what happens when we project our incorrect negative thoughts on others and what happens when we then change those thoughts.

I had a family member who was always fighting with me and seemingly seeing me in a bad light. This had gone on for years. When he and I were together, I felt anger and fear. One day, a friend who had witnessed him and me together told me that he liked me (new information or perspective). I couldn't have been more flabbergasted. How could this be? He was always angry with me and telling me what he didn't like about my personality or my behaviour. I realized that I liked him too (new thought); I just didn't always like his behaviour and I was always afraid he would get angry at me, because that was usually what happened. Once I realized that I liked him and truly enjoyed being with him when we were getting along, I handled things differently the next time he got angry with me. He was carrying on about what I had done to anger him, and I responded by saying, "Why are you always so angry with me? I love you. I don't want these challenges anymore with us" (new feelings and therefore new response on my part). You should have seen the shock on his face! He didn't say anything about my words, but we stopped arguing.

A few months passed and he called our home to speak to another family member. I answered, and while we were waiting for the other person to come to the phone, he said, "You know, Meredith, the reason I fight with you all the time is really because I like you" (new response on his part). I don't know why this dynamic happens with people but it does! Years later, he and his wife split up and he needed a place to live for a while. No one would let him live with them, not even his mother. When I meditated on whether it would be right for him to live with us, I heard the words "Show them the way." A few days later, he called our home and I offered for him to come live with us. He replied, "You, of all people, would allow me to come live with you? After the relationship we have had?" He lived with us for the better part of a year and that is when we truly came to understand one another. My feelings for him were anger and fear for over two decades. My feelings for him now are pure love and understanding.

What this example also shows us is that our thoughts, feelings and belief systems draw situations into our lives that automatically validate those belief systems. I thought this family member disliked me and I was angry with and fearful of him. My negative belief system attracted negative circumstances. But by changing my belief system, I attracted a good friend into my life.

"We can change our thoughts and this can change our feelings and our actions. However … if our thoughts are caused by unresolved, deep-seated feelings that are governing our existence, the thoughts will reoccur time and time again until we resolve the core feeling" (Truman 2003, 77).

I have known people who have spent decades believing they were unlovable, not smart or undeserving. I have observed how their lives have gone when those were their core beliefs, forming their personalities; they were lonely, didn't make good decisions for themselves and kept having bad things happen in their lives. We already discussed that our beliefs tend to become self-fulfilling prophecies. In each case, I observed what happened when some of these individuals were told by someone they trusted that they were lovable, smart and deserving. The improvement in their lives and in their belief in themselves was miraculous. We are all lovable, smart and deserving; it is only ever our belief in ourselves that is lacking.

Any belief that contradicts our innate greatness needs to be addressed if we want to meet our needs. When we catch ourselves having a belief of this kind, we can ask our belief what it wants. It may think it needs to protect us from disappointment or pain, as it might have done in the past. But each belief wants to be great and feel great. We just need to get out of its way! We simply need to change our limiting belief to an abundant belief that matches whatever we desire.

Exercise

Bob Gottfried offers a useful approach when you get frustrated or disappointed about things you cannot change (2004, 230). These steps are also helpful in *dealing with recurring thoughts or behaviours you want to let go of:*

1. Become aware of an unwanted emotion or thought pattern and observe it for a while.
2. Say with great determination "Stop."

3. Take a deep breath in and confirm "I am letting go of (state the feeling or thought pattern)."
4. Proclaim, "I choose peace instead."
5. Do a few moments of deep breathing for reinforcement.
6. Assume the observer position again and notice what you feel.
7. Keep breathing deeply until the thought or feeling subsides.
8. Repeat the process whenever the unwanted feeling or thinking pattern recurs.

How We Handle Our Feelings and Emotions Once We Have Forgiven Ourselves

We are free only after we decide that we no longer want to suffer, that we no longer want to bear a burden that we need not bear. It means deciding that we want to enjoy our life and be happy, no matter what happens. This can only occur once we have forgiven ourselves. (See Chapter Four for an exact description on how to accomplish this seemingly monumental task.)

When we are in this peaceful place, some believe that we never experience negative emotions or pain. They are wrong. We are still human, and as long as we are human, we will feel pain. However, once we have forgiven ourselves and others, we can observe ourselves as if from a distance. We simply allow the pain or negative emotions to come up and then pass through; we no longer get lost in our emotions. The time it takes us to process our emotions becomes less and less the more we forgive ourselves.

You already learned that we are not our emotions; they are just what we feel or experience. We are also not our mind or its thoughts; thinking is something we can watch the mind do. The more attention we give our mind, the faster and longer it will run. We are the ones in control of our mind. We need to remind our minds that we are in control. We can do that by changing a thought or belief or by using affirmations, visualization or meditation, to give a few examples, all of which are discussed later on.

 "The minute you are not afraid of the pain, you'll be able to face all of life's situations without fear. ... [T]his is the core of [our] work. When you are comfortable with pain passing through you, you will be free. ... [I]f you do not care, if you are no longer afraid of yourself, you are free" (Singer 2007, 106).

Once we can just witness and stand apart from our emotions, thoughts and even moods without being overtaken by them, our biggest challenges are over. We can then use our conscience and independent will in entirely new ways. We can literally transcend our past and negative stories. This means that when we are with others who used to push our buttons, they will no longer upset us. We will observe their behaviour and listen to what they are saying but not take anything personally, for we will know that nothing they do or say has anything to do with us. And we will know that they have decided to stay in their stories for now and that there is nothing we can do to wrench them away at this time. With that knowledge, we can feel immense pride in ourselves.

Exercise

This exercise summarizes the steps discussed in this chapter and will help you see yourself clearly:

1. Do you see yourself as a victim? Are you sharing a sad story of your life with others? Make a list of the people or incidents that hurt you. Put an asterisk beside the one that bothers you the most; that may be the one you work with first.

2. Make a list of the negative feelings you experience when you think of those people or incidents.

3. List the ways in which you have suffered as a result of these people or incidents. Become aware of the unhealthy patterns you have adopted as a result. (See Chapter One and Chapter Two for options.)

4. Make a list of the ways in which you contributed to each challenging relationship or event, if applicable i.e. take responsibility.

5. List the positives gleaned and the lessons you learned from each negative occurrence.

6. Determine how you want to express your negative emotions in a healthy way.

7. Determine how you want to reframe your story.

8. Determine which feelings, thoughts and behaviours you want to change in order to experience more peace in your life.

Four

Tools for Releasing and Healing Our Pain

Managing our pain is a vital skill. All of the craziness in our world comes from individuals trying to escape their pain and suffering. Individuals drink themselves into oblivion, hit their partners and children, gamble, cut themselves and even kill themselves because they have unprocessed pain.

There is another way. We need to learn to sit with our pain, listen to it for messages about our lives, process it and release it rather than run from it. By learning to write about our pain, talk about it and express it through exercise, art, dance or music, for example, we find predictable and positive ways to calm ourselves.

The Healing Process: Six Steps to Integration

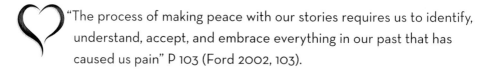

"The process of making peace with our stories requires us to identify, understand, accept, and embrace everything in our past that has caused us pain" P 103 (Ford 2002, 103).

If we allow our stories to make us feel unimportant and powerless, how can we ever feel worthy enough to live the life of our dreams? If we continue to feel bad about our stories, fail to see the gifts that they hold for us and refuse to forgive others, as well as ourselves, we cannot move beyond our stories and end our unhealthy patterns. When we follow the steps to healing, we integrate our stories (the unprocessed events of our past) with our current life. Then, our stories no longer use us; instead, we use them to create a new story, with new beliefs and better outcomes.

The qualities that arise from our pain are vital to our lives and to those who are part of our lives. Once we come to a place of peace with our stories, we can move beyond them and our love for ourselves only grows. That is when freedom sets in and we can fulfill our deepest desires. Then and only then can we use our pain and struggles from our past to make our unique contribution to the world. *When we are able to use all that we know and all that we have been and all that we are (the positives and the negatives), that is when we know we have integrated our stories and are now living our true purpose.*

There is a process each of us can follow in order to heal from our past. The process is the same whether we want to heal from a painful incident or accept a part of ourselves that we don't like or suffer from depression or any illness or feel unworthy in general. Usually, we work on healing the most traumatic events first and then the secondary traumas. After that, the less significant issues seem to just fall away. Here are the steps to healing our pain:

1. Uncover the incident, issue or emotional wound that is causing us pain and become aware of how it makes us feel emotionally and physically. Unfortunately, avoiding, distracting and disassociating ourselves from the trauma of our past is a way of life for the majority of people. It is only by uncovering and clearing the root cause of our unhealthy patterns that we can release its influence on our lives and start living the lives we want to live. In other words, we need to understand and clear our past before we can move on. We start by sitting in silence and taking a number of deep breaths until we reach a very relaxed state. Then we ask ourselves "Which incident from my past is still causing me pain, regret or anger?" Some of us are so filled with thoughts or worries that we cannot arrive at an answer. If that is the case, there are techniques that coaches or professionals can use to access the memories that are needed. You can refer to Chapter Two for insight into what areas are out of balance in your body to determine a starting point. When I went through the process with one client, she had boils all over her skin, which she knew were caused from anger boiling inside of her. I asked her what was making her so angry. Her immediate answer to the question was, "The relationships I had with the men that I dated or lived with." Now, this doesn't go back to her childhood but we can be sure there is a connection. She then discussed how frustrated, angry, tired, sad, bitter and lonely she felt when she reflected on each of these relationships. She also admitted how scared she was to enter a future relationship with a man. It's important to really feel the pain caused by our wounds (of loss, hurt,

insecurity, etc.) until its intensity lessens and we are no longer triggered by particular people or events.

2. Then we make a list of all of our beliefs, behaviours and recurring patterns that came about from the incidents that we recall. ***The meaning that we assign to the events of our lives causes our emotional pain, not the events themselves.*** My client told me that she felt unimportant as a result of her relationships with men, which resulted in low self-esteem, which made her not exercise, eat well or look into her health and often made her feel tired and unmotivated. She talked about allowing the men's needs to come before her own and those of her child. She said that she had allowed herself to be immersed in their negativity and lies even though that was not who she was. She talked about the lack of trust she now had in men (lots of negatives). For this woman, the recurring patterns were her unhealthy relationships with men and her lack of love for herself.

3. Next we look at what it is we are getting out of holding onto these incidents from the past and begin to take responsibility for our part. What choices did we make that put us in unhealthy situations? My client said, "I always chose men who needed my help, instead of choosing men with whom I could share a true partnership; it always made me feel so good to help them and to be the first person they could depend on. I chose overweight and unattractive men, hoping they wouldn't be desired by other women and therefore would remain loyal to me. Because of those choices, I am able to hold onto my belief that you can't really count on anyone and that I really am not important" (incorrect beliefs but a means of protecting oneself in the short term). Because her belief was that she couldn't trust her boyfriends, they did cheat on her. Because she didn't love herself, she didn't believe she deserved intimacy or a true partnership with an emotionally healthy man. When we become aware of the beliefs we have about ourselves and others, we can see the recurring themes in our lives that result from those beliefs.

4. Then we need to think about and write down all of the times that we contributed to similar happenings in our lives. This means looking at the choices we made. My client found that even in some of her other relationships, she felt she was unimportant and thought that others wouldn't be there for her. Her father left her at a young age and the

rest of her family didn't see her as important (connection to childhood—I told you there would be one!). They had favoured her younger sibling, always bending over backward for her but not for my client. My client perpetually put others' needs before her own and had the hardest time saying no to anyone.

5. We need to look at the positives and negatives that came from these incidents and determine the lessons or the gifts that came from the pain. Sometimes, we need help with this step. I was able to discuss the fact that my client's beliefs about being unimportant and unable to count on others were not always correct, citing various examples based on what I knew about her life. When she realized that her decision to help men who were suffering in their lives was creating pain and challenges in her own life, she understood her role in what had gone wrong and where it had stemmed from. She no longer wondered why certain things happened to her (a huge positive). In terms of the gifts that came from her pain and how those gifts were serving her in her life, my client learned to become very sensitive to the needs of others and is adept at showing others how important they are: her child, those she works with and everyone she comes into contact with are the recipients of these incredible gifts. Her commitment to others is one of the aspects of herself that she loves the most.

6. We need to close our eyes, look inside and ask ourselves what needs to happen in order to heal from and let go of the incidents that hurt us. Numerous suggestions on how to do this are included in this chapter. My client wrote a letter to her last boyfriend, who had lived with her, explaining her role in the demise of their relationship and apologizing for her part in what went wrong, making sure he knew that this letter was not an attempt to reconcile. He called her after reading the letter and apologized for his part in what went wrong. Not everyone has a perfect outcome like this, but healing can occur in any number of ways, as you will see. My client also started being more sensitive to her own needs and began to nurture herself for the first time in her life, gradually increasing her importance in her own eyes.

Each of us can look back at our lives and find the common challenges that have repeated themselves. We can ask ourselves what lessons those challenges were trying to teach us, what we have to do to fully learn those lessons and what we have to change in our thinking or let go of in order to transcend our challenges. Then, once we have completed our learning, we can watch as our lives change in a beautiful way.

Using the Healing Steps to Recover from a Death

We can use the healing steps to recover from the death or loss of a relationship, a job or a way of life. It is important to mourn any loss we undergo so that we avoid emotional pitfalls later in life, but we are not meant to mourn forever. I would like to describe to you how we can recover from loss by sharing the process I underwent when my brother died.

Once I got over the shock of Jay's death, I began to regularly and purposely recall the aspects of his death that were most painful to me. Those aspects were saying goodbye to him for the last time, imagining his actual death (I knew the circumstances, location, timing, etc.), the police coming to my home to tell us that he had died, telling my parents that their son was dead and imagining how his dead body had looked based on what my family told me (I couldn't bear to see his body). I felt the powerful emotions and pain over and over again with each memory.

I now know that certain aspects of traumatic flashbacks can heal us, and you now know that the most powerful step we can take toward healing is to feel and move through the feelings that have held us hostage. Some of us cry for a week; some of us lie in our beds unable to function; some of us writhe in pain at the helplessness we feel. It is vital that we let ourselves feel whatever comes up for us and that we have compassion for ourselves. When we are looking back, we know we have already survived the trauma, which already improves our perspective on the actual event.

When I had these traumatic flashbacks, I found myself crying, yelling and speaking out loud to my brother and to those who had raised us. Over and over, I listened and sang along to a recording of Josh Groban, singing "You Raise Me Up", which was played at the family memorial after Jay's funeral. I released the pain as much and in as many ways as I could, until it wasn't as sharp. Initially, I went over the memories daily. Eventually I could go months and then years without remembering specific aspects. Without realizing it, I wore the dark colours of mourning over the course of the next three years.

Five years after his death, I visited a naturopath, who asked me to tell her the worst thing that had ever happened to me. I told her that it was my brother dying. After asking me a series of questions, she determined that I had not got over his death. I had made some progress with my own work but had not got all the way there. She prescribed a homeopathic remedy for grief called Iamara. (To learn more about how homeopathic remedies help us move through our emotions faster and easier, please see Chapter Ten.) She told me to take two pellets when I had a considerable amount of time to be with myself. Then she asked me to journal the ways in which Jay's life had positively impacted me and the lessons his death had taught me. Being very sensitive to homeopathic remedies, I began crying within minutes of taking the remedy and then continued throughout the journaling process. The whole process was completely cathartic for me. It wasn't long afterward that my suffering over Jay's death came to an end.

Suffering ceases to be suffering once we have formed a clear picture of it in our minds. I think back to the incidents surrounding his death that were so painful for me and I find they are no longer so. Do I still miss Jay like crazy? You'd better believe it. Did writing our story for this book help me come to terms with Jay's death even further, even though it has now been over a decade since his death? One hundred percent.

Using the Healing Steps to Let Go of Aspects of Ourselves We No Longer Need

 "This is often how it works, you have a quality which has a gift for you. You call on the gift to help get something you want in life. Then because this aspect of yourself is not fully integrated into your psyche and because you've made some negative judgment about it, it takes on a life of its own, acting out in inappropriate ways. Until we embrace the qualities from which we've disassociated ourselves, they will continue to act up until their needs are met. Remember, what you resist persists" (Ford 1998, 102).

I'd like to give you examples of letting go of aspects of ourselves that no longer serve us. We might want to let go of controlling others, keeping our houses obsessively clean, responding dramatically or trying so hard at aspects of our lives that are not working for us. It is human nature to feel bad about these parts of ourselves, think about them as negative or dark, or feel ashamed of our "weaknesses". But if we resist or defend the dark parts of ourselves, they persist. Every part of us plays an important role. As soon as we accept and use these parts of ourselves rather than let them use us, and as soon as we have compassion for them, each part of us becomes a gift. We turn potentially unhealthy parts of ourselves into healthy parts.

I decided I was going to let go of pleasing others and always trying to prove my value. So first, I needed to look at why this pattern began. As a child, I felt that I was not loved for who I was and that I was not important in the eyes of others. Was that true? No. But when your mother doesn't want you, this is how you feel. When the people that raise you hit you and hurl emotional abuse your way, this is how you feel. I didn't know at the time that my mother simply didn't feel equipped to raise her children on her own and that she did not have the parenting instinct. I did not know what had happened to my nanny and step-mother and that they were still very much in pain from how they had been raised. I just knew that if I tried to be perfect, I might make them happy, and they, in turn, would give me the love I wanted so badly. I transferred this belief onto other people in my life as well. How did wanting to please others and prove myself serve me? How did this supposed weakness play an important role in my life? The answer is profound. I believe that being this way actually saved my life. If I had not been so ambitious, gone to university and then climbed the corporate ladder for ten years, I might have gone the route my brother did, got into drugs and left this earth far too early. And my corporate work made great improvements in the companies for which I worked.

By realizing the positives of the aspects of myself that I did not like, I embraced them. You now know that we cannot move beyond our past and forge a new destiny, unless we accept or embrace our past and then let it go. Eventually, I reached a point in my life where I learned how to meet my own needs and come to love myself. I no longer felt the need to seek external rewards, such as promotions and an increased salary, or work so hard to please others. *I knew I was enough, and if others didn't see that, then I knew I was hanging out with the wrong people.*

Friends used to ask me what I had planned for the day or the week and, wanting to seem extra important and busy, I would proceed to list all the things I would be doing. I really did have those plans but I wanted to drop the need for all my plans and the need to impress others with them; it was all very exhausting and I was ready to feel peace within. So I began trying to simplify my life, spending more and more time doing what I wanted and loved doing rather than what I felt I should do. The fact that I was eventually able to do this showed me that I had let go of pleasing others. In the same week, I heard two men talking. One said "It's sad how people discourage one another from relaxing and give each other such a hard time for doing it."

Exercise

Create a list of the parts of yourself that you see as weak or dark. Then find the gifts in each aspect of yourself. Elaborate.

Using the Healing Steps to Accept Parts of Ourselves We Don't Like

How do we accept a part of ourselves that we don't like? We look at all the parts of ourselves that we do like and appreciate them. We recognize that we cannot be all things and that each of us has our own unique talents.

My stepmother is the most incredible cook. She uses organic foods and home-grown herbs and spices and tries new dishes all the time. Everything always seems to turn out beautifully. I did not learn these skills from her. As you know from reading my story, I never took to cooking. After I gave birth to two girls who needed me to cook for them, I learned to cook simple, fast meals for them and serve lots of raw vegetables. It took me years to be able to admit to others that I really wasn't a great cook and that I would rather be writing. I remember when I finally admitted this to my parents when they came for a visit; it was such a relief for me to say it out loud. Then I became a nutritionist and, of course, was asked to offer cooking classes. I simply explained that there are far better cooks than me, still feeling a little guilty that I was not adept at cooking, even though I was a nutritionist. I explained how simply I cook and my feelings about that to a fellow nutritionist, even mentioning some of the healthy meals that I purchase. She reminded me that lots of people don't love to cook and are looking for simple and healthy meal ideas for their families. Now I share my simple and healthy meal ideas with others and even included them in my first book, *The Resourceful Mother's Secrets to Healthy Kids*. I am completely comfortable with the fact that I am a nutritionist with talents other than cooking.

Using the Healing Steps to Accept Aspects of Our Lives That Are Not the Way We Want Them to Be

When I first separated from my husband, there were many aspects of my life that didn't go the way I wanted them to. I missed my children badly. I had raised them almost single-handedly and being without them for any length of time was next to impossible for me. I struggled with it for over a year, particularly when my girls were having so many challenges with their dad. One day, I decided I had better start seeing the positives in the situation. I thought of how wonderful it was that they were finally spending more time with their dad and imagined their relationship strengthening; I became grateful for that. I thought of the parents who were working full-time and making lunches, dealing with their children's challenges and struggling to get their kids to school and activities on time. I thought of all the parents who were not meeting their own needs because they were always meeting the needs of their children. I then felt very blessed to have been given a reprieve from the hardships of raising children and to have the chance to rejuvenate a few days a month so that I could be better for Taylor and Paige each time I got to be with them. Every day, I felt overwhelming gratitude for this time on my own at this stage in the parenting process. I had embraced my challenge. Then, lo and behold, didn't my eldest come home one time and tell me that she didn't want to spend as much time with her dad anymore? I only had to go just over a year without one of my daughters being with me the majority of time.

I used this method to embrace all the aspects of my life that were not working for me. One by one, the challenges began to disappear, because I was focusing on the positives and funnelling my energy there, as opposed to the negatives.

There are so many ways that we can heal. There are so many tools to help us. Each individual can decide what they feel comfortable doing and when. Deciding to use any of these tools means that you are making the decision to leave the past behind, which is simply *huge*. Every tool that you put to use will help you regain your inner strength. Please keep in mind that there are hundreds of tools not even mentioned in this chapter that will help you as well.

Healing Tools

We release our pain and heal within by telling our story, releasing negative emotions, conscious complaining, choosing an enlightened witness, meditating or centring ourselves, journaling, pursuing an art form, doing housework, spending time in nature, performing exercise and movement, praying, using self-help supports, interviewing ourselves, grieving aspects of our lives, creating and repeating affirmations, and having a healthy confrontation with our parents.

Telling Our Stories

We can tell our stories in a number of ways:

- We tell aspects of our "negative" stories to others. By doing this, we get these aspects out of our bodies, releasing our stories' power over us. We also gain perspective from others.

- We can record aspects of our stories in a journal. Again, we get aspects of our stories out of our bodies and often gain perspective. Many of us find it easier to be honest with ourselves in the privacy of the written word.

- We can tell our whole negative story, in great detail, to at least one person, whom we trust implicitly. Ideally, this person is compassionate, non-judgmental and perceptive. Few people tell their stories this way. The first time I did it was at the request of my homeopath in order for her to determine the right constitutional remedy to balance my system. Her perspective alone was vital to my healing, and the remedy she prescribed was even more so.

- We can write our whole story down, as I did at the beginning of this book. When I shared this story with some friends, a few of them felt compelled to record their own stories. We all found that writing our whole story down, in all its gory detail, was extremely powerful and couldn't help but assist us in healing. The story can be written from a number of perspectives, highlighting the wrongs that were done to you, the mistakes you made and learned from, your feelings and belief patterns, and the positives or personal strengths that came out of the negative circumstances in your life.

We may need to do all of the above, sometimes over and over and sometimes over the course of many years. Once we start healing, we may find that each time we tell our stories, we tell them with less blame and less anger and more perspective on the lessons learned. Eventually, we find we don't need to tell our stories anymore unless we are trying to help others heal.

Releasing Negative Emotions Healthily

If we do not fully release all of our anger, fear, sadness and other negative emotions, these negative emotions will remain with us, creating emotional blocks as well as pain. Nothing is more draining than holding onto our negative emotions.

It is our right to feel and express our negative emotions. Healthy ways to release our negative emotions include the following:

- Writing an angry letter and sending it to the person who we feel wronged us
- Yelling at photos of the people we are angry with or having imaginary discussions with them
- Writing an angry letter about the person who wronged us or the incident that caused us pain and destroying it or sending it into the sky, attached to a balloon
- Punching a pillow or punching bag
- Crying
- Yelling or screaming in the shower, forest, car or anywhere we have privacy
- Jogging, walking, doing an aerobics class or doing any other form of exercise to release tension
- Swinging a baseball bat at a mattress
- Standing in front of a mirror, speaking our mind, pretending the person we are angry with is looking back at us
- Listing our negative emotions on paper and burning them
- Listing our burdens or challenges on paper and burning them (helps relieve the subconscious mind of our patterns and problems; this can be done daily or as needed)
- Writing a letter to the person who "wronged" us, thanking them for all the lessons they taught us and listing each one
- Altering nasty texts or emails to the wording we would have liked to have received from the sender
- Laughing (Laughter is a happy release that heals! If we do it enough, it can put things in their proper perspective.)
- Singing the words of a song or along with a song that echoes your anger or feelings about a person or circumstance
- Listing your top five biggest mistakes or regrets, describing the people involved and the circumstances, and then writing down what you learned from each mistake and how you would have handled the situation, knowing what you know now; then ask for the forgiveness of those affected and also forgive yourself (read further on in this chapter for more on this); the last step is to tear up the piece of paper with your list and never suffer from those mistakes again.

Conscious Complaining

Karla McLaren's book *Language of Emotions* (2010) encourages us to find a "complaining partner" with whom we can be in a bad mood or to whom we can complain. This partner can be a person, a room in our homes or a place outdoors.

The book advises you to "Let yourself go and give a voice to your dejected, hopeless, sarcastic, nasty, bratty self. Whine and swear about the frustrations etc. of your situation. Complain for as long as you like and when you are done, thank the furniture, the walls, the ground, the trees for listening and end your conscious complaining session by bowing, shaking off and then doing something really fun" (p 148).

The idea is to be ourselves, to express our emotions and to consciously complain, and then it's over. It's not about sugar-coating things or whining without purpose or trying to transform anything. When we are done, our body has released the pent-up emotions and tensions, our vision and focus return, and no one gets hurt in the process.

Choosing an Enlightened Witness

Our enlightened witness is someone who bears witness to our pain and struggles. This is someone with whom we feel safe sharing our deepest feelings and the circumstances of our lives. **When we bare our souls and speak from the deepest part of ourselves, with complete honesty and humiliation, we allow ourselves to heal.**

An enlightened witness is a person with depth of character and wisdom. This is someone who loves us unconditionally; they see our flaws and still love us. An enlightened witness is someone who sees beyond the obvious. They help put perspective on our wounds and, ideally, help us identify the good that has come from our wounds.

This is a person who knows us possibly better than we know ourselves. The longer this person has been in our lives, the more of a witness they have been to the unfolding of our lives. Jay was my enlightened witness. Sometimes, parents are our enlightened witnesses. Sometimes our friends are our enlightened witnesses. We can choose anyone to be our enlightened witness.

I have been amazed at how many counsellors, therapists, psychologists and other individuals whose profession it is to help others heal are judgmental. It is entirely impossible for a person to heal when they are afraid of being judged. In fact, the number one way in which I have helped others heal is by seeing every individual through the lens of my heart. I can easily put myself in the shoes of others, understand their pain and resulting "mistakes" and see their beauty. Once they see that I forgive them for their pasts, it is amazing to me how this translates into them starting the process of forgiving themselves. Sharing my understanding or perceptions of their past is also a vital aspect to their healing.

Meditating or Centring Ourselves

Meditation has been practised for at least 2,500 years around the world. The purpose of meditation is to relax physically and mentally, disengaging ourselves from our worries and challenges. It allows us to gain new perspective by opening our hearts and finding inner peace.

The term "meditation" has been overused and made to be more complicated than it is. We are told that we need to do it every day, at the same time, for long intervals, sitting in certain positions with our hands and fingers organized just so. But have you noticed that everyone seems to differ on the specifics of meditation?

We can meditate whenever we want, for as long as we want and in any position. Is it more effective when we do it at the same time each day and for longer periods of time? Yes. But it still works if we simply meditate when we can. We can do it in our offices, our bedrooms, our parked cars or anywhere we want. We can meditate in silence or to music or to a guided meditation CD; the key is to determine what we are comfortable with.

We can choose scenes to visualize that will calm us. My late father-in-law used to visualize loading all his problems onto a raft and pushing them away from shore. A friend of mine visualizes herself as a mountain and sees hurtful words or actions as dark clouds passing by her. Some people envision a mental picture of themselves days or years from now when their pain has ended and they are looking confident and relaxed.

When we are still, the two musts for meditation include closing our eyes and breathing deeply into our abdomen—that's it. Breathing is the most natural and easy way for us to centre ourselves and be in the present moment. When we first start doing this, our minds are filled with thoughts and we think about all the things we should be doing instead of sitting doing nothing. This is normal. Please don't beat yourself up when this happens. Just return to focusing on your breathing. With practice (it could even take a few months), you will eventually be able to close your eyes and breathe deeply without thinking much about anything. Some people count their breaths to stay focused on their breathing as opposed to their thoughts.

We can meditate for just five or ten minutes and feel better afterward. I recommend that parents of young children head into the bathroom to get their five to ten minutes of alone time. Even after that small amount of time, we feel better because we are more relaxed. Sometimes a new perspective comes about while we are meditating. Other times, it comes about once meditation is finished. Some people have wonderful visions or hear voices or feel things; others just hear and feel their own breath. Extricating ourselves from our chaotic lives or thoughts or fears is the key. There is always a safe, peaceful and joyful place in our minds; we just need to find it. If we can find the peace within ourselves when chaos and challenges abound, our connection will stay with us forever.

Some meditate by working in their garden or hiking in nature. You might say, "But you said we had to close our eyes. We can't garden or hike with our eyes closed!" If we are staying still, we need to close our eyes. *The idea is that we connect with our inner selves and afterwards feel calm, quiet and refreshed. The more we do this, the deeper our connection to our inner selves will be.*

Journaling

A journal can certainly take us a great distance in healing. For those who worry that their journal will be found and read, there is no need to keep your journal. Record your feelings and thoughts and then destroy the pages. The important aspect of journaling is extrapolating your feelings from your body and noticing the patterns that you want to keep or discard.

Psychologist James Pennebaker of the University of Texas has studied individuals who write down their most painful feelings and thoughts for twenty minutes a day over the course of four days. He discovered that they "experienced marked improvement in their psychological and physical well-being. They became less anxious and depressed and [were] physically healthier for as long as five months afterwards. He also demonstrated that subjects who wrote about past traumas for four days had stronger T-lymphocytes—immune cells that extinguish disease agents—for a period of six weeks. He found that not only writing but also talking about past traumas or current stress can be healing" (James Pennebaker, as cited in Domar 2000, 50).

We can write about our painful feelings and memories, strained relationships, challenges at work, health conditions or anything that pervades our thoughts. The blank piece of paper upon which we write holds no judgment. The process of writing for twenty minutes every day for a minimum of four days can be cathartic, integrative, infinitely insightful and an effective way to connect with our inner selves.

Pursuing an Art Form

We can easily see the beauty that exists in our world as soon as we begin drawing, painting or photographing it or writing or singing about it. Each of these art forms helps us release our pain and heal.

A friend of mine just told me about a book that encourages us to draw in order to heal. She explained that one of the exercises in the book is to draw a permission slip (she drew a slip that one would wear under a dress) and then fill in what we want to give ourselves permission to do, such as rest more, play more and so on. Another friend's daughter has quotes and drawings all over the walls of her bedroom; she remembers what was going on in her life almost every time she put pen to wall.

I remember when Paige was five years old and reacting to the chlorine in the drinking water at her school by breaking out into regular tantrums. The only way I could get her out of her tantrums was to have her draw her anger. She used the black, brown and red crayons and pressed extremely hard on the paper; this process never failed to diffuse her anger.

Taylor diffuses her anger or frustration by singing. She comes home from school, heads up into her room and sings her heart out, resulting in a marked improvement in her mood.

We can also use certain songs as mantras, which you can read more about further on in this chapter.

Doing Housework

Housework can be healing. **Cleaning our houses cleans our minds and allows us to slow down and process aspects of our lives.** When there is little or no clutter in our homes, we can move through them, focusing on more important thoughts.

As soon as I learned that doing housework could be healing, I viewed it entirely differently. I remember having an argument with someone and tackling the dishes right after, washing all of my frustration out and then watching it disappear down the drain. Wielding a vacuum around the house can accomplish the same thing and so can scrubbing a carpet or polishing silver, to give a few examples. It is often suggested that we clean a room or empty a closet to purge the old from our lives.

Spending Time in Nature

We all know the healing power of spending time outdoors. Some of us need to be by the ocean or in the trees or by a fire, while others need to have our feet in the sand or just be in the fresh air. Whatever aspects of ourselves need to be balanced determine what we need to spend the most amount of time doing. Ayurvedic philosophy describes this in great detail. We all reap enormous benefits from being in nature. For some, what is most appreciated is being with animals in their natural setting. Nature is one of the most healing of all the healing tools.

Performing Exercise and Movement

Exercise and movement are necessary for discharging our emotional tension, releasing our pain and growing within. Each time we get our heart rate up for at least twenty minutes, we release our negative feelings and replace them with endorphins and positive feelings. We simply need to find the activities that we enjoy the most. Examples include dance, aerobics, zumba, walking, running, biking, skiing, racquet sports, Nordic pole walking, tobogganing and swimming. Yoga, t'ai chi, qigong and brain gym exercise our minds and our bodies.

Praying

When we pray, we can free ourselves of fear, doubt and our "baggage". We stop trying to understand and determine what we need to do and turn it all over to God, Allah or other higher power. We can also receive the help we need to heal our relationships or challenges of any kind.

Until I was in my thirties, I only ever was grateful to God for various things in my life. I had never asked for help with anything because I actually didn't think I was worthy. In my first book, I wrote about the first time I asked God for help; I wanted help in healing Taylor. Within hours of my prayer, I received the message that I needed to find a book about allergies and children. I found the only book on the topic in the store; it was the last copy on the shelf, and soon after I learned that the book had gone out of print. The book played a huge role in the healing of Taylor. Subsequently, both the book and Taylor played a huge role in the healing of many people. Ironically, one of the meanings of Taylor is "God's gift".

Using Self-Help Supports

Reading self-help books, listening to self-help audios, using healing cards and attending personal growth workshops are vital healing supports that can be used regularly and often, but there is a cost associated. Each of these increases our perspective on the circumstances of our lives, gives us positive action steps and helps us come to know and love ourselves more.

Healing cards may require more explanation. Each time we are drawn to choosing a card from a deck of face-down healing cards, the card we choose has a particular message for us that we must interpret to help us understand ourselves or the circumstances of our lives better or to provide us with the right next course of action for ourselves. We only ever pull the card we need in that particular moment. There are several types of cards to choose from, depending on which ones resonate with us.

Interviewing Ourselves

In an excellent book called *Change Your Questions, Change Your Life* (Adams 2009), the author encourages us to think of a challenging person, situation, success or failure and ask these questions:

- What do I want?
- What are my choices?
- What assumptions am I making?
- What am I responsible for?
- How else can I think about this?
- What is the other person thinking, feeling and wanting?
- What am I missing or avoiding?
- What can I learn?
- What action steps make the most sense?
- What questions should I ask (myself or others)? i.e. After an altercation where you were frustrated with another and unhappy with your behaviour, you can ask yourself "Why did I do what I did?"
- How can I turn this into a win–win?
- What's possible? (p 184-185)

When we answer these questions often enough, they will become a natural part of our thinking and create the results we want in our lives.

Grieving Aspects of Our Lives

It is important and necessary to grieve for the aspects of our lives that did not work out the way we hoped they would. We may need to grieve for what we did not have in our childhood or grieve for the parents we never had but wished we did or grieve for the relationships we wanted with others but never had. When we feel and express our grief, we heal.

Susan Forward (1989) suggests a "burial" exercise as a way to help us grieve for what we lost in our childhood. We place a vase of flowers in front of us to symbolize a grave. We then say, "I hereby lay to rest my fantasy of the good family. I hereby lay to rest my hopes and expectations about my parents. I hereby lay to rest my fantasy that there was something I could have done as a child to change them. I know that I will never have the kind of parents that I wanted, and I mourn that loss. But I accept it. May these fantasies rest in peace" (p 219).

When we consciously grieve for anything we didn't have in our lives, we need to be gentle with ourselves, as if someone in our lives did indeed die. It is also helpful to make a list of ideas to help us get through our grief. The list usually incorporates ways in which we like to relax or have a good time.

Creating and Repeating Affirmations

Affirmations are positive statements about our value or potential. They help us overcome our fear of change and help us take responsibility for ourselves. Affirmations foster self-control, self-confidence and inner peace. They connect us to our positive inner voice. **They can help us break through our negative beliefs about ourselves, change our fearful thoughts and help us give ourselves the love we didn't receive as children.**

Affirmations are written in present tense and always discuss something we want for ourselves but are not quite sure we will receive, feel or accomplish. The mind is more powerful than any external conditions. If we repeat an affirmation a minimum of once a day for five weeks or more, our lives will start to look the way we want them to. We say affirmations until we believe them without a shadow of doubt or until we are living them. When affirmations don't work for an individual, it simply means that they do not feel they deserve whatever it is they are wanting. You now know that each of us deserves to be happy. Each time I help a client recognize and understand their unhealthy patterns and forgive themselves, our next step is always to create one or more affirmations for them to live by. They write their affirmations down on a piece of paper and know to repeat their affirmations every day.

Examples of affirmations you might adopt in dealing with your parents are the following:

- I am nourished by my parents' love (despite their limitations).

- I have always wanted my parents' approval; now I provide myself with the approval I need.
- My parents want me to live out their unfulfilled dreams; I fulfill my own dreams.

My friend Krystal believes that when we start an affirmation with "I allow…" we stop the subconscious parts of ourselves from sabotaging ourselves. This makes sense to me; by doing this, we are saying, "I don't know why I am unable to do this and I don't know what is stopping me but I allow the good in." Also, "allowing" implies "effortless", which makes these affirmations much more enticing to say.

Here are some examples of "I allow" affirmations:
- I allow this happiness to last.
- I allow this meal to nourish me by properly absorbing all vitamins and minerals.
- I allow my conscious mind to hear my inner voice clearly and often.
- I allow myself to release anxiety and fear.
- I allow myself to feel safe and loved.

We can also choose a song to be our set of affirmations or mantra. All we need to do is choose one that touches our soul and inspires us and sing it over and over out loud or in our head. We can do it whenever we feel insecure, worried, uncomfortable or unloved. We can sing it quietly or at the top of our lungs. Each time we sing it, we strengthen, until, eventually, we get into a new groove. Examples of possible songs include "Just the Way You Are" as sung by Bruno Mars or the classic "I Will Survive" sung by Gloria Gaynor.

I would like to tell you about the first time I unknowingly used an affirmation and its amazing power. I smoked cigarettes in my twenties. Sometimes people would tell me that I didn't look like a smoker and would ask me why I smoked. I told them that I was rebelling from my childhood and that I would stop smoking as soon as I became pregnant, believing that it would be entirely easy for me to do so. As soon as I found out I was pregnant, which luckily was in the first few weeks of my pregnancy, I did indeed quit smoking (too bad it didn't happen before I became pregnant!). I never desired a cigarette again. *Who quits smoking without ever desiring it again?* Only a person that had unknowingly used an affirmation for over a decade and come to believe, without a shadow of a doubt, that they would accomplish that task, no problem. This example also demonstrates that whatever we believe and say, in our heads or out loud, becomes an affirmation and, eventually, our reality.

Having a Healthy Confrontation with Our Parents

Having a conversation with those who have hurt us can be vital to our healing and have a significant impact on our lives. "Confronting" sounds harsh, but I use the word to describe the process of standing up for ourselves and addressing someone who has and may continue to hurt us. When we confront others, the idea is not to punish or degrade them or seek revenge. Rather, we are asserting ourselves, which, in turn, reminds us that our opinion matters and that we *are* important. We overcome our fear of facing others and speak our truth. Relaying our pain to the person we feel hurt us is extremely healing for us, even if the person we speak to does not respond in the way we hope they will. ***If we don't assert ourselves in this way, we are reinforcing our feelings of powerlessness and incompetency and undermining our self-respect.*** Confronting another is also an opportunity for us to change the balance of power between us and set new parameters for our relationship, if needed. Ideally, this eventually allows us to be more open and honest in future with those we have confronted.

 "There's one more vitally important reason for confrontation: What you don't hand back, you pass on. If you don't deal with your fear, your guilt, and your anger at your parents, you're going to take it out on your partner or your children" (Forward 1989, 225).

At some point in our lives, I believe we need to confront our parents if we feel they hurt us. I've already talked about the relationship with them being our very first and most important and the fact that it sets the tone for our other relationships.

How do we know if we need to confront our parents? Janice Berger offers the following:

There are many indications that we may be stuck and it is helpful to become aware of them. We can ask ourselves:

- Can I say no to my parents?
- Do I feel resentment towards my parents?
- Do I tell my mother or father only what they want me to hear?
- Do I need their approval when I make a decision?
- Am I afraid to disagree with them?

- Do I feel responsible for how my mother or father feels?
- Do I feel that no matter what I do it is never enough?
- Do I keep hoping that my mother or father will change?
- Do I have things I need to say to my parents but do not?
- Do I get angry and rage at my parents? (Berger 2000, 217)

Once we have decided that we do need to confront our parents, how do we prepare?

We have to feel ready. **We need to have come to love ourselves to a certain degree in order to know that we are not responsible for the bad things that happened to us as children.** We need the strength to speak our truth and deal with the possible repercussions of the conversation. Some people don't feel ready until they have had their own children or are in their thirties or forties; this is often the case. It helps to have friends, family or a professional with whom to plan, role play and discuss the confrontation before and after. If no one is available, we can rehearse or write out what we are going to say on our own.

It helps to visualize ourselves talking to our parents, observing their facial expressions and responses as we speak to them. We can even practise our steady and non-defensive responses. Most importantly, once we are ready, all needs to be calm within our own family life to allow time and patience for discussion. If we can arrange for the confrontation to take place in our own home, we will feel stronger still. Some people feel more comfortable confronting a friend or acquaintance before they confront a family member; it gives them practice for the big confrontation.

What are the steps for our healthy confrontation? (See the Compassionate Communication section of Chapter Six for more information.)

1. Share the negative events that we recall from our childhood. We do this in a calm but firm voice without anger. It helps to explain that we know they didn't mean to hurt us.
2. Tell our parents how we felt about the events and how they negatively affected our life, and discuss our current relationship with them. It is important to relay only our own feelings and unmet needs and not to make assumptions about theirs.
3. Explain the aspects of our relationship that are not currently working for us based on our unmet needs.
4. Explain how we would like things to work, i.e. set the boundaries, taking into account our differences.

We can also opt to conduct our confrontation by writing a letter to our parents. We already learned how therapeutic writing can be. A letter helps us organize and reorganize our thoughts until we are pleased with the way we are presenting them. We can even choose to write a letter and read it to our parents when we confront them in person. Giving them a letter is a safer alternative if we are concerned that we will lose our focus or our calm in a face-to-face confrontation, if we are concerned about our parents reacting aggressively or if our parents won't listen to us. If they have passed away or if we don't know how to reach them, we will also want to handle our confrontation by letter. We can read our letter at their gravesite, to their picture or to anything that was important to them.

How might our parents respond?

It is important to remember that we are doing this for ourselves, not for them. Our confrontation is successful simply because we had the courage to do it. When parents respond negatively to us, they deny what happened; pretend to forget what went on; blame their child or someone else, as opposed to accepting responsibility; become very angry, which you now know means they are fearful, usually of being caught making a mistake; accuse us of various behaviours; reject us; or create a negative consequence such as cutting us off financially or emotionally. **When parents respond positively to us, they see our pain and apologize for hurting us.**

The book *Toxic Parents* (Forward 1989) does an incredible job of explaining all aspects of conducting a healthy confrontation with our parents and even provides examples of their potential responses and ours.

I want tell you about my confrontation with my mother to help you understand this better. I was twenty-six. I had been steadily moving up the corporate ladder and, simultaneously, my confidence had been increasing. I had not read about confronting a parent nor had I practised what I was going to say to her. My mother had arrived for a week-long visit from England, and I had not taken one day off work to be with her, thinking that the weeknights and weekend would provide me with a sufficient amount of time to spend with her. You see, I had not forgiven her or myself for our past and therefore really couldn't even be around her without getting completely worked up. I wanted to be around her as little as possible. She was obviously upset at the small amount of time I had allotted to her in the week, so every night, I came home from work and told her about my challenges with her, starting from when I was a small child, explaining how much she had hurt me. If you read My Story, you know the range of challenges that I discussed with her. My mother corrected me on some of the facts, explained that some of her behaviour was due to her lack of love for herself and defended herself over and over. But when we got to the final day of her visit, my mother looked at me with complete understanding and awareness of the severity of the problems that I had perceived to exist in our relationship. She said, "I am sorry that this is the way you see me. I am sorry you feel this way. I don't know if we can fix this." She began to cry at the futility of it all but clearly wanted to rebuild our relationship. I told her that I didn't know how we could move on from this either. Soon after, I took her to the airport, and we parted ways, not knowing the fate of our relationship.

My example indicates that sometimes we have a confrontation and, afterwards, don't know how we want to proceed with our relationship or if we even want to. I did not receive an apology for being lied to, manipulated or neglected. I did receive an admission from my mother that she didn't love herself enough. She clearly saw my perspective and my pain, and I saw her desire to forge ahead in some new way with me. These results were enough for me to want to build a new relationship with her. Sometimes just wanting to forgive puts us on the road to forgiveness. That is what I ended up wanting. A few days later, we simply started talking again, and before we knew it, our relationship began to strengthen.

I felt relief and confusion immediately following my confrontation with my mother. Others might feel excitement, contentment, disappointed, hurt or out of balance. It can take a few weeks for it all to integrate and for us to feel empowered by our confrontation. Regardless of how we feel and how long it takes to adjust, it is important for us to stand our ground, maintaining our reality of how things were for us, while our family adjusts to their new understanding of how things need to change in order to proceed with our relationship. We need to be prepared for whatever consequences come our way.

Over time, I integrated our discussion and continued on my path of self-healing, helped in part by my own aging process. I also found myself being honest with my mom in sharing how I wanted our visits to go and for how long. She understood the reasons why and went along with my boundaries for many years. I discovered that I could now easily spend time with her, and we began to really enjoy being together. In fact, we had both benefited from the confrontation. I still saw plenty of evidence of her not loving herself but it no longer bothered me. At that point, it made me want to reach out to her, offer reassurance and let her know that I saw her beauty inside and out. Other than if she had directly apologized to me, this was the best-case scenario for the result of our confrontation.

Each time we take the initiative to attempt to build a better relationship with our parents (or anyone else, for that matter) we increase the potential for our relationship to become more satisfying for both parties. Our own needs become the solution to making our relationship with others more honest, easy, fun and healthy.

Another possibility is that we express our hurt and our current needs but things simply continue on as usual. We have a number of choices for dealing with this, but a common route is for us to stay in contact with the person we confronted but remain on less demanding terms (for example, reduce our visits or limit our conversations to neutral topics). When we choose this route, we are also choosing to accept the other person for who they are and accept the limitations of our relationship with them. This is a very healthy place to be. We are no longer using hope to protect ourselves from the fact that the other person is not who we wanted them to be. And remember, *our parents or other elders did not grow up in an era where many people were seeking therapy or reading a lot of self-help books, so living emotionally healthily is even less familiar to them than it is for us.*

The final possibility for our confrontation is to not see the person we confronted temporarily. Sometimes this is what is needed in order to let go of old patterns and make our relationship work. We can try having no contact for three months and see how things are without one another and then decide from there whether we want to meet one another's boundaries or end the relationship indefinitely.

As long as we hold our ground following our confrontation, we will find that we begin to let go of our past, stop seeing ourselves as victims and go on to experience tremendous strength and growth. We will begin to parent ourselves, always knowing that we are responsible for how we feel and think and thus coming to love ourselves more than ever before. We will learn to nurture *ourselves* when our parents or others disapprove of our actions. We will know when to exert control, when to re-establish boundaries and to let go of them when we have learned the lessons we needed to learn from them. We will have far more time and energy to do the things we love and can finally live our lives the way we want to.

"Making peace with your parents is at the very core of the human experience: an adventure of the heart, to love and be loved. We must make peace with ourselves and our families if we are to make peace on Earth" (Bloomfield 1983, 218).

Forgiveness: The Key to Changing Our Feelings and Thoughts and Truly Healing

You read earlier that as long as we are holding onto resentment, anger, guilt and fantasies of revenge, we remain trapped in victimhood. When we no longer harbour those negative feelings, we create space within to shift out of victimhood, see the bigger picture, heal ourselves and grow as individuals. We do this by forgiving ourselves and others. When we choose to forgive, we choose to let go of the past and reframe our story. We can embark upon this process only when we understand that we are responsible for our thoughts, feelings and behaviours and others are responsible for theirs. Forgiving ourselves and others is the way to take back our power and take responsibility for how we feel. Forgiveness is not an emotion but a decision we make, once we do our emotional work. But it is our emotions that move painful memories and imbalances into a peaceful place (for example, anger always precedes forgiveness and healing).

Forgiving Others

"The true nature of forgiveness remains misunderstood. It's not telling the person who harmed you "It's okay."… Rather forgiveness is a complex act of consciousness, one that liberates the psyche and soul from the need for personal vengeance and the perception of oneself as a victim" (Myss 1996, 215).

Forgiveness does not mean condoning the behaviours or actions of another. It does not mean that everyone suddenly gets along and lives happily ever after. It does not mean that we are weak or lacking in principles or intelligence. What it does mean is that we are no longer letting someone else take over our thoughts, make us perpetually angry or "ruin our lives"; only we can do that to ourselves. It means coming to see those who hurt us with new perspective. *It means no longer looking at what they did to us but, instead, looking at their pain.* We need to think of them as hurting and find out about their life's hardships and then try to understand why they hurt us. Now I know that some of you are reading this and thinking, "Why should I?"

Certain self-help books and counsellors believe that we do not need to forgive those who hurt us deeply. Some individuals have told me how happy they are to have read or hear that they do not need to forgive. After researching this topic for over twenty-five years, I can tell you that we *do* have to forgive. Forgiveness is the only way we can heal; we need to forgive for our own health and well-being. Forgiveness is a gift we give ourselves. The gift of forgiveness is emotional freedom. It gives us peace of mind. If we hold onto our resentment, we give control over our emotional well-being to the person who hurt us. You already know that it does not serve us to bury our anger, resentment and other negative feelings. When we hold grudges, our love for ourselves cannot grow. We remain victims and we deprive ourselves of healthy, fulfilling relationships, allowing unhealthy patterns to take hold.

 "We forgive for the freedom of our own heart"
(Brach 2003, 262).

The following example of one of the toughest situations to forgive but it provides lessons about forgiving others, as well as ourselves. I have a friend who discovered that her ex-husband had sexually abused their sons for years. The rage and pain that coursed through her body were horrific and lasted for years. Abuse toward one's children is perhaps the hardest thing to forgive. It would have been easier for my friend if she herself had been sexually abused, instead of her sons. Many months after her discovery, she told me that she could never forgive her ex for this act. Louise Hay says that whomever we have the hardest time forgiving is the one we need to forgive the most. My friend had done copious amounts of healing in her life and knew the importance of forgiveness, which is why she told me about her unyielding anger. I asked her about her ex-husband's childhood. I wasn't surprised when she told me that he had been sexually abused by his father for years. Remember that we cannot hurt another unless we have been hurt in the same way. For my friend, knowing about her ex's childhood suffering was not enough information for her to open her heart and feel compassion for him. I asked if she had released her anger and confronted her ex-husband about his abuse of their sons. She had but found that the confrontation was not enough. After ending her friendship with her ex, she made her anger at him apparent every time she ran into him. Within very little time at all, her cancer returned. Remember I told you that cancer comes about when we are filled with resentment for another?

Many experts believe that all dis-ease comes from not forgiving another. *Unfortunately, when we live with hate for another or allow our thoughts of them to consume us, we are granting them victory and only hurting ourselves.* What could my friend do to begin to forgive her ex? She could try to encourage him to open up and describe his pain to her—his pain from being sexually abused and his pain from sexually abusing his own children. Hearing about his own feelings might help her open her heart and feel compassion for him. But that is only part of what was needed. She needed to look at her boys, who were now adults, and find the silver linings in them and in their lives. One son has his own children—two daughters—and treats them with the utmost respect; he has become an amazing father. When she thinks about her grandchildren, she is filled with gratitude for how wonderful their lives have been because their father did not perpetuate the pattern that his father did. Would my friend's son have been such an incredible father had he not been sexually abused? Maybe not. Her other son studied psychology and went on to help many in his life. He treats everyone he meets with love and respect. Both boys forgave their father and have a relationship with him to this day.

Thankfully, my friend believes that everything happens for a reason. She is very close to her sons, their wives and her grandchildren and knows that none of them would be the people they have become had it not been for their past. This knowledge, coupled with time and the realization that she could not have known or stopped what went on, allowed her to forgive herself for what happened to her sons. Sometimes, when the wrongful act is so offensive, forgiving others has to start with forgiving ourselves. Does she have a friendship with her ex-husband now? No, of course not. Does she ever think of him fondly? Rarely, but she does. Does she say that she has forgiven him? No, but she has come to a level of peace, and that is all one can ask. The proof of her peace is that her cancer has not progressed. Recently, she told me that she plans to write a book to help others recognize, cope with and heal from sexual abuse. This action might just take her the whole distance in forgiving her ex.

From this example, we can see that we cannot will ourselves to forgive—forgiving is not a result of effort but of remaining open to the possibility. We can see that forgiveness begins with knowing that a real wounding occurred, which naturally unleashes anger at the perpetrator. Boundaries are then set so that no further hurt can take place (luckily, in this case, the sexual abuse had ended long ago), and then we can begin to put perspective on everything that occurred.

Eventually, forgiveness can occur, if we allow it. Forgiveness automatically follows the honourable restoration of our sense of self.

When we forgive, we do not even need to tell the person who hurt us. That is proof right there that forgiveness is a gift we give ourselves. Oftentimes, if we were to tell a parent that we forgave them, they would look at us and say, "What do you need to forgive me for?" or "Forgive me? Have you forgiven yourself for how you behaved and for how you treated me?" Most times, individuals have no idea how much hurt they inflict on others.

Because I was a child who regularly attended church, I have said, "Father, forgive them, for they know not what they do" (Luke 23:34) over and over in my head each time I have seen people operating from their pain and fear as opposed to love. I have taught the phrase to my girls when they have been hurt by others.

It would be ideal if those who hurt us would apologize to us and explain so that we fully understand why they hurt us, but that is rarely the case. *And if those who hurt us would say, "I'm sorry; I love you; please forgive me," the door to forgiveness would be open even wider.*

Sometimes we don't have the luxury of finding the reason for someone hurting us or another. This is when we need to do the counterintuitive work to come up with the potential positive reasons for why things happened the way they did. Forgiveness is the decision to see others through the lens of our heart. When we do that, we see that others don't have the life skills to behave differently or they don't fully love themselves or something else was taking priority in their lives at the time, just to give a few examples. Forgiveness is seeing the innocence in another, as opposed to their guilt. What people say and do is *not* who they are. Our goal is to accept others based on what we know to be the truth about them, even if they are not aware of that truth themselves.

It is so easy for us to see the innocence in a child. When a four-year-old girl is crying or misbehaving at the mall, many of us feel sorry for her and realize she must be tired, hungry or over-stimulated. But when a forty-five-year-old woman is crying or misbehaving, even if her pain is directly related to what happened to her when she was four years old, many of us think there is something wrong with her or that she is flawed. Why is it so hard for us to see the innocence in adults?

I would like to share another example of forgiving with you. I had a friend who was dying of cancer. Her best friend was going away on a vacation for a month and she asked my friend to wait for her to return before passing. Every day, I watched my friend struggle to live long enough to see her best friend return. She was skin and bones by the end, dying just days before her best friend returned from her vacation. If her best friend had flown home one day earlier, she could have attended the funeral. She had the money to do so. I was so angry that my friend had allowed her best friend to put her through this torture and that this woman didn't attend her best friend's funeral. My anger consumed me for a few days until I learned this: The best friend was married to my friend's brother, and he could not bear to see his sister die nor could he bring himself to attend her funeral—it was too painful for him. His wife was only supporting him. As soon as I understood their pain, I was able to forgive them. Unfortunately, we don't always have the benefit of learning what is behind a person's actions.

There are many different ways and timeframes in which forgiving can happen. For example, sometimes we can forgive our parents only after we have left home, settled into a new routine and begun to see our past with new perspective. **Sometimes forgiving happens when we have our own children and catch a glimpse of the challenges our parents went through in raising us.** Sometimes we contract a disease and a healer helps us forgive those who hurt us. Sometimes forgiving happens instantly when we gain a new insight into another. Sometimes forgiving is a gradual process that happens over many years, and that's okay.

In My Story, you read that what got me started on forgiving the adults who raised me was choosing to believe that I had selected my parents and the people in my life to teach me certain lessons. Once I believed this, I no longer saw myself as a victim but as the victor because I felt that I had learned the lessons I had set out to learn. Did I know whether I had chosen my parents? Not a chance. I just decided I was going to adopt this belief.

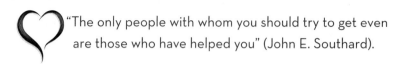 "The only people with whom you should try to get even are those who have helped you" (John E. Southard).

Over the years, I found out more information on the backgrounds of the people who raised me, allowing me to see them through the lens of my heart. Simultaneously, I was working on coming to love myself, which gave me a protective layer from taking things personally. Time spent away from the people who raised me helped me to forgive, as well. In my thirties, I felt I had reached the point where I could be with any of the adults who had raised me and not be negatively affected while in their presence. Then my brother died and my anger at them all reared its ugly head once again. Time and perspective came to my rescue, as they always do. Unleashing my anger and having conversations with each of the parties involved got me partway there. Seeing some of those adults undergo their own pain in losing Jay moved me further along in seeing them with compassion. Eventually, gathering further information on some of those adults' childhoods helped me complete my process of forgiveness.

When my girls were young, wanting them to build closeness with their grandparents, we went to visit my dad and stepmom out west. Because I had not forgiven my stepmom, I found that she pushed my buttons like there was no tomorrow, each time she tried to control me. One day, on the fifth anniversary of Jay's death, I lay on the beach sobbing, angry tears spilling down my face. A big voice came into my head and asked, "Who controlled *her*?" Who controlled her the way she was controlling me and the way she had controlled Jay, as well as others? I did not know the answer but I suddenly realized, deep within my soul, that she must have been controlled and badly, badly hurt to treat us the way she had. A wave of compassion, tears and then relief, washed over me. Sometimes we can't forgive our parents until we have cried for them. A little while later, I went inside and saw my stepmom working way too hard on making us all supper, like she always did, looking completely exhausted. I put my arms around her and thanked her for how hard she was working, each day of our vacation, to please us. She was shocked that I would hug her out of the blue— we did not do that. My eyes saw her in a whole new light. As a result of whatever had happened to her in her childhood, she did not love herself nor had she forgiven herself and that is why she was the way she was. This moment in time completed my process of forgiving each of the adults who raised me.

From the various examples that I have shared, you can see that there are many facets to one's process of forgiveness. It was easy for me to forgive the nanny who cared for my brother and me when she discussed her treatment of us, described her past to me and apologized to me over and over. The way in which I forgave my mother was by having a healthy confrontation with her. My father and I had a number of discussions that helped me see him through the lens of the heart. My hope is that you will be open to the possibilities for yourself now that you understand the various ways in which forgiveness occurs.

 "Forgiveness is a state of grace, nothing you can force or pretend" (Orliff 2009, 348).

Alternate methods for forgiving others

Here are some other methods for forgiving others:

- When you are feeling hurt, angry, closed down or unforgiving, take a deep breath in and simply connect with your pain. Notice where you feel it in your body. Feel the pain. Keep breathing. Know that your feelings are natural under the circumstances. Remind yourself to stay open to healing one day. Remember that your desire alone can create forgiveness.

- Each night, look at a happy, flattering picture of the person you are trying to forgive. Think of their challenges and their strengths and imagine hugging them. Then say, "Thank you for teaching me _____. Thank you for playing an important role in my life. I love you."

- Letting go of our usual ways of defining others can help us see their innocence more easily. Every person is new depending on how we perceive them at any given moment.

- Most of us have watched a child sleeping and seen their innocence. You can picture others as children.

- You can also imagine that you are seeing someone for the last time or that they have already passed away.

- Some of us picture the people who hurt us towering over us, particularly if they are an adult and we were a child. Picture yourself standing tall and the person who hurt you becoming smaller and smaller in your mind's eye until you feel they are powerless over you and you are overcome with compassion for them. No one is ever as powerless as when they hurt another.

- Picture putting the person you have challenges with in a pink dollhouse. Pink is the colour that represents love. Make a room for them there, putting their tiny body in a hammock or in front of a fireplace or however you picture them being comfortable. Imagine yourself, larger, blowing love at them through the window.

 "It's easy enough to love those who agree with us and treat us well. We must learn to love those with whom we do not agree and who have not necessarily treated us justly. Just as we work to build up our muscles, we must work to expand our capacity to love" (Williamson 2010, 157).

How do we know if we have forgiven another?

We have forgiven another when we can be around them or speak to them without being negatively affected by them. We no longer let what they do or say to us control our self-respect or well-being. The state we reach is called detachment. When we are detached, we can disagree with another but still love them and simultaneously feel a kind of numbness. We no longer feel that we have to defend ourselves nor do we fear that they will trigger our old hurts. We can see them with compassion, often coming to the realization that they don't love themselves. *If we can eventually reach the point where we no longer blame another but say instead, "I don't believe the part of you that hurt me is who you really are," then we know we have forgiven.* And amazingly, once we forgive, we forget a lot of the details of our unhealthy relationship because we are not constantly reliving the bad memories in our minds.

Just because we forgive someone who hurt us does not mean that we need to remain in a relationship with them. If we set our boundaries with them and they do not comply (they are still doing hurtful things to us), the relationship can safely end. (More on that in Chapter Five.)

"Know that the best revenge is your success, your happiness, and the triumph of not giving vindictive people any dominion over your peace of mind" (Orliff 2009, 351).

When we view our lives on earth as the best course we could enrol in to learn how to open our hearts, we realize that the people and experiences that are in our lives are absolutely perfect for helping us learn and grow, making forgiveness that much easier. When we understand that our own thoughts and feelings, as adults, create our destiny, forgiveness becomes even easier.

Let me explain what I mean by these last few points. At nineteen, when I met the man I married, I was extremely insecure because I had not received the love that I needed as a child. Oh, I did a fantastic job of hiding my insecurities, but they were there, trust me. When we don't love ourselves, we attract someone else who does not love themselves to a similar degree; it's one of the laws of our universe. I ended my marriage because my thoughts about myself had changed; I had opened my heart to myself. My love for myself had grown to such a degree that I now required a partner who loved himself just as much as I loved myself, so that he, in turn, could provide me with the love I now knew I deserved. Was I angry at my husband for not being able to provide me with the love I deserved? You bet! Did I say nasty, hurtful things to him because I was hurting? You bet! We are only human. But once I understood that he was one of my major teachers and that he had been instrumental in helping me come to love myself like never before, I called him and thanked him from the bottom of my heart. My marriage was not a failure ending in separation; it was a gift.

> "True forgiveness is when you can say
> 'Thank you for that experience'" (Oprah Winfrey).

Forgiving Ourselves

"Self-compassion is the ability to believe that, no matter how terrible your mistakes, love and forgiveness are part of your birthright and humanity" (Coleman 2008, 31).

Usually forgiving ourselves is harder than forgiving others, but sometimes that is where we have to start. We need to forgive ourselves no matter what we have done, just as we need to forgive others no matter what they have done. There is nothing more crucial to our overall well-being than making peace with ourselves. If we do not do this, we continue to use our past to beat ourselves up and sabotage our biggest dreams.

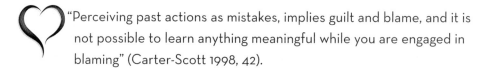"Perceiving past actions as mistakes, implies guilt and blame, and it is not possible to learn anything meaningful while you are engaged in blaming" (Carter-Scott 1998, 42).

It is easy for us to dwell on our regrets, the things we lack, the things we missed out on and the things we could have done differently. Forgiving ourselves is a little more difficult. It means letting go of blaming (judging or disliking) ourselves; none of us deserves blame. It means bringing compassion to the pain we are feeling; each of us deserves compassion. It means making a commitment to loving ourselves. It means being sensitive to our own suffering and coming to understand why we are the way we are, why we have certain beliefs, why we feel the way we do and being okay with all of it. It is only when we can accept our stories (whatever happened to us in our past) and forgive ourselves entirely that we can obtain the wisdom that our stories hold for us. Forgiving ourselves and coming to trust our innate goodness can take a long time; each of us needs to decide when we are ready to start the process. Once we do forgive ourselves, it is so much easier to apply this same thought process in forgiving others. We can continually exercise our minds to see the innocence in others, as well as in ourselves.

When we are forgiving ourselves, we are forgiving ourselves for:

- the things that were done to us a child
- the times in which we underperformed, behaved without integrity or failed to be grateful for the people or things that were once part of our lives and are no longer

How do we know that we have not forgiven ourselves?

I remember the day I realized I had not forgiven myself for what had happened to me as a child. I was well into my thirties, already had both my children and was crazy busy. I had, a few years prior, forgiven all those who had hurt me. Yet I was still painstakingly trying to prove myself to others and to myself.

When we are constantly trying to please or prove ourselves, we have not forgiven ourselves. Similarly, when we are not treating ourselves with love and respect, we have not forgiven ourselves. When we are always feeling the need to defend ourselves, we have not forgiven ourselves. When we are punishing ourselves in any way, we need to find the part of us that needs healing and begin the process of forgiving ourselves.

When I came to the realization that I had not forgiven myself, my mouth opened in disbelief. How could I blame myself for how I was treated as a child? Yet that is what we do until we learn another way, isn't it? Many adults gain perspective on their own childhoods when they see how innocent their children or grandchildren truly are at the very age they were when they were mistreated by an adult. I thought about the circumstances that made up my childhood and I thought about the adults who raised me and all of their emotional wounds, and I cried. I cried for a good hour, releasing all the blame and guilt that I had held for over three decades, for I finally knew that I had done nothing wrong. This demonstrates the concept I explained earlier: Sometimes just wanting to forgive can begin the process of forgiving. For others, forgiving themselves for what went on in their childhood could occur from reading self-help books, from seeing a therapist or counsellor, or from talking to a trusted friend.

In order to forgive ourselves for the mistakes we made in our lives, something else is required. We need to take responsibility for the times in which we underperformed, behaved without integrity or failed to be grateful for the people or things that were once part of our lives and are no longer. We take responsibility by apologizing to those we hurt by our mistakes. There is nothing that tests our willingness to take responsibility more than saying, "I'm sorry." When we say those words, our egos take a backseat. We have to let go of being right or upholding a certain image. Apologizing means describing our mistakes in enough detail to the person we hurt that they know that we truly understand what we did wrong and why we did or said what we did. And then, if we are able, we resume our relationship with them and treat them with love, respect, integrity and gratitude. The person we have wronged will also want to see us, if possible, treating others with love and respect and living our lives with integrity. If we cannot make amends with those people because they are no longer in our lives, we ensure that we do things differently with new relationships. Admitting the mistakes we made to that new friend or lover or a trusted third party goes a long way toward healing ourselves and preventing us from making the same mistake again. **Admitting our mistakes and "making things right" also helps us make peace with our stories and, subsequently, feel better about ourselves.** The faster we recognize our mistakes, apologize fully and without hesitation, and make amends with the person we hurt, the faster everyone heals.

We grow up in a culture that teaches us that it's not okay to make mistakes. We are human; we are going to make mistakes. Amazingly, part of being human is that we always know when we have been wrong or made a mistake. Anyone who says they have not made mistakes is not telling the truth. When we do make mistakes, we are usually judged, chastised or abandoned, which makes the mistake seem even worse. But sometimes it is us doing that to ourselves. However, if we learn from our mistakes or they become opportunities for speaking our truth, they are not mistakes. Mistakes are caused by an error in our thinking at the time we made the mistake. "When we make a mistake, it's because in the moment we make it we forget who we are" (Williamson 2012, 61). We make mistakes based on the perceptions we had at the time, and the experiences relating to those choices only serve to bring us to a higher level of awareness. Mistakes provide us with feedback about what works and what doesn't work.

Another way of looking at mistakes is that "all mistakes are a call for love", as described by Marianne Williamson in *Enchanted Love* (1999). You see, they are only made when we are operating from the ego (more on the ego in Chapter Five). *No mistakes are made when we are operating from our heart and from the love that emanates from within each of us.* Making and admitting our mistakes keeps us humble. When we truly apologize for our mistakes, we are dropping the ego and our defences and speaking from our heart. The heart provides us with a deeper level of awareness than the ego could ever deign to provide.

Alternate methods for forgiving ourselves

Maybe we have hurt our child and have an exceedingly hard time forgiving ourselves for that, even knowing the stress or pain we were experiencing at the time. The techniques that we have available to us for healing ourselves are truly amazing. In *Radical Acceptance* (2003), Tara Brach explains that instead of trying to forgive ourselves in a case like this, we can look at the shame we are feeling and send a message of forgiveness to our shame. We ask ourselves, "Can I forgive the shame for existing?" We can do the same for the guilt, fear or any other negative emotion we are feeling. In this way, we are forgiving each feeling and the experiences with which they are identified, which creates loving, compassionate feelings within ourselves that allow our emotions to come out and change, thereby facilitating forgiveness.

Sometimes we need to take other steps in order to forgive ourselves. We can simply set the intention for ourselves that we let go of blame and be kinder to ourselves. We can think about the people who love us and see ourselves through their eyes, increasing our appreciation of ourselves. We can also write a letter of forgiveness to our younger selves; in the process of writing it, we may realize that we did what we did because of where our thinking was at the time. Often, it is only with time or repercussions that we learn that we made an error in our thinking. If the letter contains the lesson we learned from our "mistake", it is even easier to forgive ourselves.

Exercises for forgiving ourselves

1. Make a list of your regrets for the actions you took or didn't take. You could make a list pertaining to each of the important people in your life. The more specific the regrets, the more pain can be felt and released. Beside each regret, write an explanation about why you took the action you did or why you didn't take an action. Then, write the good that arose from what you did or didn't do or the lesson learned. The goal is not to dwell on our guilt or blame ourselves; it is to release our pain and forgive ourselves. When we share our regrets with a sibling who has similar regrets, we help each other heal. When we share with our partner, we release ourselves from our emotional isolation and intimacy builds.

2. We can visualize or imagine sharing our regrets with the person involved, seeing them understanding our feelings and then expressing their forgiveness. We can imagine that person hugging us, holding our hand or patting us on the back. By imagining them accepting our apologies and receiving our love, we can release the remaining guilt from our system.

3. We can also think about the words or feelings we have always wanted to hear from our parents or other individuals but never heard. We can close our eyes and imagine them saying or doing what we most wanted. We can imagine this many times. Feel the relief that comes from finally being understood and appreciated by that person.

4. We can also write a letter to a parent or other individual telling them how we would have loved them to have responded to us instead of the way they did respond to us.

5. Kathy Preston (2003) provides us with further ideas for forgiving ourselves: Call someone you've wronged and make amends. Clean out your closets as a symbol of purifying your internal energy. Do a cleansing diet to detoxify the body. When you are in the shower, visualize all the old patterns being washed away with the water. Give up a bad habit (e.g., smoking, eating sugar, biting your nails). If there is a particular situation that requires your attention, commit to dealing with it within three days. Address it within that time, and then let it go (p 119).

How do we know if we have forgiven ourselves?

When we forgive ourselves, we know that our imperfections don't take away our innate goodness. When we forgive ourselves, we replace self-rejection with self-acceptance. When we don't like ourselves, we attract people and events that reflect those negative feelings about ourselves. When we start taking responsibility by forgiving ourselves, we start feeling worthy of receiving what we desire; we let go of our unhealthy patterns and decrease the frequency and intensity of the negative experiences in our lives. This results in greater self-control and a calmer existence. That forgiveness leads to accepting, respecting and eventually loving ourselves—even when we act crazy or feel jealous or sad. When we can truly love ourselves for who we are, that is the beginning of our freedom as humans and that is when everything good comes into our lives; we literally reprogram our future.

"What all of us need, at bottom, is the same: to be free of the past, free to start over, free to feel that we're good and decent people, and free to feel there's something good and true and beautiful we can contribute to this world. Our learning how to see others that way is the greatest contribution we can make to their lives. And the person who makes us feel this way is a gift beyond rubies or gold" (Williamson 1999, 206).

Five

Parenting Ourselves by Coming to Love Ourselves

"❝ I find that when we really love and accept and approve of ourselves exactly as we are, then everything in life works" (Hay 1999, 100).

When we are born, we are filled with love and an innate goodness. Who we are as young children is who we really are—loving, trusting, free, imaginative and completely accepting beings. ***The love within us is real and therefore cannot be destroyed, but it can become hidden by the fear we learn here on earth.*** When we come to love ourselves again, we experience the love and understanding that we missed when we were growing up. When we come to love ourselves, we gradually let go of our fears and open our hearts. We find that it is more natural for us to love and have positive feelings than to fear and experience negative feelings. When we rediscover our inner beauty, we come alive again and our biggest needs are met. We are able to relate lovingly to others and know how to embrace the present moment as well as the beauty and pain that is within and around us.

What Is Self-Esteem?

Coming to love ourselves is about cultivating our self-esteem. In 1890, William Jones, a psychologist, devised the term "self-esteem" and defined it as "feeling good about yourself and your accomplishments" (Orliff 2009, 4).

Judith Orliff, in her book *Emotional Freedom* (2009), lists the following factors that contribute to our self-esteem:

- The quality of our womb experience—a nurturing experience cultivates self-esteem. When a mother is sick or overcome with stress, anger or fear during pregnancy or doesn't want her pregnancy, her baby's self-esteem suffers.

- Our inborn temperament and biochemistry—children share the same characteristics as their parents; usually they share the temperament of one parent more than the other. If a child's inborn temperament is moody, irritable or explosive, self-esteem will be a greater challenge for them.
- Our parents' attitudes and acceptance of us. And as we mature, others' attitudes and acceptance of us also affect our self-esteem.

Some of you may read this and think, "Well, I don't have an ounce of hope for having a healthy self-esteem." Maybe your mother didn't want you and gave you up for adoption. Maybe you have been angry for as long as you can remember. Maybe you haven't had a good relationship with anyone your whole life and loneliness has pervaded your soul. Every one of us has the opportunity to build our self-esteem and transform our lives. There are no exceptions!

 "I have never met anyone who was born with a strong sense of self-esteem; this form of power must be earned" (Myss, 1997, 43).

We build our self-esteem by regularly understanding, identifying, accepting and expressing our feelings and thoughts in a healthy way. The more we do this, the more we think about ourselves in a healthy way and the more love and attention we give ourselves. The more love and acceptance we receive, the greater our intrinsic worth. Every one of us is in various stages of working on understanding, loving, accepting and trusting ourselves once again, whether we are aware of it or not. Everything we experience and every relationship that we have brings us closer to knowing and loving ourselves. Some of us think we love, accept and trust ourselves, but our actions beg to differ. Some of us, a rare few, will admit to absolutely hating ourselves. Some of us are so insecure that we have developed arrogant, know-it-all personalities to convince others of our confidence. Some of us are so insecure that we allow our every move to be controlled by another or we allow others to treat us badly. Some of us are so insecure that we control others or treat others badly. Some of us trade self-respect for praise and the reputation of being known as a nice person. Each of these ways of thinking or being come about when we operate from our ego or our fear-based mind.

The second way in which we build our self-esteem is by making things happen for ourselves. This means having the ability to see what we want and going for it. When we can do this, we can create the life we want to live.

Meeting Our Needs: Externally or Internally?

We were taught that we are worthy when we clean up after ourselves or obtain high marks. We were taught that the more attention we received by getting gold stars, ribbons or trophies and the more competitions and special awards we won, the more approval we would receive. We were taught to evaluate ourselves by how well we met the expectations of others or by comparing ourselves with everyone else. Not many of us were taught that we are inherently good. Not many of us were given unconditional love and approval for being who we are, as opposed to what we do. This leads invariably to feeling undervalued and incompetent and believing that there is no point in doing our best, because it's never enough. We end up fighting for our own identity by becoming apathetic, defiant or rebellious.

 "Unconditional love is a full love that accepts and affirms a child for who he is, not for what he does. No matter what he does (or does not do), the parent still loves him. ... Conditional love is based on performance and is often associated with training techniques that offer gifts, rewards, and privileges to children who behave or perform in desired ways" (Campbell and Chapman 1997, 17).

Every human being wants to feel safe, valuable and loved. We all want harmony, cooperation, happiness and freedom. Many of us take the route of seeking external gratification (looking outside of ourselves) in order to acquire these feelings. We obtain nice homes, cars, clothes, vacations, money, credentials or power. We struggle ceaselessly—working, acquiring, achieving, over-committing and rushing—in a perpetual quest to prove ourselves. But when we take this route, we are operating from our ego and are never satisfied because we are motivated by not having enough. Oh, temporarily we are satisfied, but not in the long run; instead, we find our lives rife with challenges and pain.

"Our culture wanted us to learn early that we are what we acquire (money, possessions, power), and if we have or want very little, then we are of very little value. Furthermore, we are what others think of us, so if our reputation is sullied, we're of even less value!" (Dyer 2006, 28)

In order to take the route of internal gratification (looking inside ourselves), it is helpful to understand how our ego affects our thinking and reclaim the power that our ego has taken from us. Whenever we operate from our ego, we can never be at peace. It is the ego that causes us to seek immediate pleasure and make bad choices rather than act with integrity. It is the ego that needs to feel important by competing, winning, judging or being right all the time. It is the part of us that feels we need to struggle to get ahead and that there is only so much success to go around. It makes us feel separate from others, fearful, unhappy, insecure, resentful, hopeless or jealous or believe that we are superior to others. It is the ego that has us overthink things. It rushes us and makes us feel as though there is never enough time or that we are wasting time or that we made a mistake. It is bothered by the little things in life and gets stressed easily. It causes regular challenges for us, is always calculating and needs to know everything. The ego is insatiable; it focuses on what we don't have and always wants more. The ego does not like making mistakes, never mind admitting to them; it is really not comfortable taking responsibility. It seeks approval, security and control. It doesn't know its own value so tries to convince others of its value. Those operating from ego use guilt and fear to motivate others. Whenever our actions are motivated by fear (of loss of approval, security or control), we are operating from our ego.

"The ego wants us to regret our past ... and ego loves guilt. Such negative energy fabricates an excuse for why our present moments are troubled and gives us a cop-out ... and thinking about where we have been or what we did wrong in the past are great impediments to an inspired life" (Dyer 2006, 32–33).

The *only* real route to acquiring and maintaining harmony in our lives is the route of internal gratification, which comes about by being motivated by peace and love, as opposed to fear. **There seems to be little value placed on the experience of inner peace.** Experiencing inner peace means surrendering our ego and operating from our hearts. You just read that the ego handles insecurity through external gratification. In contrast, the heart handles insecurity by looking inward to find the causes of insecurity and heal them. We don't need to draw attention to ourselves or try to be better than others. We simply need to recognize that deep within ourselves, we are naturally peaceful, joyful, creative, intuitive, loving, pure and good, each with our own unique talents.

It is important that you understand that I am not suggesting we surrender our ego entirely. You now know that every seemingly negative aspect of ourselves has a positive purpose. Without our ego, we would all be couch potatoes. Our ego provides us with our drive. Each of us needs our ego to fulfill our individual purpose.

"There are two types of classes in the Earth School—classes about fear and classes about love. Anger, vengefulness, sadness and greed are classes about fear. Joy and gratitude are classes about love" (Zukav and Francis 2001, 45).

What Is It Like When We Don't Know and Love Ourselves?

When we don't know and love ourselves, we are disconnected from our true selves. We feel emotional pain and loneliness. Our lives don't go in the direction we want them to go. We often don't know what we need or want. We forget who we are because we have hidden the parts of ourselves that others have disapproved of and have continually taken direction from others. When we feel disconnected from our true selves, we cannot feel essentially good about ourselves. This initiates the process of always looking outside ourselves for our answers.

"Only when we stop pretending to be something we are not—when we no longer feel the need to hide or overcompensate for either our weaknesses or our gifts—will we know the freedom of expressing our authentic self and have the ability to make choices that are based on the life we truly desire to live. When we break out of this trance and are no longer preoccupied with fitting in, with what other people think of us or what we think of ourselves, we can open up and take advantage of the opportunities that might just pass us by when we are trapped inside our story line or behind the mask we wear" (Chopra, Ford and Williamson 2010, 106).

When we don't love ourselves, we feel we don't deserve love, so we subject ourselves to pain and sacrifice. Every single challenge we undergo stems from not loving ourselves enough. Every single experience of jealousy, resentment, anger and insecurity points us in the right direction to finding and healing parts of ourselves that need healing. Challenges in every aspect of our lives—relationships, jobs, health and finances—can diminish, if not disappear, when we come to love and accept ourselves and, eventually, others. Each and every experience exists to teach us love and forgiveness.

"When you feel worthless, you are terrified by your life, and when you are terrified by your life, you are continually in the pain of trying to shape your life as you think it needs to be. When that pain is acute, you cover it with anger. You strike out at friends and perceived adversaries. You mistake kindness for weakness. You cannot imagine that others care for you because you do not care for yourself. You imprison yourself in a cell that you have created. You blame everyone else for being there" (Zukav and Francis 2001, 137).

When we don't love ourselves, we don't see our value. We are incapable of imagining that we can make a major difference in the world. We deny our beauty, our power and our responsibility for the consequences that we create. People treat themselves and others badly only when they are in their own pain. We can only treat ourselves and others well when we love ourselves. When we eat badly, don't exercise or don't do things that make us feel good inside, it is simply because we don't love ourselves enough. Now, there are times in our lives when it is impossible to do things to make ourselves feel good inside, such as in the first few weeks of a new baby coming into our home or when someone in the family is really sick and needs our care. The majority of time, however, we are free to do things that make us feel good inside, but we must first realize we are free and that we deserve to feel good.

Coming to Know and Love Ourselves

Ironically, we already are what we spend our lives trying to be; we just don't see our own magnificence. We come to love ourselves and heal all wounds by connecting with who we truly are and where we came from. Specifically, we come to love ourselves by connecting with our younger selves, determining which needs were not met and which parts of ourselves we shut down or hid from the view of others and eventually ourselves.

Earlier in this book, I spoke of the importance of parents allowing their children to have control and encouraging them to be themselves and express themselves freely. Children raised that way see their own magnificence, know they are free, deserve to feel good inside and usually know how to go about achieving just that. Unfortunately, somewhere along the line, most children are taught that their larger purpose is to meet the needs of others, that it's not right to ask others to help them and that it's selfish to prioritize their own needs. That's why they end up feeling guilty when they pursue pleasure.

Thankfully, some of those children eventually come to a junction in their adult lives when they discover it is time to start doing things differently. We each need to become aware that we are hurting, that our needs are not being met and that maybe, at this moment, we do not have the freedom for ourselves that we would like. It is impossible to obtain the freedom we desire without first realizing that, at this moment, we don't have it. Usually, when we reach the point where we have had enough, a breakthrough occurs, and that is when our new awareness kicks in. And then if we gain the awareness that our adult lives are the result of what we believe and that sometimes what we believe is not real. Then we can begin to change our beliefs and improve our lives.

"What we don't realize is that our ultimate unconscious goal is to come to understand who we really are" (Truman 2003, 48).

Events That Crack Us Open

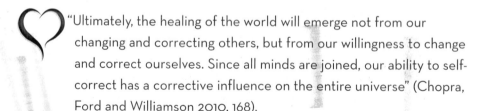

"Ultimately, the healing of the world will emerge not from our changing and correcting others, but from our willingness to change and correct ourselves. Since all minds are joined, our ability to self-correct has a corrective influence on the entire universe" (Chopra, Ford and Williamson 2010, 168).

There are a number of different ways in which we can first become aware that it is time to do something differently in our lives. Certain events seem to crack us open:

- Any kind of loss, such as the death of someone to whom we were close, divorce or loss of a job, cracks us open. Divorce entails more than the loss of our partner; it involves grieving the death of a dream and the loss of hope for that relationship. And any losses remind us of the other losses we have suffered.
- Pain, sickness or disease can get us searching for answers.
- The birth of our child and the raising of them are revelatory. Sometimes it takes raising a child to find out how angry or impatient we are or that we ourselves are in need of healing.

- We can be in the midst of chaos and disarray, and one day it hits us and we find ourselves saying, "I am not happy."
- We approach forty or fifty years of age and are accused of going through a mid-life crisis or menopause. Both stages of life present opportunities for us to notice our feelings and learn about ourselves; instead these pivotal times in our lives are often used against us.
- We go on a vacation or do something that takes us away from our regular thoughts and ways of doing things.

Events that crack us open allow us to step back from our lives so that we can see ourselves with new perspective. There doesn't need to be a big event for us to step back. We can meet up with a friend or book an appointment with a counsellor and find the perspective we need there. We can simply close our eyes, listen to our breath and sit in quiet contemplation. We can consciously decide to slow our lives down so that we can gain the perspective we need.

Generally, our modern lives are too noisy: We watch too much television and spend too much time on our computers. Generally, our lives are too busy: We make too many plans and are reluctant to say no. Consciously slowing our lives down means looking at whether we are getting enough sleep and relaxation time, whether we have too many commitments or whether we have too much noise in our lives and then taking the necessary steps to cultivate more time for ourselves. Our overscheduled lives leave us no time to think or gain new perspective, never mind heal. Ironically, sometimes the moment in which we most need to slow down is exactly when it feels most excruciating to do so. Slowing down when we are in a rage, overwhelmed by sadness or filled with desire may be the last thing we want to do. But it is when we cultivate quiet that we cultivate our healing. With quiet, we can journal our thoughts or listen to our own breathing or employ any of the healing techniques discussed earlier. Those of us who are able to spend a month alone learning to enjoy our own company can make peace with ourselves even faster.

Regardless of *how* we get there or *when* we get there, the more time we spend doing what we love, the more likely it is that we will ask ourselves, "How can I do more of this?" and "Why haven't I been doing more of this?" And the more we do the things we love, the stronger we become deep within. We can start taking responsibility for ourselves and identify, understand, feel and express our feelings. And then we can make the necessary changes in our lives needed to come to love ourselves more. Our self-esteem grows when we graduate from an educational program, do well in our jobs or determine how to meet the many needs of our child, our partner or others. ***It is when we become aware that we are on a journey to love ourselves more or feel happy more often that the rewards become much greater.*** How quickly we do this depends on how open we are, how vulnerable and honest we are prepared to be, how much we allow ourselves to let go and how much time we dedicate to the process.

I remember when my conscious journey of coming to love myself began. I went to a counsellor for help with recurring kidney stones, knowing that the emotional connection to kidney stones is lumps of undissolved anger and that the kidney represents our partnership. I mentioned earlier that the counsellor told me to have a love affair with myself. Well, I didn't have a clue about how to go about such an affair. I had been raising my children and caring for family members and friends; the only thing I did for myself was get to the gym about three times a week.

I started by taking ten minutes a day to do nothing. Eventually I was able to spend hours, one day a week, doing nothing, just lying in the grass or in the sun or on the hammock, listening to my own breath! The day I told a good friend that I had just spent hours lying in the sun, doing absolutely nothing (what a luxury!) was the day that my true progress in coming to love myself was demonstrated.

"If you can spend a perfectly useless afternoon in a perfectly useless manner, you have learned how to live" (Lin Yutang, as cited in Dyer 2007, 269).

Steps to Coming to Love Ourselves

 "Every moment is an opportunity to exhale old energies and breathe in new life; to exhale fear and inhale love; to exhale littleness and inhale magnitude; to exhale grandiosity and inhale grandeur" (Williamson 2008, 45).

We are living at a momentous time on earth when our capacity to find the best within ourselves is larger than ever. In most countries, modern technology has created conveniences that have eliminated our need to spend hours and hours doing the manual labour that our ancestors spent their lives doing. We no longer need to churn butter, grow our own food, cook from scratch or write on paper with feather pens. We have the luxury of having time to focus on our physical and emotional growth and well-being. It is easier for us to focus on each moment that we are alive and view it as a gift. When we do view our moments as gifts, we find that we spend our moments differently. Here is a list of how we can spend our moments in order to come to love ourselves more. There is no correct order for following these steps. The only requirement is that we work on each of these steps on a regular basis. Earlier chapters explained other steps that we need to take in order to come to love ourselves more.

Important: If you read through these steps and want to follow them but are unable to, you may still be sabotaging yourself because you have not forgiven yourself for aspects of your past. Please refer back to Chapter Four and reread the section called Forgiving Ourselves.

Do More of What You Love

"Practice doing what you love and loving what you do each day. If you are going to do something, then give yourself the benefit of not complaining about it and, instead, loving the activity. This puts you 'in spirit' and literally provides you with the enthusiasm for being a worthy recipient of God's grace. The word enthusiasm comes from the Greek root *entheos*, literally, 'to be filled with God'" (Dyer 1997, 87).

It is no coincidence that I discuss this concept with you first. It is the most important step that we can take in coming to know and love ourselves. It sounds so easy, but for most people, it is one of the hardest steps to take. ***It is cherishing ourselves that makes us strong, but, unfortunately, many of us were taught that being hard on ourselves makes us strong.*** The more we allow ourselves to do what we want to do, the more control we have over our own lives and our ultimate happiness and the better job we do of parenting ourselves. When we afford ourselves the luxury of playing, we have a good time and regenerate ourselves and our suffering eases. What is amazing is that the more time we take to do the things we love, the more effective we find ourselves to be in the rest of our lives.

We need to take time to be with ourselves in a place where we feel safe and can relax. Give yourself permission to do things like the following:

- Take a bath in the dark with candles surrounding you.
- Take an afternoon nap—yes, you can do it!
- Purchase a selection of herbal teas and make a different one each day of the week.
- Listen to music and dance in your favourite room of the house.

- Spend hours exploring your local bookstore.
- Fly a kite.
- Clean a closet: organize clothing by colour, use, type or season.
- Make a photo album or scrapbook with a particular theme: Christmas, "my friends", "my favourite scenery pictures", etc.
- Take fifteen minutes each morning and write about whatever comes to mind.
- Make a list of the things you like to do that fill you up with joy and peace. What did you enjoy doing as a child? It's time to make the younger you happy once again.

We need to take time to be with others and in a group. Our self-esteem builds when we feel that we belong and are supported. You already learned that the more connected we are to others, the safer we feel and the more we operate from our hearts. Give yourself permission to:

- join an exercise class
- join a sports team
- join a meditation group
- join a discussion group
- join a support group
- sign up for a course

There are unlimited benefits to laughing more, as well. Humour helps us detach from our circumstances and gain more perspective. Watching comedies or being with others who make us laugh counts as doing more of what we love.

Exercise
Make a list of the things you enjoyed doing as child and choose one that you haven't done in years to do again. Or stand in front of a mirror and ask yourself, "What would you like to do today [tomorrow or this week] that will make you happy?"

Start Saying No to the Things You Don't Love
"Every baby knows what feels good and what doesn't feel good, and up until about the age of six, a child will automatically go toward what feels good and away from what feels bad. This capacity is seen in its purest form in a two-year-old child who has just learned how to say no" (Northrup 1998, 61).

Children love saying no when they first learn the word and then after that because they know what they want and don't want. It is we, the adults in their lives, who tell them that they shouldn't say no so much.

When we are always saying yes to everyone or rescuing people in need, we are hoping to earn their love. We cannot come to love ourselves unless we become assertive. When we are assertive, we stand up for ourselves in order to get our needs met. We are taught to put ourselves last because that is what good people do. *But the truth is, if we truly loved ourselves, we would never give all of our time and energy away to others; that only breeds exhaustion and resentment.* When we stay late at the office instead of going home and having a bubble bath or we forgo eating because our child wants us to play with them or we decide to make a pie from scratch for a party in an already busy week, we are definitely not loving ourselves.

A key step in finding time to do the things we love to do, is saying no to others when we don't really want to do what they are asking us to do. I remember being asked out to lunch by various people in my corporate days and saying yes each and every time, whether I gained enjoyment, knowledge or business from that person or not. Then when I had my children, of course I helped out at their schools. Isn't that what a good mother does? Once I came to love myself more, do you think I was going to lunch with people I didn't adore? Not a chance. And I no longer spend my time fundraising for my girls' schools; instead, I offer to teach the students, teachers or parents about proper nutrition or emotional healing because I now know that this is what I am here to do. Parents want to contribute their time to their children's schools for a number of reasons, but the key is that it needs to be a mutually beneficial relationship. If a woman enjoys and is adept at raising money and is at home raising her children, her skills are badly needed at schools, so this would form a mutually beneficial relationship. If volunteering is causing a parent to be more stressed than they already are or if the politics are troubling them far too often, then volunteering is not making that parent feel better about themselves. Everything we choose to do needs to make us feel better about ourselves. When we don't want to do something and we say no, we might initially feel guilty, but once we say no a few times we feel empowered and proud of ourselves. For when we can say no whenever we so desire and without shame, we have found the truth of who we are.

Some would respond to this example by saying, "If I don't volunteer at my child's school, what would the principal or other parents think of me?" or "What will they do without me?" If you are worrying about that, you care more about the thoughts and well-being of others than you do about yourself. "Isn't that what we are supposed to do?" you ask. Ah, that is what most of us have been taught, isn't it? Guess what? Just as we have been taught to keep our emotions in check, we are taught to put others before ourselves. There are times when we need to keep our emotions in check and there are times when we need to put others before ourselves. The important piece to understand is that if we do either of those things too much, we will be in trouble. Our bodies may become sick or we may become miserable; there simply are no other results.

Generally, when we spend much of our time pleasing others, we are avoiding the conflict that might ensue if we tell the truth about our feelings, needs or desires. Many women get tired of spending so much of their time pleasing others yet they have little respect for their our own needs and opinions. **Once we start saying no, we begin to understand and trust ourselves. As a result, we become more dependable and trustworthy to others.** Many men often become numb and lose their ability to feel, which leads them into living as shells of their former selves. Many individuals create a sickness, at a subconscious level, to say no for them. When these individuals consciously start saying no they begin to feel human again and become more open, empathetic, happy and healthy.

There are other times in which we must say no. We need to say no to acting weak. We need to say no to acting less than who we are. We need to say no to those who don't respect us. We need to say no to the aspects of our lives that are not working for us. We need to say no to the negative ways in which we view ourselves. We need to say no to the things that drain us and yes to the things that replenish us.

Another aspect of saying no to the things we don't love is starting out each day asking ourselves, "What do I *need* to do today?" or later on, ask yourself, "What do I *need* to do now?" Really think about your answer. So many of us have great big to-do lists, but when we just do what we *need* to do each day, it frees up all sorts of time for us to do what we *want* to do. Each of us is entitled to be ourselves and, in fact, that is one of our most important objectives.

Exercise

Ask yourself if the time and energy that you are investing in various activities are contributing to living what you deem to be a meaningful life. Try to determine your motivation for extending yourself in areas that do not fit into your vision of a meaningful life. Then say no to the people who ask you to do things that you don't want to do, and feel good about it!

Stop Criticizing or Judging Yourself and Others

"It's easy to be cynical. In fact, it's an excuse for not helping the world" (Williamson 1992, 275).

Criticizing is always a bad thing. Our goal is to convert that criticism into compassion. Judgment and being judgmental are two different things. *Our judgment marries our thoughts to our emotions and helps us discern who and what is right for us so that we might set appropriate boundaries.* There are some people in our lives who teach us the lesson of discernment, which is recognizing who to turn away from. We need to be able to discern who can meet our needs and who cannot. Being judgmental, on the other hand, is attacking oneself and others; it is projecting our own views onto another person or situation; it is often name-calling or single-minded categorization of the world shared in an angry tone, and it always results in misunderstandings and exclusion. Like criticizing, being judgmental needs to be converted into compassion. We really have no right to judge another; if it is inappropriate for them to be acting the way they are, they will eventually suffer the natural consequences of their behaviour.

When one of our friends starts partying all the time and drinking too much, we have two choices in how we respond. We can think to ourselves, "What's got into them? They are a mess! How irresponsible is that; she has children to raise! I am having nothing to do with her anymore." Or we can ask her, once she is sober again, "Are you okay? Is something troubling you? Is there anything I can do to help you?" Many of us would immediately judge her behaviour, which is quite a normal reaction. The solution is to open our hearts and look beyond the inappropriate behaviour to what is really going on with our friend. There is *always* a reason behind what we deem to be inappropriate or uncharacteristic behaviour.

When we judge or criticize others, we are not seeing ourselves in others. We are not living the lives they are living. If we were, we would probably be acting similarly. Each of us makes the best choice available to us given our awareness and needs at the time. Whenever we harshly judge and criticize,

- We are only hurting ourselves.
- We interfere with loving ourselves.
- We are unable to be empathetic or compassionate to those in need.
- We don't understand the other person; it's impossible to judge another if we understand them.

- We cannot help those we judge, and often they are the ones who need it the most.
- Our bodies suffer. Remember, criticism can physically manifest as arthritis.
- We temporarily feel superior to those we judge, but we also feel a loneliness because we are distancing ourselves from them.
- We are prevented from connecting with others, not just the ones we judge but others in general.

Even if we know a course of action that would benefit another, we do not know when the time is right for them to take that course of action. If we can put ourselves in another's shoes, we can connect to their essence and their pain. Our harsh judgment and need to change them will disappear. Not unlike forgiving ourselves and others, we stop ourselves from judging or criticizing by opening our hearts and allowing compassion to take over our senses. Judgment initiates in our mind, whereas compassion initiates in our hearts. Compassion is also the secret to not judging. When there is compassion, there is just appreciating and honouring. Others heal in the presence of someone who sees their innocence. Remember, we are all innocent at our core, and it is that innocence and purity that are real, not our self-destructive behaviour. When we have compassion for others and ourselves, we understand and accept ourselves; this is the essence of self-esteem. If we make a mistake and we forgive ourselves, we have reasonable expectations for ourselves.

In order to avoid feeling that we are not good enough, we see others as not good enough. When this is the case, we offer others unsolicited advice or opinions. We also lash out at others before they can lash out at us or reject us. We assume they will give us a hard time because we give ourselves a hard time, so why would others be any different? When we judge others, we deny ourselves acceptance and intimacy. And we give our power away to those we judge. We often don't realize that when we see the goodness in ourselves, we see the goodness in others and receive the acceptance and intimacy we all need.

Sometimes it is our beauty or our sparkling personality that attracts other people's judgment. When I was in my twenties, whenever I met a beautiful girl around my age I felt insecure, simply because I had not come to love myself yet. Instinct would have me judging her, trying to find fault with her before she could reject me. To counteract those negative feelings, I would usually start talking with her if the opportunity presented itself. I usually found her to be friendly and saw other positive traits about her, which would then turn my thoughts about her around so that I was only feeling positively toward her. Sometimes, we even became friends. If I delve deeply into this scenario, I realize that if the beautiful girl liked me, I was okay with myself. If I didn't get to talk to her or if she wasn't friendly, I liked myself less. Once I started coming to love myself, I no longer thought negatively about others, never mind need to be liked by them. Love for ourselves provides us with such freedom and peace.

Now here is a key concept: Whatever we criticize or judge in others is actually a disowned or rejected part of ourselves. ***We cannot love or hate something about another person unless it reflects something we love or hate about ourselves.*** We become angry or disappointed in others in order to avoid feeling our own pain or shame. If we don't have the characteristics we dislike in others, we would not react to them. Our reaction to others is our signal; each time we analyze the criticism or judgments we make about others, we find clues about how we can heal ourselves and become whole. We need to feel the pain we are trying to mask by judging others. When we embrace the aspects of others that bother us, we will no longer be bothered by them. We will probably notice them but we will no longer be affected by them. (For more on this concept, please see Chapter Six.)

The same concept applies when others criticize us. If someone insults us for having green legs, we are not going to be bothered by that because we know we don't. However, if someone tells us that our legs are big, that could get us worked up, particularly if we were worried about the same thing. We are only supersensitive to criticism that gets close to our own thoughts and insecurities. When others criticize our personality or our actions and we get worked up, it is because they are getting close to our wounds or injuries.

 "We must forgive ourselves for being imperfect. Because when we judge ourselves, we automatically judge others. The world is a mirror of our internal selves. When we can accept ourselves, and forgive ourselves, we automatically accept and forgive others" (Ford 1998, 6).

Criticizing ourselves does not help us release our unhealthy patterns or help us grow; only acceptance does. The paradox of personal growth is that we need to come to love ourselves exactly as we are in order to implement long-lasting positive change. If we are trying to lose weight because we hate ourselves every time we stand on the scale, any weight loss will be short-lived. Self-hate creates negative self-fulfilling prophecies. Conversely, if we were to buy a few clothes to fit our overweight bodies and we appreciated our beauty, knowing that at some point, we would have the self-discipline or gain the knowledge of how to eat healthily or cleanse our bodies, we will lose weight. When we let go of our self-hate, we free up our thoughts and our energy for making the positive changes we desire.

Lastly, when we stop judging others, we create the opportunity for others to see the good inside us. Likewise, when we come to love and accept ourselves, we see the good inside others, which allows them to stop defending and protecting themselves. By accepting people, we are not condoning their weakness or agreeing with their opinion; we are simply affirming their intrinsic worth.

Exercise

The next time you want to criticize someone's behaviour, find something good to say about them instead. Even better, spend some time thinking about what might have made them behave the way they did.

Stop Taking Things Personally

Taking things personally is believing that everything is about us. This is the maximum expression of selfishness. Sometimes we agonize over what others think of us and we seek approval from them. There is little we can do to ensure others' continual approval because, in reality, it has little to do with us but lots to do with them. **Even if someone directly insults us, it actually has nothing to do with us.** Others may even share their opinion, but that does not mean that they are right, either. Others can only say or do something that matches their beliefs, and we know that beliefs can be wrong.

Unfortunately, we assume that everyone sees the world the way we do. We presume that others feel, think, judge and punish themselves the way we do. This is why we are afraid to be ourselves around others. We think others will judge and punish us as we do ourselves. Even before others have a chance to reject us, we have already rejected ourselves. But everyone sees the world through different eyes because we all live different lives.

"Your point of view is something personal to you. It's no one's truth but yours. Then, if you get mad at me, I know you are dealing with yourself. I am the excuse for you to get mad. And you get mad because you are afraid, because you are dealing with fear. If you are not afraid, there is no way you will get mad at me. If you are not afraid, there is no way you will hate me. If you are not afraid, there is no way you will be jealous or sad. If you live without fear, if you love, there is no place for any of those emotions. If you don't feel any of those emotions, it is logical that you feel good. When you feel good, everything around you is good. When everything around you is great, everything makes you happy. You are loving everything that is around you, because you are loving yourself. Because you like the way you are ... you are happy with the movie that you are producing, happy with your agreements with life. You are at peace, and you are happy. You live in that state of bliss where everything is so wonderful and everything is so beautiful. In that state of bliss you are making love all the time with everything that you perceive" (Ruiz 1997, 52).

When we take things personally, we suffer needlessly. I had a pivotal moment in my corporate career when I was in my twenties that I would like to share with you. I used to regularly write reports for one particular lady. She would bring me the material on which to base my reports, and each time she would be nasty to me. One day, I asked her point blank, "Why are you mean to me? Have I hurt you in some way?"

Much to my amazement, she was shocked to her very core. She said, "No, I just hate my job. It has nothing to do with you!"

If you are in doubt about whether something is about you, I encourage you to ask! Asking questions can stop us from making assumptions. Not everyone is as clear as this woman was about what was bothering her, but many can attest to the fact that it is not personal. I encourage my girls to ask fellow students why they are behaving in certain ways; usually, the troubling behaviour stops once the root cause is discussed. *I have reached the point now where someone can insult me, right to my face, and I simply know that they don't love themselves, for if they did, they would speak only from their heart.* But it hardly happens anymore, only with the odd stranger, because people who know me know I operate from my heart and they do the same with me.

You can see from this example that there is a large amount of freedom that comes to us when we stop taking things personally. When we follow our hearts, we don't need to place our trust in others or be responsible for what others think, say or do. Thankfully, one of the benefits of aging is that we care less about the opinions of others. We need to trust only ourselves to make responsible choices.

I want to discuss something now that is hardly ever discussed. I find it amazing, to this day, the number of people who won't accept the love of others. The people who are loving and adoring of others end up getting hurt many times over because their love is rejected or unrequited. The people who are rejecting or not returning the love simply don't love themselves or feel that the person offering their love is not the right person for them based on their belief systems. I remember the first time I heard someone say that they didn't feel they deserved their spouse and then another time heard someone else say that one day their spouse would leave them. I was shocked! In each case, the spouse chose to marry that person instead of anyone else. Why would these people feel so undeserving? What ends up happening is that these beliefs or fears become self-fulfilling prophecies when the person making the statements doesn't come to love themselves. And the person who was married to them walks away from the marriage taking everything personally, when really their spouse simply doesn't feel they deserve to be truly loved. It happens time and time again.

Exercise

The next time someone insults you and you are tempted to take it personally, ask yourself what you now know about that person.

Speak with Integrity

Don Miguel Ruiz reminded us in *The Four Agreements* (1997), of this important concept; we are the only animal on the planet that can speak; our word is the most important tool we have as humans. "We use the word to curse, to blame, to find guilt, to destroy. Of course, we also use it in the right way, but not too often. Mostly we use the word to spread our personal poison—to express anger, jealousy, envy and hate" (p 33).

It has become commonplace for people to swear when speaking to one another, and many are impolite to others, particularly strangers. Swearing and being impolite simply don't make us feel good about ourselves. Well, the odd swear word can actually provide some relief from pent-up emotions, but swearing as a regular part of our conversation can only affect us negatively. The next time you have a conversation, refrain from swearing and see how you feel afterward. When you say please or thank you, also pay attention to how you feel afterward.

"If only our tongues were made of glass, how much more careful would we be when we speak?" (Shane 2011)

We tell little white lies regularly or sometimes pretty big lies. For many, lying has become a habit. When we lie, it is impossible to feel good about ourselves. Many of us lie because we feel we are not enough and we lie to make ourselves sound better. Many of us started lying because the truth was not deemed acceptable to others. I used to lie to my stepmom because if I told her the truth, even about minor things, she would punish me. Punishing a child for telling the truth does not teach a child to be honest. (To learn how to teach children honesty, please see Chapter Eight.)

When we become conscious of the fact that we are lying or saying things we don't mean, we can begin speaking with more integrity. We can begin to notice when we are saying bad things about ourselves or to others directly and practise keeping our lips sealed. Our word is powerful. Imagine if we all used our words to spread truth and love?

Something else accompanies speaking with integrity. When we use our words to speak only truth and love, we take responsibility for our actions. It is then that we come to love ourselves enough to admit our mistakes and our vulnerabilities rather than judging or criticizing ourselves or others. The ironic thing is that once we heal ourselves, we no longer have the need to lie, say things we don't mean or try to convince others that our opinion is right and theirs is wrong. We usually find that we spend more time listening and less time speaking. Often, those who are always speaking aren't tapping into their silent knowing.

When we practise speaking with integrity, others mirror us. Action produces a like reaction. If we speak loving words to another, they will speak more loving words to us. If we insult others, they will likely insult us. Speaking lovingly and being gentle with ourselves results in others being gentle with us.

Exercise

The next time you are about to lie in order to make yourself look better, try admitting your perceived weakness.

Operate with Integrity

 "More than declaring something or theorizing about any truth, it is your actions that tell the universal mind who you are and what should come your way. You may find that you make small changes such as not going to the gym anymore but hiking in nature. You may choose to talk on the phone less and keep a journal more regularly. Whatever it is, be conscious of the soul's impulses to grow and direct you to love and make your choices according to the love that guides you" (Preston 2003, 178).

When we make choices that go against our values or hurt those we love or don't listen to our intuition, we fail to operate with integrity. Not only does everything we say matter but everything we do matters, right down to how we perform a mundane job or treat an employee with a low-paying job. Many of us feel that having a bad day gives us licence to mistreat another—why? **When we choose behaviours and perceptions that are of a higher calibre, we have a reverence for life and can only feel better about ourselves.** Being the best we can possibly be is a rocket ship to self-love.

I remember being eighteen years old and dating a guy for eight months, at which time his best friend told me that he was cheating on me. The best friend did not want his friend to know that he had provided me with this information. Upon hearing it, I was obviously angry and hurt. Most girls would tell their boyfriend they knew what he had done and be itching to make him feel absolutely miserable for acting without integrity. But if I had done this, I would not have been acting with integrity, would I? I was given this information in strict confidence. As I reflected upon our relationship, I realized that we were very different people and that it was time to say goodbye. I ended the relationship by explaining our differences, without ever saying I knew the truth about what he had done. I felt elated! I had acted with integrity and without drama. That way of responding was far more powerful than any other way of responding. You should have seen the guilt and shame written all over his face. He knew what he had done was wrong; somehow we always do.

The choices we make each day can either diminish our confidence in ourselves or make us feel powerful and suffused with love for ourselves. Each time we feel happy, we know we are making the right decisions for ourselves. Each time we feel bad, we know we are not operating with integrity. When we don't operate with integrity, we erect barriers between ourselves and others and also between ourselves and the fulfillment of our dreams. Bottom line, we end up feeling guilty. **When we feel guilty, we expect punishment, consciously or subconsciously, and therefore prevent ourselves from receiving the love and success that we want.** Our outer world always reflects our inner world.

Some of us were never taught to operate with integrity. When this is the case, we can act in a certain way, in a way that matches the person we want to be, as opposed to the person we have been. After we spend time acting the way we want to, we often find that it becomes easier to automatically operate with integrity. Eventually, we will reach a point where nothing will dissuade us from operating with integrity. For example, if we are given too much change by a cashier, we will point out the error and give the money back. We will simply apologize for being late without giving an explanation rather than making up a reason.

"Until we have integrity, we will never feel deserving or worthy of living our highest life" (Ford 2002, 140).

Exercise

The next time you find yourself being impatient or mean to another, immediately apologize to them or begin treating them with respect. Surprise them!

Speak Your Truth

Speaking our truth is different from speaking with integrity. It is feeling comfortable enough with ourselves that we can express our truth and our authentic selves with others. It is getting out of our head and speaking from our heart. It is no longer worrying so much about what others think or trying to impress others. It is saying "It hurt me when you spoke that way to me" or "I missed you when you couldn't make it to watch the play with me" or "I feel so happy to have built this closeness again with my son." It is a deep sharing of ourselves with others. It also involves sharing our stories or aspects of our stories, including our mistakes, with others. Each time we speak our truth, our heart opens up, our body thanks us, and intimacy builds with others, provided they are not suffering or in pain so much themselves that they cannot receive our truth.

Many people are comfortable with sharing numerous aspects of themselves but maintain certain big secrets that they have never shared with anyone. I have a friend who held onto a big secret for years until she finally shared it with a counsellor. The counsellor told her she was lying and refused to believe what she shared with him. At the age of four, her father had forced her and her brother to hold her mother down while he knocked out all of her teeth and raped her before their very eyes. My friend lived with the guilt of having allowed this to happen to her mother until she was almost fifty years old. She eventually decided to confide in me. She was shocked and relieved by my reaction. I knew enough about her dad, at this point, that I asked her, "Did your dad threaten to kill you and your brother if you did not do as he asked?" She told me that is exactly what he had done. I then proceeded to explain to her that she had absolutely no choice but to do what she had been told, as is usually the case with children. I explained that her mother had chosen her husband and we discussed some of the lessons her mother might have learned from him. My lack of judgment and my outpouring of compassion for my friend and what had happened to her opened the door to her own self-forgiveness. Within the following months, I found that she began to speak her truth more and more to others and even began clearing people out of her life who had not been treating her with respect. She began doing things that she loved to do. She was coming to forgive and love herself.

 "We are only as sick as our secrets. These secrets make it impossible for us to be our authentic selves. But when you make peace with yourself, the world will mirror back that same level of peace. When you're in harmony with yourself, you'll be in harmony with everyone else" (Ford 1998, 62).

There is a way to speak our truth to minimize conflict with others. It involves stating how we are feeling inside, never assuming we know how another feels or blaming them. So we say, "*I feel sad* that you choose not to be with me" as opposed to "*You make me sad* when you choose not to be with me" or "*You are being mean* to me each time you choose to be away from me." No one can make us feel anything. Only we can experience the feelings that arise within us, and those feelings most likely arise because of the circumstances wherein we felt sad in our past. If we label someone "mean", that is not the truth; that is only our perception. The person who chooses not to be with us might be processing something, be in emotional or physical pain, have to take care of the needs of another or simply need time alone.

There is a time to speak our truth to minimize conflict with others, just as there is a time to speak our feelings. We don't want to tell our friend that we are upset about something they said to us when they just made it to the finish line of their craziest week of work ever. We need to gauge where others are before we add to their load. The better we know others, the easier it becomes to choose the right time. There are also certain times that are more powerful for us to speak our truth. When we are already in a fight with our partner, for example, it is not the ideal time to speak our truth. It is far more powerful to speak our truth or even write our truth when things are calm and we are getting along well with them.

When we speak our truth, we find we have renewed energy, newfound clarity and have an easier time living in the moment. Because we have honoured ourselves, we gain pride and come to love ourselves more. Speaking our truth increases our trust in others and, in turn, encourages others to speak their truth. "Finding and living our own truth—not telling others what theirs should be—is the greatest gift we can give to others" (Williamson 1999, 127).

Exercise
Tell someone something that you have been too afraid to express. Start with one of your smaller secrets. Don't be attached to their response.

Set Boundaries with Those You Love, if Needed
You now know that when we don't love ourselves, we attract others into our lives who do not love themselves. Sometimes, those people do not treat us the way we want to be treated. As we come to love ourselves more and more, those people need to reflect our love for ourselves or we end up in conflict with one another. When others do not treat us the way we feel we deserve to be treated, we need to tell them how we want to be treated. One of the ways in which we do this is by setting boundaries.

Examples of setting boundaries include telling others to call us rather than just dropping in on us, seeing someone once a week as opposed to three times a week, asking someone not to talk about natural health with us anymore because we are truly not interested, and so on. When we set these boundaries with others, we need to do so with love and sensitivity to their needs. Our boundaries need to be healthy and helpful for ourselves, as well as for the person we ask to honour them.

After my girlfriend's father-in-law passed away, her mother-in-law wanted to be at my friend's home far more than she and her husband wanted her there. We discussed the fact that her mother-in-law was alone for the first time in years and afraid of being alone, of aging and of feeling left out. She had to learn a whole new way of existing and making herself happy. Understanding all of this softened my friend's feelings toward her mother-in-law and assisted her in helping further. I explained to my friend that setting healthy boundaries with her mother-in-law would help both of them. Her mother-in-law was not allowing herself to heal and find a new way of existing if she was always at their home. My friend explained this to her mother-in-law, which made it much easier for her to accept the boundaries my friend had proposed. She understood the reasoning and that this was for the higher good of both parties. She also knew that she could still be with her son's family some of the time, but the rest of the time she needed to focus on finding her own enjoyment.

When others cannot meet our boundaries, their respect for us is not there and we end up continuing to be unhappy in our relationship with them. Anyone who continually makes us feel unhappy is not good for us. When we have tried to set boundaries and they have gone unheeded, we can keep our distance from those people or, if we are being hurt badly enough or over a long period of time, we can safely end our relationship with anyone, and I mean anyone.

Exercise

Practise setting a boundary with someone in order to bring love and strength back into your relationship.

Let Go of Those Who Don't Appreciate You

"Don't you dare, for one more second, surround yourself with people who are not aware of the greatness that you are" (Jo Blackwell-Preston).

We are taught that we need to remain friends with everyone, even those who criticize, judge, tell us what to do, mistreat us or don't support our growth. We are taught to put loyalty to others above loyalty to ourselves. We stay in relationships because we are "good" people. And "good" people do not walk out on marriages or stop talking to a sibling. We are particularly frowned upon and looked upon with eyes of blame when we choose to break ties with a family member. Once again, we have been taught incorrectly. ***If anyone is failing to treat us with love and respect, is not accepting our boundaries or hinders our success, we do not need to spend another moment with them.***

But some of us feel that ending relationships, particularly with family members, would not be operating from our hearts. We cannot continually open our hearts and be supportive of people who do not want to receive our love and who continually hurt us. It is also impossible to come to know and love ourselves when we surround ourselves with people who do not see our value (which is simply because they don't see their own value). When we continue to spend time with these people after becoming aware of how detrimental they are to us, we are leaving the door open for our old negative ways to proliferate.

"Humans are addicted to suffering at different levels and to different degrees, and we support each other in maintaining these addictions. Humans agree to help each other suffer" (Ruiz 1997, 56–57).

As you know, I forgave my mother for what went on between us in my early years. We had many years of love and friendship as a result. You may be surprised to learn that, as of four years ago, we are no longer in each other's lives. Her family members had long ago decided to keep her at arm's length. For most of her life, my mother has borrowed money from others, including me, and never paid them back. As adults, she and I spoke every two or three days for over twenty years, and the majority of our conversations would involve her telling me about her latest business ideas or the people she had met who were going to lend her money or invest in her ideas. I always listened to her and supported her. To be fair, I spoke to her for almost nine years about my unhappiness with my husband but I always filled her in on other aspects of my life, as well.

The first boundary I set with her was telling her that I was no longer going to give her money; she understood that. Later, I asked her, more than once, to stop talking to me about her business (set another boundary), but she never did. I then started tuning her out somewhat (new response, on my part) when she shared the names of the people with whom she met, the locations in which they met and the details of their conversations. This new response of mine worked for me. When I decided I was finally ready to leave my husband, I was amazed to learn that she didn't support me. I was very surprised, particularly since she, of all people, knew how unhappy I had been with him for so many years. A couple of weeks later, she asked me if she could ask him for a loan. After all of these years, the only reason I could think of that she would do that is because she knew he would do anything to get me back and she knew she would probably get the amount she sought if she now asked him for money. I asked her explicitly not to ask him for money (setting another boundary). She did it anyway. I told my ex not to lend her the money but he did, knowing he would never be reimbursed but probably secretly hoping I would reward him for it.

Shortly after that, while I was revelling in pleasure at having finally surrendered my unhealthy marriage, I found myself listening to my mother tell me about one more deal that had fallen through for her. I decided to write my mother an email to explain to her how to surrender what was no longer working for her (speaking my truth and trying to help another), so that she could feel the pleasure that I was now feeling at having escaped from my self-made prison, knowing she was still in hers. I sent her what I thought to be a lengthy, descriptive, helpful and loving email. Her response was abhorrent to me, on many levels, and she told me that she never wanted to speak to me again. It was at that moment that I realized she would never surrender the aspects of her life that were not working for her, that she would never live with integrity and that she was filled with anger, which I knew stemmed from fear. I was actually relieved when she told me that she wanted me out of her life. Every once in a while she makes an attempt to reconcile, but I have not capitulated.

When we are supporting another in a relationship and they are not living in integrity or supporting us (and often don't realize it), it is difficult to continue the relationship, but when they then openly attack us, the relationship is no longer healthy for us. When we are in a relationship and we realize that there is very little that we would miss if we were not in that relationship, that relationship is no longer serving us. Here is the key: We can't just end relationships that are not the way we want them to be. There are two requirements. First, we have to have reached a point of complete acceptance of the other person. That means that we can be with them, watch them lying to others or to themselves, not living in integrity, making poor choices and so on, and know that their behaviour has nothing to do with us and that they are only behaving in this way because they don't love themselves. When we reach that point of acceptance, we can continue a relationship with them and enjoy their wonderful aspects, still loving them. But if we reach that point of acceptance and we tell them how *we* want to be treated (set a boundary) and they continue to mistreat us, we can safely end our relationship with that person. That is the second requirement for ending a relationship with another. And to tell you the truth, if we do not end a relationship of this kind, we are disrespecting ourselves. When my relationship ended with my mother, I had come to a point where I loved myself too much to be mistreated and I loved myself enough to know that her challenges had nothing to do with me. It was easy to let go of and forgive my mother. It is very easy to let go of and forgive others when we reach that place of peace within ourselves.

Here is the final piece to understand. If a family member or friend whom we love but are estranged from genuinely changes their ways, comes to love themselves, apologizes to us and then asks that we resume our relationship with them, we need to renew our relationship with them. If we do not, we have not forgiven them, and that will only hurt *us* in the long run.

Letting go of unfulfilling or destructive relationships of any kind is paramount to coming to love ourselves, but the loneliness that can set in afterwards can threaten to change one's mind. Be aware of this but stay strong! When we let go of unhealthy relationships, we open the door for people who will love us the way we deserve to be loved.

Exercise

Ask yourself if you are investing your time and energy in the people who matter most to you. Make a list of the people who improve your life, brighten your day or see your greatness and those who don't. Then decide who you want to let go of first and how and when you are going to go about it.

Surround Yourself with People of Integrity, Who Love and Appreciate You

As we come to love ourselves, ending or limiting time spent with certain people in our lives is part of our natural evolution. We no longer want to be part of the drama and the people who create it. We want to surround ourselves with people who understand us, see our beauty, share our belief in the possibilities and lift us up.

In time, as we come to love ourselves more, we find that more and more emotionally healthy people show up in our lives, and some of our old relationships may even become stronger than ever before. I have experienced this myself and witnessed it many times. As we live with integrity, we attract others doing the same—it is another law of the universe.

People say that you can never choose your family. In *Making Peace with Your Family* (1983), Harold Bloomfield suggests taking care of our own needs for emotional support by building a surrogate family. He explains that the more our needs are met and the happier we are, the more we can accept and love our parents without trying to change them.

Just prior to my separation, I found a surrogate family for myself and my girls. These beautiful people have become my "adopted parents", the parents I always wanted. I met Pat while learning Nordic pole walking with a group of women. She and I connected so easily. In time, she introduced me to her husband, George, with whom I equally connected. Fast forward two years and we were spending every Mother's Day, Father's Day and special occasion together, not to mention the regular days of the year that we enjoy together. Pat told me that after she had her two sons, she had wanted to adopt a girl because she had wanted a daughter so badly, but it never happened. I cannot tell you how special this couple has become, not just to me but to my children as well. They know my girls and me far better than some of our own family members do and love us exactly as we are. They are interested in every aspect of our lives; they guide and support us in everything we do and even stick up for us! They help us maintain our home, bring us meals and take my girls places when I cannot. The level of care they show us is something the girls and I had never experienced before. If I go more than a couple of days without contact with them, I miss them terribly, and they feel the same way.

The bottom line is that we need to choose people with whom to surround ourselves who make us feel good inside, who see our beauty, who make us laugh, who help us when we need it, who encourage us to speak our truth, who want success for us and who see the wonder in this world alongside us.

Exercise

Think about which of your friends loves and respects you and arrange to spend more time with them. If you don't know anyone who treats you with love and respect, you know you need to work on loving and respecting yourself more. You can read books or watch movies to see the qualities you want to experience in yourself or another.

Let Go of the Aspects of Your Life That Are Not Working for You

I briefly touched on this topic already but feel that further elaboration is needed. We have all heard the saying "Never give up." Guess what? We have been taught incorrectly once again. As much as I have talked about taking responsibility, there are times in our lives when we need to give up. But I prefer to call it "surrendering" or "letting go". Surrendering usually signifies defeat in war but, in life, surrendering signifies transcendence.

"Our resistance is triggered whenever we make ourselves, others, or the world wrong" (Ford 2002, 65).

When we experience stress, we are resisting the flow of life. **Stress is not caused by the circumstances of our lives but by our reaction to the choices we have made that result in the circumstances of our lives.** When the circumstances of our lives or people don't meet our approval, we focus our energy on trying to control or change the circumstances or people in our lives. Why are we giving our power away? We expend a massive amount of energy trying to conceal the pain of our past and change our external circumstances or other people, hoping that one day we will finally be happy. Some of us stay in this pattern for our whole lives. Anything we want to change or we're afraid of or angry about or refuse to accept will keep us attached to our negative stories and the beliefs that go along with them. Resisting what is will never make it disappear. We know we are resisting when we experience physical manifestations such as a stiff neck, clenched jaw, headache, sighing and tightness in the chest, just to give a few examples. Once we recognize where our resistance is anchoring in our body, we are able to identify it and the triggers more easily.

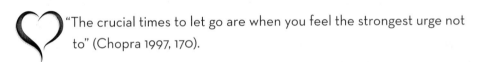 "The crucial times to let go are when you feel the strongest urge not to" (Chopra 1997, 170).

Once we accept that this is the way it is going to be with this job or this situation or this person or this quality about ourselves that we don't like, we can stop resisting and let things flow effortlessly. Then we can determine what we need to do to create what it is we desire. Our ego mistakes surrendering for failure and the end of power, but when we surrender, we transcend our ego and let go of control of circumstances over which we really never had any control anyway. We can stop forcing things and simply allow things to happen. We are most powerful when we are working with life rather than against it. Surrendering is stopping ourselves from doing the things that make us miserable, crazy or self-hating. When we stop abusing ourselves, love and healing can move in. Surrendering to what is, requires us to let go of our expectations that arose from our stories and accept the wisdom of life's experiences and the resulting joy. If we have resisted throughout our life, then we will need to learn to surrender; it will be one of our lessons.

"Something amazing happens when we surrender and just love. We melt into another world, a realm of power already within us. The world changes when we change. The world softens when we soften. The world loves us when we choose to love the world. Surrender means the decision to stop fighting the world, and to start loving instead. It is a gentle liberation from pain" (Williamson 1992, 61).

The example I want to share with you to explain this concept is not life altering but it is profound. When in Mexico with my family, my girls and I went horseback riding late in the day. While riding, Paige and I saw a giant turtle in the sand. When our ride finished, the two of us wanted to go back and get a closer look at the turtle. Taylor rejoined her dad while Paige and I embarked on our quest. We walked and walked and walked for almost an hour. In her eagerness, Paige walked far in front of me. When we were long past the spot where we had seen the turtle, I wanted Paige to turn around and return to our hotel with me, but she kept on walking. I was tired, hot and hungry and desperately wanted to go back but had no way of conveying my feelings to Paige; she was too far ahead of me and the waves were crashing in noisily beside us. Eventually, I just stopped walking. I didn't want to. I didn't want to lose sight of Paige. But I had no way of reaching her. I turned to the side and stood with my arms and legs all in a straight line, so that if Paige looked back she would see that I was no longer following her. And I waited. It seemed like forever, but eventually she noticed me and ran back. You see? I struggled and struggled, trying to catch up to Paige, hoping she would change her mind and call off the search for the turtle. All I needed to do was surrender. I wished I had done it sooner. And that, interestingly enough, is often how we feel once we surrender.

Sometimes, we struggle and struggle and get nowhere. We think and hope we are getting somewhere but we are not. It's like a hamster in his wheel; he is not going anywhere. When that is happening in our relationships or in our jobs or in any aspect of our lives, it takes incredible courage to say to ourselves, "Enough of this struggling! This is not working for me." They say the definition of insanity is doing the same thing over and over again, hoping for a different outcome. Stop the insanity!

Surrendering is not sacrificing who we think we are; it is remembering who we truly are. *We are not angry people who fight all the time and criticize others; that is not who we are. We are not the people who work ourselves to the bone to prove ourselves to others and get no appreciation in return; that is not who we are. We are not constant complainers who can't get anything to go the way we want it to in our lives; that is not who we are.* Complaining is just wanting someone else to be responsible for what we are experiencing and to make things better for us. We really are just peaceful, loving and happy individuals.

What makes us continue struggling? Why don't we surrender? A part of us feels we deserve to struggle; that is the only reason. It is always fear that lies behind those feelings of not deserving. We are afraid of what will happen if we surrender. We are afraid that if we surrender, we can't prove ourselves to others. We are afraid that if we don't accomplish what we are trying to accomplish, we are a failure or we will be rejected or ridiculed by others or there will be repercussions with which we cannot live. Or maybe we see the good in the person we are struggling with in a relationship but they don't see the good in themselves. Ironically, if we saw the good in ourselves, we would know that we deserve more for ourselves. We need to look carefully at the beliefs, habits, perceptions, judgments and excuses that we are desperately holding onto that keep us in our unhealthy, repetitive patterns. There can be any number of obvious reasons to continue the struggle, but we can only face our biggest fears once we come to love ourselves enough. That is the only time we really know we do not deserve to struggle anymore and the world truly can be a peaceful place.

We need to stop fighting when things continually don't go our way, when we get sick or when we are mistreated or misunderstood. We need to slow down, feel our pain, see ourselves clearly and surrender to our uneasiness and uncertainty. The majority of us who surrender do so when the pain of holding on is even greater than the fear of letting go. Ideally, we would avoid despair of such magnitude and take our leap of faith into the unknown sooner, because when we surrender, the struggle ends, relief washes over our bodies and opportunities abound. And guess what? Courage and confidence automatically follow when we surrender; it's an amazing phenomenon.

When we surrender a relationship, it does not mean that we stop caring for another; it means that we finally understand that we cannot change or control another. When we surrender, we are no longer trying to tell others what to do; we are allowing them to learn from natural consequences. When we surrender, we are no longer trying to fix things for others; we are being supportive. When we surrender, we let go of criticizing or blaming others and decide to focus on loving ourselves instead. When we surrender, we are fearing less and loving more.

"And sometimes in those moments of surrender, you will get to see how much you get from staying stuck in the way you see yourself and other people; how much you have invested in making someone else wrong, so that you don't have to accept your own culpability; how you idolize others so that you don't have to claim your own power, take a stand, be your most noble and reliant self" (Lesser 2005, 270–71).

Exercise

Here is an exercise to help you surrender, cultivate more peace in your life and become aware of when you are feeling peaceful.

Notice when it is that you feel peace. Is it during specific activities? Is it when you are alone or with others? Is it at home or at work? What makes the peace end? How frequently do you feel it? What beliefs do you hold that are preventing you from feeling peace more often? What do you have to let go of in order to transform?

Face Your Fears

In order to surrender, set our boundaries and do the other things we need to do to come to fully love ourselves, we need to face our fears. Each time we face a fear, we open a door to enlightenment and our love for ourselves grows. Fear is our emotional GPS; it alerts us to the negative emotion that is no longer serving us. **Whatever we are most afraid of is our biggest clue about what we need to do.** If we fear commitment, we really desire a happy, healthy and long-term relationship but we are scared that we will never have it. If we fear failure, we really desire success. It reminds me of when we are trying to determine the food that is behind our most severe or pervasive physical symptoms, we need to look at the food that we are most afraid of living without and that is usually our biggest culprit. (My first book expands on this concept.)

A woman in her early fifties came to see me before she was to go in for knee surgery. She had previously had hip surgery. Both of these joint problems represented a fear of moving forward. One of the first things the woman said to me was "And don't tell me I need to leave my husband because I refuse to do that." Well, guess what she needed to do? But because she was not ready to go there, she left my office without ever discussing leaving her husband.

"You might have heard the adage 'What you resist persists.' Understanding this statement is the key to embracing your fears. Resisting, judging, and hating your fears only allows them to have a tighter grip. When you ignore, judge, or hide them, you are actually handing over your power to them. … [Y]ou need to open your heart to the wounded part of yourself" (Ford 2012, 34).

In order to access our courage, we need to acknowledge, accept and become friends with our fears. Our fears are born from our misunderstandings of our past experiences and create the challenges that we are destined to overcome. When we acknowledge that we are scared or insecure or admit to regrets from our past, we can receive the gifts that fear has for us. When we overcome our fears, we break free of our past, come to love ourselves more and receive the courage we need to be who we really are inside.

Our fears remind us of the child each of us has within us that needs our love and focus. When we face and overcome our fears, we provide that child with what they need. *We need to thank our fears for the role they play in helping us evolve and find the love and happiness we all deserve.* Love trumps fear every time.

A family member was born of a very controlling mother, married a very controlling woman and worked for a very controlling father. He lived under their control until he was about forty years old. He was desperately unhappy and had no idea who he was. He was scared out of his mind to stand up to these people he had allowed to have such a hold over him. He was scared for his children and their future if he did anything to rock the boat. He believed that his freedom would not only hurt but damage everyone he loved. He worried that he could not make the income he needed to on his own. Some would say, putting a negative spin on what happened, that he went through a mid-life crisis. I believe that when many of us approach forty, we reach a point where we have had enough of not living our lives authentically and we know we don't want to spend the next forty years living the same way. So what did this man do? First he divorced his wife, then he stopped working for his dad and started his own business in a similar line of work but took on more of the creative aspect of that work. And the *coup de grâce*? He had a huge tattoo imprinted onto his back of a rising phoenix with massive wings spanning his shoulders. Overall, it was a monumental set of moves. Did it all go smoothly for him after that? His parents gradually adjusted to his decision, and he remains close to them to this day. It took a few years, but his business flourished, and he loves doing what he does. His wife was belligerent to him for years but finally calmed down. His children rebelled but are now happy and they remain close to both their parents. What a tremendous example of transcendence; I am thrilled to have had the opportunity to be a witness to it all.

"Pain can burn you up and destroy you, or burn you up and redeem you. It can deliver you to an entrenched despair, or deliver you to your higher self. At mid-life we decide, consciously or unconsciously, the path of the victim or the path of the phoenix when it is rising up at last" (Williamson 2008, 50).

Exercise

What are you afraid of? Make a list of your fears and then circle your greatest fear. Spend some time contemplating what life would look like for you if you no longer had that fear.

Trust Yourself and Your Intuition

"A true gut feeling will always be born in love, and will be an activity that meshes with your natural talents and interests. Your gut will always direct you toward activities that benefit other people, and never toward those that involve dishonour or deception" (Virtue 1995, 228).

Many of us are taught to not trust ourselves. It starts when our parents tell us not to feel a certain way. It continues when our parents teach us that we can't do things our way. As adults, we are told by others not to do the things we feel compelled to do. Even when we are parents, we are dissuaded from following our instincts. Mothers often tell me stories of their children not having bowel movements for days on end. Their instinct is that something is wrong, so they take their child to the doctor and are told "That's normal. Don't worry about it." No, it's not normal! How do we, as adults, feel if we go a few days without a bowel movement? We need to expel the waste from our bodies or the waste builds up inside us and we become sick.

 "We see, hear, taste, touch and smell—and we have a 'gut reaction.' All six senses provide information on which we make decisions. Intuition is also a talent each of us is given and is a capacity we can develop. Unfortunately, we often hold back our intuition. We hold back because intuition is looked on sceptically by our culture—at least compared to the scientific and empirical methods of knowing. Because of that, we don't get much practice using our intuition as we grow up—so our intuitive 'ear' is not well trained. Sometimes we hold back because we're not sure our intuition is 'right'" (Howson 2010, 15).

Our conscience is our friend. It is the part of us that helps us stay on track and do the right thing. It always operates from the highest integrity. *Our inner voice always speaks to us in a language we understand.* When we start to trust the messages we receive, we find we are always guided for our highest good, and our lives only get better and better. Think back to the times in which you trusted your instincts and were led to the right course of action, and my hope is that you will receive a gentle reminder to do this more often. Each time we honour our inner knowing and follow our hearts, we are rewarded. All answers do lie within us, if only we will take the time to listen. Spending time in nature, writing, doing art or listening to music are just a few of the ways in which we can hear that inner voice that guides us more clearly.

Many of us have a hard time trusting our inner voice when we do hear it. Sonia Choquette (2010) is excellent at explaining how to do things like this because she writes in such simple terms. She suggests speaking the advice your inner voice gives you out loud and then observing how the words affect you. If they are true guidance, your body will feel good inside, especially your heart area. If it is not your true inner voice that you are hearing but your hope or your fear speaking, you will feel some agitation in your body. These feelings can be subtle, but the more you practise, the more you will know when something is off.

The more we come to love ourselves, the greater our intuition becomes. This is because we are no longer surrounded by chaos or overcome with pain and we are becoming more used to heeding the advice of our inner voice.

"Examine your thoughts carefully. See if those thoughts are totally congruent with your actions. To say 'I believe in a healthy body' and to practise eating in unhealthy ways dissolves trust in yourself. Congruent thought, emotions and behaviour are strong indicators of your self-trust" (Dyer 1997, 33).

Exercise
Sit with a piece of paper and a pen and ask a question out loud to which you want an answer. Begin writing down everything that comes to mind. You might

be surprised to find your answer in that writing, even if you don't see it until you reread it at another time.

Be Grateful

"When you stop comparing what is right here and now with what you wish were here, you can begin to enjoy what is" (Cheri Huber).

Most of us have been told since we were young children to be grateful. We hear it time and time again, "Think of the starving children in Africa. Be grateful that you have a meal in front of you." Being forced to be grateful, as with anything that is forced, is not going to make us grateful.

Why is being grateful so important? Gratitude connects us to what feels right about ourselves and what is going well in our lives. Giving thanks for what we have actually augments its value in our mind. Gratitude is the secret to opening our hearts. When we are grateful, we lower our defences, become humble and replace criticism, judgment and perceived lack with love and appreciation. Gratitude soothes our souls and sorrow always moves into gratitude once we heal. Whenever we find ourselves having negative thoughts and we replace those thoughts with all the things we are grateful for, we feel better inside.

When we do replace the negative with gratitude, what is lacking in our lives seems far less important. ***When we are thankful for the things that go right in our lives and see our lives as abundant, we find that our energy goes to abundance rather than to scarcity and more goes right in our lives.*** It is another law of the universe. When we complain about what we don't have and are negative about our life circumstances, we invite more to go wrong. Think about the people you know who are like that. Every errand seems to go awry, they break things all the time, each job seems to be a "make work" project. Is abundance surrounding them? Impossible. I find that some of the most intelligent of people overthink things and can easily foresee everything that could go wrong with their plans for a day. More times than not, their plans become thwarted. In contrast, think of the fictional character Forrest Gump. He was so grateful for the simplest things in his life and saw things so simply that he ended up accomplishing the most incredible feats. Think of how you feel when you give a gift to someone who is appreciative; all you want to do is give that person more gifts. The more grateful we are, the more blessings come our way—it's just the way it works.

Gratitude helps us focus on the present moment. It is pretty difficult to think much about our past and future and things we cannot control when we are simply feeling grateful for where we are at this time. Gratitude increases our feelings of pride in ourselves, which helps us come to love ourselves more. It increases our zest for life because we are not wallowing in self-pity or regret over our past or worrying about our future. When we feel gratitude, we feel so good inside that we want to pass the feeling onto others. This makes us kinder and more generous. Then the people around us, touched by our generosity, want to be kinder and more generous and want to pass the feelings onto others. This is how we pay it forward.

Exercises

Here are a number of exercises to cultivate gratitude. These are excellent ideas to do with children, as well:

1. Relay your positive experiences or achievements to others. Their enjoyment can only add to your appreciation of those experiences and achievements.

2. Write out a list of everything for which you are grateful. One list can include the big things such as your relationships, home or job. Another list can include individual circumstances that made you feel good inside; write down those good feelings. Another list can be your accomplishments, such as achieving a high grade in a course or graduating from a program or running a marathon. Another list can include your different positive attributes and then the positives that can be gleaned from your negative traits. Another list can include tinier details, such as seeing the dew sit on a bright green plant or seeing a baby's face light up when they see a puppy or feeling someone touch the skin on the other side of our elbow. You can feel grateful just to be able to breathe or be alive.

3. Create a gratitude jar. Each day, write what you are grateful for on slips of paper and add them to the jar. At the end of each week, review everything and feel your heart fill up.

4. Spend time helping those who are less fortunate, so that you gain perspective on what you have in your life.

5. Practise seeing the gift in each challenging incident in your life. Before you know it, you will start to be able to see the gifts quickly and easily every time and see that you are continually receiving and experiencing gifts. For example, if you experience digestive challenges, be grateful that your body is letting you know what foods or aspects of your environment are not good for you. Seeing the gifts in our challenges is

actually the key to overcoming our challenges. When we see only what we are lacking or how we are hurting inside, our energy becomes focused on the negative, and the negative will perpetuate.

6. Write thank-you letters to the five people who have made the biggest difference in your life.

7. Scrapbook or journal your positive experiences. This is a way to ensure that you spend more time reliving and enjoying your memories of those moments.

8. Celebrate your successes. For example, as adults, when we graduate from an educational program, we often don't celebrate our achievement, but we wouldn't think of not celebrating our child's graduation. When we start a new job, turn a year older or end a marriage that was holding us back, celebrating increases our gratitude. I have a friend who hosted a party to celebrate her divorce and invited everyone who supported her throughout the process.

9. Write a fan letter to yourself and mail it to your home.

The highest form of gratitude is being thankful for the good we currently *have* in our lives and for the good we *want* in our lives before it has even appeared. *When we reach a point where we are so overcome with gratitude for what we have in our lives that we actually cry, we have felt the gratitude that literally shifts our perceptions and subsequently makes unimaginable improvements to our lives.*

Think and See Positively

"The measure of mental health is the disposition to find good everywhere" (Ralph Waldo Emerson).

The more we love ourselves, the greater our outlook on life in general. The more we open our hearts, the more positively we are able to think and see. Why do we need to think positively about ourselves, others, the circumstances we experience or witness, the possibilities or the world we live in? Positive thinking is crucial to producing positive emotions. Positive emotions such as love, joy and gratitude reduce stress, increase order, bring balance to our nervous systems and bring harmony to our lives. As with gratitude, when we think positively, more positive things happen in our lives, which results in us having more joy and appreciation. We receive what we think about, whether we want it or not, so we had better think positively! When things are continually not going the way we want them to, we begin to expect that things will continue that way; if we don't change our attitude, our worst fears *will* come to fruition.

I would like to share an example of this with you. Taylor was fourteen years old. Her life was not going the way she wanted it to, yet the people and circumstances around her were ripe with promise. One night, she explained to me how down she felt. I asked her to describe what led her to having these feelings. She explained that when she thinks positively and things go well for her, a little voice in her head tells her that it won't last. She admitted that she is afraid of being disappointed, so she stops herself from thinking positively. I asked her what it feels like to be disappointed. She started to cry and said that when she feels disappointed, she feels sad, frustrated and lonely and that she is not making the difference she wants to in the world. I then told her that our thoughts determine our reality and pointed out that her fear of being disappointed was causing her to experience the very feelings that she didn't want. She cried really hard when this knowledge sunk in, and the crying was a great release, for she realized that she had created her own pain. I asked her if she was scared of anything else and even gave her specific examples, but she wasn't scared of anything else. I asked her if she was done feeling disappointed, and she said she was. I asked her if she felt that she deserved to be happy, and she said she did. I asked her if anything was stopping her from being happy, and she didn't think there was. I asked her if there was anything for which she had not forgiven herself. She then relayed an incident that she had felt ashamed of for the past four years. We discussed it at length; I normalized it for her so that she was able to forgive herself. We determined that there was nothing else for which she needed to forgive herself. I asked her to describe to me how it would feel when she is happy and perpetually feeling positive about life, so that she could start to visualize the way she wanted things. She then came up with an affirmation to help her think more positively about her life. Her life turned around from that night on.

For some of us, thinking positively comes naturally. For others, we need to be taught how to think positively. Interestingly, the people who adopt an unfailingly positive attitude usually have had the most struggles and pain in their lives.

I invite you to spend one day listening to the voices in your head. The more you can witness your negativity, the less negative you will be. **Negative thoughts create a low self-esteem. Positive thoughts create a high self-esteem**. Are your thoughts predominantly positive or negative? Do you believe that you deserve good things to happen to you? Is anything stopping you from being happy?

Those of us who grew up with constant negativity may never entirely get rid of our negative inner voice but we can increase the strength of our parallel positive inner voice. So when we are telling ourselves that we can't accomplish a goal, we can literally say out loud, "Cancel that thought." And then we can replace the thought with "I am doing the best I can; anything is possible." As our positive voice gains strength, it responds more quickly, more strongly and with more conviction to the attacks of our inner critic.

When someone around us is positive, we learn by their example. When we don't have that example, self-help books are a wonderful way to learn. Sometimes, in order to be positive, we need to extricate ourselves from negative influences in our lives such as the nightly news, the newspaper, groups of gossiping neighbours or co-workers, other people's dramas, web surfing and so on. When we do this, we free up all sorts of time to learn new things, to think, and to nurture ourselves. We automatically become more positive because we are no longer bombarded with negative information or fear-inducing media. ***Our job is to learn to keep our minds disciplined enough so that they do not trick us into feeling sorry for ourselves and thinking that we are badly off; that is the easy route for our thoughts to take and for ourselves to head down a slippery slope.***

"Endlessly unchallenged negative thinking can sometimes lead to a self-fulfilling prophecy" (Domar 2000, 49).

We become anxious when our thoughts continually tell us that something bad is going to happen. We become depressed when our thoughts tell us that we are worthless and that our lives are hopeless. When we are always afraid of being abandoned, that is usually exactly what ends up happening.

 "You may not think you can talk to your DNA but, in fact, you do continually." For instance, if a person is always saying, 'I'm sick and tired of ...' they shouldn't be surprised if they are tired a lot or become sick" (Deepak Chopra, as cited in Truman 2003, 273).

Cognitive therapy (you will learn more about this in Chapter Ten) includes four questions that help us become aware of negative thought patterns, challenge their logic and replace them with more positive thoughts:

1.   Is this thought increasing my stress?
2.   Where did I learn this thought? (It is usually from someone we know or it is our own fear.)
3.   Is this thought logical?

4. Is this thought true? (Sometimes a thought is illogical but has some truth and sometimes a thought is logical but not entirely true.)

When we see things positively, we see that every challenge can be turned into an opportunity. Someone's bad day becomes an opportunity for us to treat them with kindness. A misdemeanour becomes an opportunity to forgive another and open our heart to them. A friend's mourning becomes an opportunity for us to tell them how much they mean to us.

 "Keep your thoughts positive because your thoughts become your words. Keep your words positive because your words become your behaviour. Keep your behaviour positive because your behaviour becomes your habits. Keep your habits positive because your habits become your values. Keep your values positive because your values become your destiny" (Mahatma Gandhi).

Exercises

1. Each time you answer the above questions, try replacing each negative thought with a positive, more realistic thought. Think about all the things you have done right in your life instead of the things you feel you have done wrong. Think about how hard you have worked to become a better person.
2. Whenever you have a negative feeling, shift your awareness, right in that moment, to thinking of the opposite feeling. For example, if you are feeling tired, remind yourself of what it feels like to be rested. This will provide you with a sense of balance and being at peace with yourself.

Treat Your Body with Love and Respect

We love and respect our bodies when we adopt good nutrition and regular exercise, when we work our bodies but also allow them to relax, and when we choose ways to look our best.

When we look around these days, we see that people are dressed more casually than ever before; we tend to think how great it is that we can be comfortable so much of the time. Did you know that with the influx of casual Fridays into the workplace, productivity has gone down? The more casually employees are dressed, the less some of them care about doing their work. They are used to dressing casually when they are relaxing in life and so that is the attitude they adopt every time they are dressed casually.

Let's transfer that way of thinking to other aspects of our lives.

A first-time mother often can't fit into her nice clothes and has nowhere to wear them initially anyway. She is tired and stressed from getting to know her newborn. If there is no date night with her husband or other function to get ready for, she relaxes into months, maybe years of caring for her child without ever bothering to dress nicely. It may even reach a point where she is invited to a function and determines it is just too much work for her to even contemplate attending. This is how unhealthy patterns begin. Some of you would say, "Good for her! Why should she get out of her comfy clothes? She has a baby to raise. That is her top priority." Yes, she could live her life this way, *but* it would be at her expense. And years later, when her child is off at university, this mother would realize she doesn't even know herself. She may even be out of shape or sick by then because she had ignored her own needs for so long.

I remember mothers saying to me in an insulting way, "How can you even find the time to apply makeup with a newborn?" or "Don't you ever wear sweatpants?" My response was always, "It makes me feel better about myself to look nice. My daughter sits in her vibrating chair beside me while I get ready and I sing to her." Now you probably read earlier that for years I couldn't be seen in public without my makeup because I didn't like myself. That extreme is obviously not good. But wearing makeup or dressing nicely some of the time can increase our respect for ourselves, and that is always a good thing. In fact, our appearance expresses how much we care about ourselves and others.

When Paige was only two, she would pick up a food and ask me, "Is this good for my body?" We can teach children to love and respect their bodies starting as early as eighteen months old. My first book, *The Resourceful Mother's Secrets to Healthy Kids*, outlines how to take care of our bodies nutritionally (it applies to adults as well) and through exercise and movement.

We need to feel a certain amount of love for ourselves to treat our bodies with love and respect, but the more we do it, the more the love flows. You will notice that the more your life is in alignment with what you want, the better able you are to treat your body with love and respect and the more able you will be to follow all the steps in this chapter.

Exercise

Make a list of what you want to do to treat your body with more love and respect. Set realistic goals for what you want to do to turn things around. Don't be afraid to seek outside help.

Find Your Passion

We usually have a number of passions. Many of us do not know what we are passionate about because we are so busy doing what we are "supposed" to do. We each have the responsibility to discover our various passions. Our passions bring us joy and help us make our unique contribution to the world. Our passions can be anything from dancing, skiing or hiking in the trees to improving the look of the world by becoming architects or putting smiles on the faces of seniors. Sometimes our biggest passion determines our purpose.

When we think about our talents or what we liked to spend time doing as children, we can usually uncover our passions. When I was a child, I was asked, as all children are, "What would you like to be when you grow up?" I remember saying, at one point, that if it was determined that we could live on another planet, I would like to be the person who teaches people what they would need to eat and how to care for themselves on that planet. Well, that is basically what I am doing now! But I teach people how to do things differently on our own planet. The majority of people are not living joyfully each day; my passion is to help as many people to live joyfully as I can. Each time I learn a lesson about doing this, I think, "How will I teach others or write about this?" *When we know our passions, life is always exciting; others do not need to entertain us; we are never bored; we are not easily let down by others when our plans fall through or when our relationships end because we can always focus on our passions.* The more we spend time doing the things we are passionate about, the more we come to love ourselves. Once we reach that point, we usually find ourselves making a promise, consciously or subconsciously, that we will never betray ourselves again by denying ourselves time spent focusing on our passion.

 I like this quote from Marianne Williamson: "Success means we go to sleep at night knowing that our talents and abilities were used in a way that served others" (1992, 179).

Exercise

Earlier I described how our stories provide us with experiences and lessons that teach us valuable information that we can use to make our contribution to the world. If we are trying to uncover the contribution we might make in the world, it is helpful to look at our lives and wonder if our lives had been training us to do something in particular. For you, what would that be?

Spend Time Being Creative

When so many of us are over-stressed, it is often time spent pursuing our creative endeavours that is lacking. Sometimes following our passion involves unleashing our creativity. When we do anything creative, we uncover our ability to play and unleash our imagination. We also express our own individuality, and the more pleased we are with the results of our labours, the greater our enthusiasm for life and the more we come to love ourselves. This can involve doing ceramics, finger painting with lots of bright colours, making home movies, singing at the top of our lungs, making jewellery, woodworking, making a snow angel or taking pictures of beautiful aspects of nature in your neighbourhood.

Exercise

Sign up for a class to learn how to do something creative. Or choose a day and record it in your calendar to do something creative. Sometimes asking a friend to do it with you ensures you do it!

Help Others and Allow Yourself to Receive Help

Some people's passion is helping others. When that is not the case, we need to find ways to give our time, energy and attention to others while maintaining a balance between meeting their needs and our own. And we need to help others without expecting anything in return.

When we commit to our own emotional healing and come to love ourselves, we can't help but desire to make the world a better place by helping others. The more we experience our own personal power, the less helpless we feel in helping others. Our empathy expands, and taking charge of our lives translates into making a difference in the world.

When we are helping others, not only are we connecting with others but we are making their lives easier. It is impossible to be as consumed with our own challenges when we are helping people. Helping others teaches us about the world and puts perspective in our own lives, often encouraging us to be grateful for what we have and appreciative that we don't have the challenges that others have. More than anything, helping others puts meaning and value in our lives and makes us feel good about ourselves. Really, our giving to others is the greatest illusion because every time we smile at another or put forth effort for another, we are the ones who receive the gift.

"When we decide to allow our lives to be used, we are released from the torture of our individual dramas, flaws and stories" (Ford 2012, 54).

When we can both give and receive, freely and happily, it is a big sign that our hearts are open and balanced. It is also the highest form of self-love. When someone helps us, it can both open and touch us. We will allow ourselves to receive help from others only when we feel worthy and deserving. Individuals who regularly refuse the help of others often think that they are doing the right thing, remaining independent and not being needy, but, in fact, their unwillingness to receive is only a sign of their lack of love for themselves. Fear, guilt and other negative emotions prevent us from receiving help from others. We would not be the people we are today had we not had the love and support of others. If we did not give back to others, the way they had given to us, we would be out of balance, and it would be impossible for us to fully love ourselves. But the most significant way in which we can help others is to help each other be who we are; that is the greatest gift we can give another.

 "You get to know yourself by your giving, and you get to know others by how they give. The more you give, the more creativity opens up for you. The more you give, the more answers unfold and the more you feel yourself reaching heightened levels of awareness. Giving is a doorway to vision. It's a happy sharing of what you have and what you are. Giving is the key to enjoying feelings of expansiveness, and a sure recipe to transform any situation" (Spezzano 2002, 15).

Exercise

Make a list of the people you have helped over the past week. If there is no one on your list, choose a person or organization that you want to help and set a goal for getting started. Remember, you need to be in a good place yourself before you can even contemplate helping others.

Always Ask Yourself, "What Would Love Do?"
"The longest journey you will make in your life is from your head to your heart"
(Zukav and Francis 2001, back cover).

Our heart is our most precious and wisest guide. When we cannot accept our life experiences, our heart has hardened in fear and blame. When we feel peaceful and calm, we know our heart is open and love reigns. We open our hearts by being willing, authentic and vulnerable; by forgiving ourselves and others; by refraining from judging ourselves or others; by surrendering; by having faith; and in all the other ways described in this chapter. When we continuously listen to our hearts, we are aligned with our greatest good and spread love with our thoughts, words and deeds, continually making the world a better place. We have healthy relationships and abundance in our lives.

We cannot choose all of our circumstances, but we do have the power to perceive them with love or fear. When we perceive them with love, we can be surrounded by chaos and negative circumstances and still experience inner peace and happiness. We often don't think to be compassionate when we are in the heat of anger, but when we focus on being compassionate, we become less reactive and more insightful, which results in healthier responses to people and circumstances. This doesn't mean that we won't get angry or feel other negative emotions; we know this is healthy. But compassion helps us convert every negative emotion into a positive one, if we allow it. Compassion eventually turns into forgiveness, whether it is for ourselves or another.

We have all experienced what happens when we are upset and someone shows us they care, whether through a look in their eyes, a ready ear or a gentle touch. Often, we find ourselves breaking down and expressing our emotions. Someone showing us compassion can literally open the floodgates to our healing. For many of us, it is easy to readily offer care to others but so difficult to offer the same level of care to ourselves. Yet if we learn to be gentle with ourselves, we can reverse years of pain. If we were abused as children, becoming compassionate toward ourselves and understanding how emotionally tormented our abusers must have been to harm an innocent child will eventually help us recover. When our teenagers lash out at us, determining what they fear and what their unmet needs are, helps us respond to their anger with love and gentleness.

"Love is a way of knowing, a mode of perceiving, a way of seeing. Ultimately it is the way of seeing. Anything less than love is not knowledge; it is opinion or belief, and it is always mistaken. Love is the accurate perception of the nature of the truth of being and our oneness with it. Love is intelligence. Intelligence is love" (Berends 1983, 17).

If we want loving relationships, we need to fill our minds with thoughts of love and our bodies with loving actions. One way to operate from our hearts more is to lay our hand on our heart. We can do this when we awake each day, in meditation, before spending time with someone difficult or while talking with someone we are having a hard time understanding. We can even ask our heart a question out loud and say the answer we receive out loud, while our hand rests on our heart. This works best when we ask the question at night; when we awake, we usually have our answer. An example of how to do this is to ask ourselves, "What is the most self-loving way that I can respond to [state the challenge]?"

I remember a time when my ex-husband's family was against me for feeding Taylor differently; I knew that they felt I was threatening their way of doing things. There was a wedding in the family, and as a result of everyone's new dislike of me, I was rather fearful of attending. I ended up going but wore a diamond heart necklace, smiled often (Taylor was doing really well as a result of my nutritional changes, so I actually was very happy), pulled my shoulders back to open my chest and heart and visualized radiating love to all of the attendees. Lo and behold, didn't a family member approach me who had made nutritional changes for her dog and experienced great results? Not one person gave me a hard time at that wedding. When we keep expanding our hearts, our efforts are always rewarded.

Some might ask, "How is ending relationships with family members operating from a place of love?" If our family members are too damaged or dissimilar from us for our relationship to work, we may decide to stay away from them but we *don't* stop loving them. When we take this step, we are loving ourselves more than ever before, and when we love ourselves, we are infinitely more loving to others who can receive our love. We are also more energetic and effective at doing the things we want to be doing.

Once we have come to love ourselves, we find ourselves wanting to open our hearts even further. We become more loving with others and perceive circumstances with more love than we did in the past. We smile, compliment and help strangers and find ways to easily turn negative circumstances into positive experiences for everyone involved.

Recently, I *consciously* decided to infuse love into everything I think, do and say. I could hardly keep up with the positive results I began seeing in my life! I ended up purchasing a blank journal with the title "Love Often" inscribed on the pink cover, so that I could record all of the abundance that began entering my life. What would it look like if you began infusing love into everything you think, do and say?

Exercise
Think about a relationship that you are struggling with and ask yourself, "What would love do?"

Set Goals and Intentions

Each of us has the opportunity to live the life we want—it is another law of the universe. And if we follow the steps laid out in this chapter, we find that we do have the time to do what we want. What a precious moment it is when we realize that we can do whatever we want with a block of time! When we are in relationships with people where we feel unhappy, we can't even see the options available to us. When we are stressed from doing a job that is not right for us, we are too tired to see our options. When our children are young and we have no help in caring for them, we are in survival mode and cannot see our options.

Really, it only takes a second to come up with a goal that can change our lives forever. Following through on accomplishing just one goal can fill us with pride in ourselves, build our self-esteem and fill the emptiness in us that might have existed for weeks or even months or years. Once we start to fulfill our own dreams and goals, we automatically become less interested in what others do and say. Each time we take action steps toward the future we desire, we are aligning with our own desires. We feel on top of the world because we are being called to express the best of ourselves.

Our goals need to be realistic, achievable, specific, measurable and time-limited. We can set small, short-term goals first to get us started moving in the right direction and then add in larger, longer-term goals. We can have daily goals, weekly goals, monthly goals, yearly goals and goals to achieve five years from now. We can have goals in any increments to help us fulfill our larger goals.

We need to look at what changes we want to put into place in order to live the lives we want to live. A goal can simply be to spend more time doing things we *want* to do as opposed to the things we *should* do. ***It is extremely important to become clear about what we want; it all begins with holding a vision for ourselves despite what we see around us at this moment.*** It needs to be a positive vision for ourselves, and we need to feel that we are deserving of achieving that vision for ourselves. The key to helping us understand that we deserve to achieve our visions of a new life is coming to know and love ourselves. We do this by developing our character, so that there is congruency between our inner and outer selves.

However, sometimes we set a goal but don't know how we are going to accomplish it. I remember saying that I would have my first book published within a year after writing it. I had no idea how it would be published—not a clue! People warned me of how long the publishing process took. But I held fast to my goal and accomplished it, entirely pleased with the outcome. Another law of the universe is that when we set a goal, believe in ourselves and work toward our goal, we receive exactly what we need. It might be a friend telling us about someone who can help us or a stranger sharing an idea with us that is just what we needed.

Once you decide upon your goal, feel the blessing of even having the opportunity to set that goal for yourself. Some people are just trying to determine how to get their next meal or how to get off the streets or how to heal their sick child. Then feel the gratitude now that you will feel in accomplishing that goal in the future. How will you feel when you are exercising three times a week? How will you feel looking at your slim, muscular body in the mirror? How will you feel when the man or woman you attracted into your life looks at you with love and admiration in their eyes?

And then, each time you get closer to meeting your goal, be thankful that you have made it that far. Be thankful for how good you are feeling inside at having taken the steps you have already taken to meet that goal. ***When you have reached your goal, feel the joy of your accomplishment permeate your whole being.*** Don't diminish your accomplishment and don't let others diminish it. Celebrate it! Most importantly, feel the gratitude wash over your body. Notice that the emptiness is gone. Notice that you are truly blessed. We are all truly blessed.

Once we achieve certain goals, such as acquiring the necessary education or finding a good company to work for or embarking on a career we are passionate about, we need to let go of trying so hard and simply become immersed in what we are doing, without concern for the outcome. When we love ourselves and are doing what we love, failure is impossible. How can we fail at being ourselves?

Setting intentions differs from setting goals. Setting intentions is implementing a certain mindset or expressing a goal without needing to take steps to achieve what we want. For example, we can set the intention to heal the frightened parts of ourselves that feel they don't have enough and consider the possibility that we are loved and internally abundant.

Exercises

1. Envisioning: Take a mental picture of your life. Is there something you don't like? If so, close your eyes and imagine the life you want. See yourself behaving or looking differently. Take a few minutes to breathe deeply and take in your vision. If you believe in God, ask God to help you imprint the vision on your subconscious mind. Do this for many days in a row, if possible.
2. Make a list of ten ways in which you plan to nurture yourself over the next three months and set weekly goals for implementing the ideas.

Have Faith

"I love looking into the eyes of someone who is inspired
by a vision greater than herself" (Ford 2012, 166).

Low self-esteem demonstrates our lack of faith in ourselves as well as in a higher power. That higher power can be God, Allah, the angels, spirit guides or whomever we believe in. We are in a state of grace when we trust ourselves and our higher power. When we believe in a greater power beyond ourselves, we understand that we are not alone, that there are larger aspects at play and that we are always given what is right for us. And if we believe in possibilities for ourselves, miracles will happen in our lives regularly. I see this in my work all of the time. Wayne Dyer reminds us to thank God for everything, even if that is all that our prayers consist of.

Exercise

Pray for something small to happen in your life. Believe that it will happen. Give thanks before it happens. Watch it unfold.

What Is It Like When We Start the Process of Loving Ourselves?

When we begin the process of loving ourselves, we are finally taking responsibility for our lives and protecting and valuing them with our hearts and minds. We start making positive and loving choices for ourselves and for others in more and more situations, and the self-sabotaging finally ends.

Earlier, I told you that I used to drink too much at parties and throw up for hours the next day. I remember the day that I was throwing up and actually looked at myself in the mirror and asked, "What is doing this to you?" The voice in my head answered, "Your relationship with your husband." Because I had already made the conscious decision to come to love myself more, this new insight was all I needed to stop drinking to excess and stop sabotaging myself in this way. It took me years of working on my relationship with my husband before I ended it and came to love myself like never before. But that is the way it goes; our growth is a very gradual process.

A few months after I stopped drinking too much, I started looking at my other unhealthy patterns. We can look at each area of imbalance in our life and use it to determine the next step we need to take in order to heal. The idea is for each of us to grow so gracefully that a childhood friend thinks we are the same as we always were. I have a friend from Grade Three who would tell you that I am the same now as I was then.

In the process of writing this book, I addressed the final area of my life that I felt was out of balance. I knew how to avoid unhealthy food options and did this the majority of time, but I found that I really wasn't consuming enough healthy food, such as fruits and vegetables, and this was causing certain symptoms in my body. When I finally started infusing my body with vitamins and minerals, I felt so much better; I had taken another step in my own growth. The day I realized that I had brought balance to all areas of my life, I cried with great relief. Through my tears, I spoke out loud saying "I have finally done it, haven't I?" My inner voice told me that there would still be more lessons to learn, which brought me back down to earth very quickly. I still allowed myself to celebrate the successes I had experienced and feel pride in the work I had done on myself.

When we are coming to love ourselves, we find that in addition to speaking and acting differently, we begin to think differently, and this results in a lot of uncertainty in ourselves and in those who know us. That's okay! Coming to love ourselves requires us to push past our comfort zone. ***Sometimes, we find ourselves acting the way we want to be until we are that person.*** That's okay! If we are trying to be a more loving person, we might find ourselves complimenting another. If we are trying to speak with integrity, we might find ourselves letting go of swearing or being dishonest and stopping making up excuses about why we don't want to do things. If we want to operate with integrity, we might find ourselves leaving a party early, rather than staying to the end and witnessing or partaking in all of the tomfoolery that happens at the end of a party. If we want to operate from our hearts, when we find ourselves waiting in line, instead of feeling impatient and lashing out, we might find ourselves taking a deep breath, noticing as our body relaxes and listening to the positive voices in our head. We might hear those voices saying, "I am going to wait patiently and enjoy the peace I feel within; I might even daydream." Or we might find ourselves smiling and chatting with the people in line. When we do this, we are cutting our negative feelings short and focusing on the positives, knowing that a delay or challenge doesn't need to ruin our whole day. In fact, we find ourselves choosing to spend our time in ways that bring us peace more and more often.

When we are coming to love ourselves, we might find ourselves improving our appearance, as well as that of our surroundings. Everything about ourselves and around us reflects what we feel we deserve and how much we love ourselves. The appearance and condition of our homes also affects our mood and motivation. As we come to love ourselves, we might find ourselves cleaning up the clutter that has been in our home for years, making our home more comfortable, brightening up some rooms, putting a bouquet of fresh flowers in the kitchen each week or hanging motivational verses or sentences on our walls. Each of these steps provides us with further inspiration to live our lives the way we want to.

What do all of these ways of being have in common? They involve doing things differently from the majority. That's allowed! We need to do things differently from the majority when it comes to our physical health, as well.

When we first start loving ourselves, we find that we begin observing ourselves, seemingly from a distance, and we notice the contrast between how we are behaving or responding to another now compared to how we operated in the past. Sometimes we might feel the need to tell others about the parts of ourselves that we suddenly love or how we interacted with someone in a new way. Sometimes we feel as though we are learning to speak a brand new language.

Coming to love ourselves is different from bragging, and when we do it right, we could never be described as conceited.

When we first start loving ourselves, we can feel exceedingly lonely or even lost. And let's face it, healing can hurt in the short term. We might be leaving family members, partners, friends or acquaintances behind. We might be confronting others who hurt us, which is never easy. Others who used to take advantage of us or engage in petty arguments with us may remove themselves from our lives when they realize they can't do that anymore. We might be leaving jobs behind that no longer fulfill us or make us feel good inside. We are definitely leaving behind our old sense of self and old cherished mindsets that no longer work for us. Things can be tough initially, and we can end up questioning ourselves over and over. But no matter what, if our answer is no when we ask ourselves, "Is this person or circumstance making me feel good inside?" or "Can this person meet my boundaries and treat me the way I want to be treated?" then we know that we needed to make the changes that we made. *The pain of healing is always more desirable than the pain of remaining in our unhealthy patterns.*

There is not a lot of support in our culture for taking the steps to emotional health, so we might feel even lonelier when we try explaining the changes we are making to others. Just as when we decide to eat healthier than the majority, we need to find others who are on a similar path and talk to them. Each of us wonders, "Will I still be loved if I become everything that I am meant to be?" The answer is always yes, but we might be loved by different people than we expected.

 "All personal growth requires that you leave some people behind, but such growth also brings new people and new experiences into your life. Soon you'll have the support you need to maintain your changes" (McLaren 2010, 65).

On our journey to loving ourselves, we *are* going to be tempted to do the wrong things or return to our old patterns—it seems to be another law of the universe. We need to become aware that this is a temptation and then to recognize the temptation as an opportunity for us to choose differently. Each time we are tempted, we need to consider the potential consequences of doing the wrong thing. We then need to remind ourselves that it is completely up to us whether we challenge the frightened part of our personality or not. We can say yes or no to each temptation because we are always the ones in control of our response. We can ask ourselves if making a certain choice will create peace within ourselves or our lives. Lastly, we can remind ourselves that our temptations are not stronger than who we want to become. Each time we successfully sidestep a temptation, it is important to notice how we feel inside. ***The positive feelings we experience will propel us into making further good choices for ourselves.***

What Is It Like When We Come to Truly Love Ourselves and Are Healed?

"Success is the freedom to be yourself" (Kathe Kolbe).

We spend our lives coming to love ourselves; it's an ongoing process. Bestselling author Debbie Ford describes the process of coming to love ourselves as battling with our universal enemy—self-ignorance. Herein lies a description of what it feels like to be winning that battle.

When we come to love ourselves, we come to love all aspects of ourselves— our past, the things we are not good at, the aspects of our bodies that are not our favourite, our fears. We have the courage to be who we truly are in every single moment, no matter who we are with or where we are. It is a lot of work to hide our true feelings, thoughts and beliefs and to watch what we say and do all of the time. We can feel tense and nervous when we hide away. When we come to love ourselves, we don't have to be someone we are not; we are free and our lives are infinitely easier. When we actually come to a place where we enjoy being with ourselves more than with others, we know we love ourselves to a great degree.

 "The renowned seventh-century Zen master Seng-tsan taught that true freedom is being 'without anxiety about imperfection.' This means accepting our human existence and all of life as it is. Imperfection is not our personal problem—it is a natural part of existing" (Brach 2003, 21).

Some people believe that coming to love ourselves and being healed means that we are always cheerful and always sure of ourselves and that we never need anyone. Some believe that when we love ourselves, our lives are perfect, we are perfect and we no longer feel negative emotions. And they would be wrong.

When we love ourselves, our self-doubt, self-consciousness and self-attack dissipate but don't disappear. We are still human and therefore we may feel low at times; we may feel insecure; we may become angry, anxious or sad. However, we don't blame others for these feelings; we look inside ourselves. When we have these feelings, they are no longer as intense and we find that we are now able to accept them with patience and understanding and express them freely, as opposed to letting them control us. Some believe that coming to love ourselves means that we never make mistakes. And they would be wrong. We still make mistakes, but we make fewer mistakes of lesser severity and we learn from them faster than ever before.

We don't feel as though we are lacking in any way because we know we are overflowing with abundance. We remain humble and simply want the best for everyone. We don't compete with others, toot our own horn, try to prove ourselves to others, covet what others have or want big things to happen to us in order to instil worth. If our parents don't approve of or agree with us, we are okay with that because we no longer need their validation. We are more self-defined.

We are fully aware and focused in the present moment rather than distracted or disassociated. We don't have avoidance behaviours, addictions or excessive practices of any kind because we have forgiven ourselves and others. Rather, we are able to deal with life as it is because we are connected to ourselves and our surroundings. When we love ourselves, we see the beauty in ourselves, in others and in the world around us. We understand ourselves and see the value and innocence in ourselves and others, giving value and love to others by giving them our warm attention. When we allow our true selves to be seen, our inner beauty shines through and we light up the room wherever we go. It is our human-ness that is so attractive. Ironically, if we were perfect, we wouldn't be nearly as attractive. When we live our lives with truth and integrity, our beauty has no bounds and therefore has no choice but to radiate. We feel so alive and our eyes sparkle with love and appreciation. Others, even strangers, want to be with us, want to share in our joy and want our eyes on them so that they can bask in that love and joy, if even for a short while. People we barely know tell us that they love us or offer to help us without us asking! We are excited and happy to be part of every aspect of life, and our genuine smile demonstrates that.

When we love ourselves, we don't spend time trying to change the things we cannot change. We have clarity and peace of mind, control over our own lives, confidence in our own decisions and an inner strength that allows us to look into another's eyes and hold their gaze without turning away. We no longer have the need to be right and we no longer need to defend ourselves or make excuses, because we know the truth and will no longer expend energy trying to convince others. We are not hard on ourselves or others but accepting and loving instead. We know how to set boundaries with others and do so readily and lovingly, if need be. Even our capacity to love those who are not nice to us increases. We see the world as a friendly place instead of a hostile place. We like to be with the young and the old. We see all people as equal. I am not saying that we will never notice something that seems out of balance in ourselves or another, but our love will take precedence.

 "We no longer bestow love when people are good to us and withdraw it when they are bad. Instead love becomes a constant in our lives. It just is. People who have reached this stage are in true possession of their love stories" (Chopra 1997, 45).

When we love ourselves, we refuse to be treated badly or disrespectfully or be controlled by others. We wouldn't deign to mistreat, be disrespectful to or control another. When we love ourselves, we care much less about how we are perceived by others; true self-esteem is independent of anyone's opinion, meaning it cannot be diminished by criticism nor increased by praise. When we love ourselves, we no longer seek approval, praise or credit. If someone insults us, we don't feel a rise in our body; we don't become inflamed. We just know that they don't love themselves. Conversely, when someone compliments us, we accept their words and see what they see. Others show us more respect and appreciation than ever before because they clearly see the loving energy that we exude.

"Those who care the least about approval seem to receive it the most" (Dyer 2007, 272).

When we love ourselves, we feel safe and others feel safe with us. We are approachable. We don't have to say "Your secret is safe with me"; others know it just by being in our presence. ***Think about the people in our own lives with whom we feel most comfortable; those are the people who take responsibility, work with their emotions and set boundaries.*** The ones with whom we don't feel comfortable have challenges in relationships because they have what is called "poor psychological hygiene"; they are loaded with unhealed traumas and misunderstood emotions and lack focus.

When we love ourselves, even when we feel vulnerable, we can share that vulnerability with others, allowing them to feel more comfortable in our presence and in the world. When we admit our vulnerabilities to people who care about us, we feel better about those vulnerabilities and not so vulnerable after all. When we expose our not-so-charming aspects of ourselves and laugh about them with those who love us, everyone has a good time! We might still have fears or self-doubt but they are few and far between because when we operate from a place of love, we operate from a place of strength.

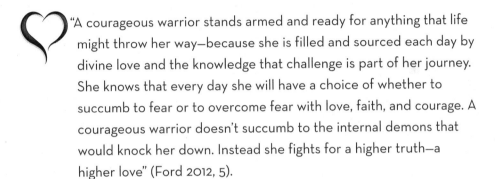

"A courageous warrior stands armed and ready for anything that life might throw her way—because she is filled and sourced each day by divine love and the knowledge that challenge is part of her journey. She knows that every day she will have a choice of whether to succumb to fear or to overcome fear with love, faith, and courage. A courageous warrior doesn't succumb to the internal demons that would knock her down. Instead she fights for a higher truth—a higher love" (Ford 2012, 5).

We move away from conflict and drama, no longer needing it to fill our egos. We are not blown to and fro by each new circumstance but instead choose to remain calm and grounded. Our inner peace determines our experience of life, so life becomes more peaceful. Once we reach a certain point of loving ourselves, we realize that our challenges simply don't matter the way they used to. So this means that if anything is removed from our life, our happiness would not be removed. Our happiness and peace are no longer attached to people behaving in a certain way or things going our way. We are happy, peaceful and in a state of grace, even if things don't go the way we want them to. We don't become immune to pain but we become better equipped to handle it. And we are clearer inside to make decisions on how we are going to transcend pain or turmoil faster because we know how to apply love to each situation, as opposed to fear or anger. I am not saying that we won't initially see our circumstances or someone else's as bad, but when we love ourselves, it doesn't take us long to see the gift in every circumstance. When we see life as a gift and we are grateful for that gift, life delivers.

We listen more than we speak without feeling the overpowering need to make our point. We don't lecture others; we wouldn't deign to think we know what is best for another person. We can't understand when others don't see their own value because we can see their value so clearly, but we can remember when we felt the way they did. We are open to and accept new ideas and opinions, even if we don't agree with them. We love to learn and be the student, as well as the teacher. We look for ways and take pleasure in serving others, without expecting anything in return.

When we love ourselves, we experience less sickness. We need to get sick every once in a while; it's a sign that our immune system is working well. But when we get sick, we see it as a temporary setback, knowing we will be well again soon. A happy, emotionally healthy person doesn't engage in destructive habits, such as eating poorly (every once in a while is fine!) and therefore doesn't attract perpetual sickness; they exercise and experience movement regularly. When we love ourselves, we attract and exude health.

When we love ourselves, we hear our inner voice more clearly and quickly and can read the minds of others more easily. We feel more in touch with everyone than ever before. We find ourselves having strong feelings about taking certain courses of actions without knowing why. We receive and recognize many signs that reassure us that we are on the right track. We notice synchronicities more often, such as when we think about something and then it happens.

Once we have come to love ourselves, we have found balance, or, at least, the most of balance we have ever had. We are more patient and less interested in knowing the date or time. We generally have enough time to sleep, rest or meditate, play, be creative, perform meaningful work, exercise, eat healthy food, do housework, learn new things, reflect and spend quality time with others. Yes, there will still be times where we are out of balance, but the majority of time we will feel as though we are in balance. When we are self-deprecating, we hold ourselves back from enjoying ourselves. When we love ourselves, we allow sheer abundance to enter our lives. We allow ourselves to sleep if we want to, do nothing for long periods of time, socialize more than we used to, buy something that we don't need and simply enjoy ourselves. ***When we know we deserve it, we can luxuriate in the richness of life.***

When we love ourselves, we become engaged in our work and love what we do; that's how we know that we are in the flow of life. We feel that our work is one of the most important uses of our time because we finally know our purpose and are fulfilling it. Our most important job though always remains becoming a magnificent person—our own hero. When we do the best that we can, we reach our highest potential and become the person we are capable of becoming; this is one of our greatest callings.

Amazingly, when we come to love ourselves, we feel good inside without anything in particular happening. We are in a peaceful place. We are free and soaring. We have more time and energy to offer our biggest gifts to the world. This is another one of our greatest callings, sharing our unique talents with others so that they too may become more balanced and joyful. **Once we come to love ourselves, we have cleared our subconscious mind so that only love can live there and we end up dedicating our lives to teaching love through our thoughts, words and deeds.** And in turn, we find that our heart's desires gradually come to fruition and we experience the highest possibilities for life.

Once we have come to love ourselves and have learned how to parent ourselves, we have learned how to reach deep within ourselves to meet our own needs. When we have met our own needs for a period of time, we find, amazingly, that our needs subside. We do not see our lives as a struggle anymore, regardless of what we experience because we are at peace. *The amount of inner peace we experience becomes our measure of accomplishment.* Eventually, we are left with one need: to experience all moments in life to their greatest depth. When we can do this, we can see the beauty in every moment and the depth in the mundane and are overcome with gratitude and appreciation for every aspect of ourselves and our lives.

When we come to love ourselves, we can stand naked in front of a mirror and say, "I love you," and mean it.

 "Completion allows you to be present with everything as it exists right now. It gives you superhero vision, because when you are complete, you commit to no longer looking through the eyes of your wounded self, through the eyes of your past, through the eyes of fear. Instead, you turn the corner, stand in the present moment, and declare yourself complete" (Ford 2012, 145).

Exercises to Help Us Come to Love Ourselves More

Journaling

There are many exercises that can be done with a journal. When I was a child, I recorded every compliment that I received and read the list over and over again, wanting to believe that the compliments were true. I did this again for many years as a young adult. It can make a big difference to confidence levels. You can make a list of:

- All of your accomplishments—big or small—to remind you of the amount and magnitude of your achievements.
- Everything that you love about who you are. Write down your strengths, talents and aspects of your appearance that you appreciate.
- The times in your life when you've been courageous.
- The times in which you helped someone or made a difference in the world.

Affirmations

Examples of affirmations you might adopt to increase your self-confidence and improve your future, in general, include the following:

- I deserve to be loved and am loved.
- I am beautiful inside and out.
- I accept where I am at this moment and am open to accepting the possibility of change.
- I have everything I need to create the life I want and am now living the life I want.
- I make plenty of money doing what I love to do.
- I release all fear, anxiety and self-doubt.
- I encourage you to create your own affirmation—don't be afraid to come up with more than one!

Actions to Take

1. Each morning and night, stand naked in front of a mirror for five minutes. Feel the negative feelings that come up and then find the parts of yourself that you like. Gradually learn to like everything that you see in the mirror.

2. Obtain help in making your beauty even more apparent. Change your hairstyle, enjoy a manicure and pedicure, go through your closet and come up with new combinations of clothes or splurge on something you have never splurged on before.

 "The greatest challenge of the human experience is discovering who you really are. The second greatest is living in a way that honours what you discovered" (Lisa Villa Prosen).

Healing Our Relationships, Healing Ourselves

"I sincerely believe that the word 'relationships' is the key to the prospect of a decent world. It seems abundantly clear that every problem you will have—in your family, in your business, in our nation, or in this world—is essentially a matter of relationships, of interdependence" (Clarence Francis).

I chose to dedicate a chapter to discussing relationships because relationships are our biggest catalyst for emotional healing; everything we need to learn is revealed by our relationships. Relationships are one of the most important aspects of our lives. They can be the source of our greatest joy or our greatest pain. If we understand how to have successful relationships, we achieve harmony, creativity, good health, abundance and love. The more we are nourished by our relationships, the more love fills our hearts and the less room there is for fear.

Without others, we could not be ourselves. Others love us, help us accomplish our goals, allow us to see ourselves more clearly, help us grow within and bring us joy. Conversely, many of us have others in our lives who don't love us, who prevent us from accomplishing our goals, who bring out the fear within us and who seemingly just make our lives miserable. We now know that it isn't them making us unhappy, it is actually our perception of their actions. Once we accept the responsibility for our own feelings, true healing can begin. The truth is, the more we come to love ourselves, the more we attract people who love and respect us for exactly who we are. Our relationships are only as emotionally healthy and happy as we are.

If we cannot understand ourselves, how can anyone else understand us? If we cannot be comfortable with ourselves, how can we be comfortable with anyone else and how can others be comfortable with us? If we cannot give ourselves the love, appreciation, nurturing, time and patience that we need, how can we do the same for others? ***Others treat us the way we treat ourselves.*** The best relationships take place when both parties come from a place of comfort and peace, which means when both parties have come to know and love themselves and are truly themselves. This is where honesty, integrity and courage flourish. And this, interestingly enough, is the place where we connect with our children.

As you have read, we are all coming to know and love ourselves more and more, whether we are conscious of it or not. Our relationships are a gauge of how much we love ourselves. If we are struggling with our partner, family members and friends, we haven't come to love ourselves enough. Conversely, if all of our current relationships are harmonious, we have come to love ourselves a tremendous amount. If no one can ever "push our buttons"—not even ex-spouses or parents-in-law—we love ourselves even more. What this tells us, once again, is that the quality of our relationships is entirely up to us, just as how our lives turn out is entirely up to us.

 "The love you get is limited only by your ability to receive it" (Chopra 1997, 85).

Some of you would tell me, "But my brother is impossible! It's not me! I am powerless to improve our relationship." I would ask you, "Why would you give your power away to your brother like that? You just don't know how to turn things around. You have not been given the tools. That is all." When we are open to finding the tools to heal our relationships, they are always provided. The more we love ourselves, the better equipped we are to use those tools in the way they are meant to be used.

How Do We Cope with Our Differences?

We cope with our differences by
- understanding that there is a purpose for each of our relationships
- seeing ourselves through the lens of our heart
- seeing others through the lens of our heart
- changing the way we view another's "faults"
- changing our response to another
- increasing our understanding of why others treat us the way they do

- accepting others for who they are, recognizing that they are not going to change
- increasing our understanding of how we allow others to affect us
- using compassionate communication to express our needs for our relationship
- setting boundaries with another so that our needs are met by our relationship

Understanding That There Is a Purpose for Each of Our Relationships

At our core, we are more alike than different. Each of us wants to give and receive love and live peaceful and happy lives. We each have our own interests and talents that need to be uncovered and exercised so that we can make our own unique contribution to this world and to one another. However, our sameness does not heal us; it is our differences that heal us. Usually, the fact that we see things differently in our relationships is a strength, not a weakness. If we were all the same, the world would be a very boring place.

"We keep looking for sameness when healing requires tolerance, acceptance, and unconditional love of complementary differences. If the on-time person marries a person who is always late, they get the opportunity to teach and heal each other" (Williamson 2008, 277).

We enter into relationships with many others throughout our lives—whether it be our family, friends, lovers, teachers, colleagues, bosses, service providers or acquaintances. Some relationships help us discern what is right for ourselves. Some relationships bring more balance, peace or joy to our lives. Some relationships bring anger, frustration or sadness to our lives. All relationships trigger the unhealed parts of ourselves. All relationships have the potential to heal the parts of us that are wounded and teach us lessons. All relationships help and support us, whether we are aware of it or not. And we always attract the relationships we need.

"The universe always guides us back to embracing the totality of ourselves. We attract whomever and whatever we need to mirror back the aspects of ourselves that we've forgotten or rejected" (Ford 1998, 34).

We can be attracted to another only if we are in many ways similar to them. They say opposites attract, but the basic natures of the two individuals who come into a relationship together are always similar. There will also be aspects of the two individuals that are opposite to one another. Whatever aspects of ourselves that we don't like or that we had shut down as children will be the aspects of another that they did not shut down because they were not hurt in that particular area as a child. To summarize: *We are attracted to people who share the same traits that we have and like, only more so. We are repelled by the very people who reflect the traits back to us that we don't like in ourselves.*

Here are some examples of how relationships reflect our feelings for ourselves and the aspects of ourselves that we have rejected. If we feel guilty about some of our behaviour, we will find ourselves attracting people into our lives that see our guilt and condemn us for what we have done. Interestingly enough, if we see ourselves with compassion and are just fine with our behaviour, no matter how shocking it is, others will usually view our behaviour similarly. If we deny, dislike or are uncomfortable with our own anger, we will find ourselves attracting angry people into our lives and judging them for their anger. If we deny, dislike or are uncomfortable with our own impatience, we will find ourselves attracting the people who take forever to cross the road in front of us, while we sit in our cars waiting to proceed. If we see, understand and heal our own guilt, anger and impatience, we won't be upset by the condemnation, anger or impatience we see in others; we might notice it but it won't affect us. It is only when we are lying to ourselves or disliking parts of ourselves that we end up being negatively affected by someone else's behaviour.

 "Acknowledging that our current relationships are influenced by unconscious, unresolved pain from our past is the major key to understanding the dynamics of human relationships" (Berger 2000, 216).

Relationships can bring us more balance. Extroverted individuals benefit from learning how to be more quiet and cautious. Introverted individuals benefit from learning how to be more dominant and inspiring. Individuals who stick to the rules all the time benefit from experiencing the freedom of breaking the rules sometimes and rebellious individuals benefit from following the rules.

"The purpose of an intimate relationship is not that it be a place where we can hide from our weaknesses, but rather where we can safely let them go" (Williamson 1999, 32).

Relationships always reflect the amount of love we have for ourselves. When a person emotionally abuses us, we know they are doing so because they do not love themselves. If an adult accepts or tolerates the abuse, there must be something that they are still not loving about themselves. Others can only put demands on us when they are reflecting the demands we put upon ourselves. *If we have not forgiven and let go of our past and previous feelings, we will continually see evidence of behaviour similar to that which we experienced earlier in our lives.* Instead of suffering abuse at the hands of another, as we might have as a child, we might find that now we are being neglected in our relationships.

Here is an example of how relationships reflect the amount of love we have for ourselves. A woman doesn't see or value the feminine aspects of herself because male attention has been missing from her life. She is easily taken in by a great performance by a man because she wants what he portrays so badly. However, subconsciously, she doesn't truly believe that she deserves to be loved and honoured by a man; she has never had that, so therefore she feels that she must be undeserving of it. The man puts on airs of being loving, caring and romantic, but he subconsciously feels that he does not deserve to be loved and honoured by a woman because he has never had that. As the two come to know one another, the two can re-open each other's wounds or they can heal each other's wounds. Each individual has a choice about whether they seize the opportunity to heal or not. They can do the work of healing their wounds and come to love themselves or they can stay clear of building intimacy and remain unhappy within. If the woman's sense of self strengthens, she will forgo false romantics and choose authentic love. If the man feels badly enough about acting a part and hurting others, he will ask for help and change his behaviour. The one who heals and grows as a person will enjoy much love and happiness in their life and cherish the experience of growing old. The one who doesn't do the work will live with regret, experience much less love and happiness in their life and just grow old. It sure is nice when both parties choose to do the work and cherish the experience of growing together and growing old together. Sometimes, a subsequent relationship teaches the individual what they need to learn. Lessons keep presenting themselves to us until we learn them—it is another law of the universe.

"Once your mind and heart are realigned—when the broken self you became in childhood is no longer manifesting broken relationships—then you're ready at last to love again. Compassion, integrity, truthfulness, generosity, and graciousness become key elements in your new romantic skill set. You come to see what you did wrong in the past and to forgive yourself, to understand other people's actions and where necessary forgive them too. You are humbled at last into your purity and grace" (Williamson 2008, 111).

We also attract relationships into our lives that help us grow into the people we want to be. We might be attracted to certain traits in various well-known people in our society because we can see our potential in them. We might be attracted to a person's courage; that person helps us see the amount of courage we are capable of having. Actors and athletes are revered and paid large amounts of money because we are searching for heroes—we want them to act out our unfulfilled desires.

"If you admire greatness in another human being, it is your own greatness you are seeing. You may manifest it in a different way, but if you didn't have greatness within, you would not be able to recognize that quality in someone else" (Ford 1998, 50).

Here are some examples of how our romantic relationships mirror our love for ourselves and our beliefs. I was fascinated by the various men I attracted into my life after I left my husband. I found that each man was better for me than the previous one, as I embarked on the journey of coming to love myself more and more. The first couple of men I dated, within months of my marriage ending, didn't love themselves enough to bestow much love on me. I was pleased to have arrived at this conclusion as quickly as I did and content to move on; I only went on one date with each of them. The next men I attracted, a year later, were very kind to me and clearly operated from their hearts, something I was not used to. Initially, a part of me thought that they weren't being real with me, as I had never experienced men like this before. These men were either too young for me or visiting from different countries, so I was obviously putting it out there that I was not ready for a relationship and still needed healing. A year after that, I met two men who were kind and loving to me and remained in my life for a while but didn't love themselves enough to receive my love; they were both still healing from past relationships where they had been criticized incessantly by their ex-wives. These men showed me that I, too, must still need to come to love myself more. I went another year without dating anyone, just being with friends and doing things that made me happy. Three years after my separation, I started meeting men who fit my description of what I wanted in a partner. So far, I haven't met one where there is a physical connection or spark, but that's okay. Meeting these men showed me that I had come to love myself enough to attract a completely different type of man then I had in the past.

Some people have told me that there is never a spark once you hit middle age, that there is no longer an overwhelming sense of excitement in the early months of first spending time with someone of the opposite sex, but I know otherwise. So many of us stay in unhealthy relationships or relationships without a spark because we think we cannot do better, that we do not deserve better or cannot believe that our ideal mate is out there. Whether we meet the partner of our dreams is determined by the amount of love we have for ourselves, by our belief that we will meet that person and by our belief that we deserve to meet that person. The partners we attract are always our mirror. *The more wounded we are, the more wounded our partners are. The more healed we are, the more healed our partners are.*

 "When we are very clear that we want to shine—and if we want to know the Goddess, we want to shine—then we attract into our lives the kinds of relationships that help us do that. Until a woman has given herself permission to be fabulous, she will not find herself with partners who promote her ability to be so. As long as she tears herself down, she will attract others who tear her down; she will find people who agree that she is undeserving and lacking as long as that is how she thinks of herself" (Williamson 1993, 59).

Seeing Ourselves through the Lens of Our Heart

"Our pain doesn't come from the love we weren't given in the past, but from the love we ourselves aren't giving in the present" (Williamson 1992, 128).

Every relationship is an opportunity to challenge and change our self-defeating belief systems. The more we operate from our hearts, the more we allow each relationship to heal us. Operating from our hearts involves accessing and expressing our feelings and needs, coming to love ourselves, understanding others and being compassionate with others.

What automatically happens when we come to love ourselves more is that we are able to meet more of our own needs and rely less on others to meet those needs. When we approve of ourselves, we don't need our father to compliment us as often. When we are feeling good about ourselves, we don't get so defensive the next time our mother is unhappy with us about not remembering to call her. When we are spending time doing the things we love to do, we won't be as uncomfortable with our spouse working long hours. The happier we are with ourselves, the happier we are with everyone else and the more love we are be able to spread. Meeting our own needs reduces conflict in all of our relationships with others.

I would like to share with you some examples of how many of us think at a subconscious level:

- When we have a partnership where our partner is perpetually failing us, we feel we are winning the hidden competition and are victorious as the better person.
- When we don't love ourselves, many of us are afraid of intimacy and therefore are quite pleased when we don't need to proceed to the next step in our partnership.
- We all know that many females are attracted to the "bad boys". The women who enter into a relationship with these men do not love and respect themselves to a great degree and subconsciously feel they deserve to be treated badly. Once a woman comes to love and appreciate herself, she will find herself attracted to a "good boy", who loves and appreciates her.

The more we heal and become whole, the more we free ourselves of our limitations and disappointments and the deeper we experience love.

Seeing Others through the Lens of Our Heart

If we want our relationship with anyone in our lives to improve, we need to focus on their innocence, as opposed to their guilt. When others don't see their beauty or their goodness, we help them most by seeing and pointing out their beauty and goodness. For example, when they are angry with us, we need to see their underlying fear and realize that their behaviour is simply a call for love.

"Everything should be interpreted as love or as a call for love. When someone has not shown us their love, our power lies in knowing that they would have, had they known how. They are not wrong so much as they are wounded, and our role is not to judge them but to heal them. It is in cleaving to our own love that we awaken it in others. In any situation where love does not rule, affirm that only love is real. Say it, repeat it, chant it like a mantra. Allow it to cast out all thoughts of blame and judgment and fear" (Williamson 2002, 160).

Here is an example of how to do focus on the good in others. A co-worker takes credit for your ideas. Only a very insecure person, who sees the emptiness in themselves and does not love themselves, would steal credit from you. They may be afraid of losing their job, of not being seen as worthwhile or of not being seen as making a contribution to the company. They must have really thought your ideas were great to want to take credit for them. You can ask them in a loving, caring way if they are afraid of any of these things and see if they need help dealing with these fears.

It's all about being willing to see each situation with new perspective. When we focus on doing this, the behaviour that previously bothered us now ends up filling us with compassion; the behaviour doesn't change but we do. It's a kind of miracle when it happens. Each time this miracle occurs, our awareness increases, our love expands and we see the beauty in the other person.

Let me give you another example. When my daughter Taylor was a toddler, she became very sick. I did everything I could think of to help her get well. I changed what I fed her and what products I used on her and started giving her supplements and natural remedies. My in-laws witnessed the changes I was making over a period of time and eventually told me that they didn't want to see Taylor or me for a month. If Taylor got better, they said they would resume their relationship with us. Instead of supporting us when we were struggling, they turned on us. I was extremely angry, deeply hurt and I blamed them. I couldn't understand why they didn't believe in me or at least recognize that I was only trying to help their grandchild.

Taylor was healthy and happy for the whole month we were apart. I, on the other hand, wasn't faring so well. I lost ten pounds that month and I don't lose weight easily. It was time for me to become an observer and extricate myself from the situation so that I could look at it more objectively. I asked myself if I had all the facts to understand our difference in opinion. I tried to understand their feelings about what I was doing with Taylor. I knew that what I was doing differently did not make sense to them as they were old-school thinkers and I was sure they thought I was crazy. I knew that I was threatening their way of doing things. Meanwhile, all I knew was that their lifestyle—the typical lifestyle—wasn't working for Taylor. I knew that the circumstances of their lives had not made them question their lifestyle up to that point but my circumstances were different.

Those facts would probably be enough for anyone to change their thoughts and therefore their feelings about their in-laws. At the time, I needed something more. I went to a healer whose job it is to help people see things with new perspective. She told me that my in-laws were my teachers. At the time, I struggled to understand what they were trying to teach me. By the end of the appointment, I was finally able to see our situation with clarity. What my in-laws were teaching me was the way the majority of people view doing things differently. If everyone had supported me in doing things differently, how good of a teacher would I be? I needed to learn how to teach the non-believers about the power of food. And that is what I did. I ended up teaching my in-laws by our example. Really, the most effective way to teach others is to continually learn our own lessons in the presence of others.

Years passed, and one day my mother-in-law said, "Whatever you are doing with Taylor, keep it up." She didn't want to hear the details but she saw how happy and healthy Taylor had become; she knew that what I had done was right for her. I came to feel grateful for the lessons my in-laws taught me about the way others react when they see things differently. If I had continued to judge and blame my in-laws, we never could have repaired our relationship and my girls never could have become as close as they became to their grandparents.

Judgment and blame generate fear, distrust and conflict. Being the observer and finding the lesson generate love, respect and gratitude. This is how our toughest obstacles can become our greatest treasures. Judgment and blame don't help us find the treasure. Observing and staying open to possibilities and the hidden wisdom in any situation help us find the treasure and feel peace within.

 "We are not here to fix, change or belittle another person. We are here to support, forgive and heal one another" (Williamson 1992, 116).

Exercises for seeing others through the lens of the heart and insights

The following exercise is designed to help you see another through the lens of the heart when you are finding someone difficult to deal with because of their negative attitude or complaints. If someone is sitting beside you on a plane and is complaining about how cramped the seats are, you can compliment them on having the good sense to choose an aisle seat. If they complain about the food, you can congratulate them on having the intelligence not to eat it. In time, as you continually do this, not only can you help the other person see themselves with new perspective (see the good in their thoughts or actions) but you might just see them relax or possibly even begin enjoying themselves, which in turn, helps you enjoy yourself in that moment.

Here is an exercise to help you see another through the lens of the heart when looking at a recent event or conversation with someone you are close to that has caused you anguish. Take twenty minutes and write down your thoughts and feelings about the circumstances. While you write, try to determine the cause of your conflict. Then put yourself in the shoes of the other person and write what you believe to be their thoughts and feelings on the conflict. This will help you go beyond your own needs and suffering and tap into their needs and suffering. This also helps you place importance on both your feelings and theirs.

One of the very best ways to see another through the lens of the heart is to put ourselves in their shoes and enter their world. When we are empathetic, we have the ability to see and understand the perspective of another person through our shared feelings, i.e. we feel the way they do. Our feelings are universal. The ability to find the humanity in another is the best way to improve the way we relate to them. Find out about their past. Were their needs met? What happened to them? What suffering did they endure? Sometimes just uncovering this information fills our hearts with compassion and augments our patience and appreciation of them as we look at what they have survived. Understanding their suffering and then potentially sharing that understanding with them can automatically bring two people closer to one another.

Another exercise to help you see another through the lens of the heart is to take a break from your conflict and take turns describing something you like about:

- the other person that you have never told them
- yourself that you have never told them
- your relationship that you have never told them

You each take turns answering each question without interrupting one another. It's amazing how incredible a person can feel after a discussion like this, which subsequently opens their heart to the person with whom they were just engaged in a conflict. One of the most common causes of challenges in relationships is a lack of acknowledgement and appreciation for one another; these are basic needs for every one of us.

An additional exercise to increase your appreciation for your partner involves writing down three things you love and appreciate about your partner and sharing one with them each day, once a week or once a month. It can be a character trait, an aspect of their appearance, something they said or something they did: "I love how often and how hard you make me laugh!" or "I love the fireworks displays you put on for our family!" or "I appreciated that you emptied the dishwasher today."

Another exercise to help you see the other through the lens of the heart, particularly someone you are very close to, is to go shopping. Hard to believe I am suggesting this, I know! As you shop, think about the things the other person likes and you will find that your positive thoughts for that person can't help but return. Then, purchase them something you think they would enjoy; it might cost only a few dollars or it might be something more expensive. The idea is to generate positive feelings for that person. Do not give your gift to them at a time of discord between you, but later, once you have reconciled or at a special occasion.

Changing the Way We View Another's "Faults"

You know now that when we criticize or judge another we are seeing aspects in them that we have rejected in ourselves. We come to love ourselves by loving the parts of others that we reject in ourselves. But how exactly do we do this? I gave you an example earlier of letting go of aspects of ourselves that we no longer need. The book *Giving the Love That Heals* (Hendrix and Hunt 1997) explains this process in more detail. The book states that, first, we need to see that the disliked aspect of another person is a projection of a part of ourselves that we dislike. Second, we need to see that this trait or behaviour helps the other person survive, just as it helps or helped us survive. We need to see that the "negative" trait serves a positive function. Third, we need to accept that the trait is functional in the other person and come to value it for the purpose it serves. When we come to understand, accept and love the trait in the other person, we come to understand, accept and love it in ourselves.

When we accept and embrace our differences, we reap the rewards from our relationships. There is something else we can do to change the way we view another's perceived faults. We can literally decide to focus on the good qualities in another, rather than on the faults we perceive in them. When we pay attention to the strengths in another, our attention to those strengths amplifies them. *When we make another aware of their strengths, they become aware, too, and find themselves wanting to showcase those strengths more and more.* You read earlier that our children believe what their parents tell them. When we tell our son he is inconsiderate of others, inconsiderate of others he is! When we compliment him on helping the lady at the grocery store who dropped her groceries, do you think he won't want more compliments? Conversely, when others don't display the positive traits we would like to see, we can practise seeing them. Remember, what we see as a fault may be a strength in another situation. A child who is really intense and tenacious can be hard to cope with day in and day out, but imagine that child running their own company one day! The goal is to see the good in another, as opposed to seeing their faults and trying to change them.

The only person who doesn't see the good in themselves or want compliments is the one who dislikes themselves so much that they think others are being untruthful or naive when they give a compliment. What if we see the good in another but they refuse to see the good in themselves and continue to disrespect us or lash out in anger?

Accepting Others for Who They Are, Recognizing That They Are Not Going to Change

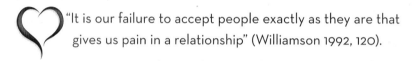 "It is our failure to accept people exactly as they are that gives us pain in a relationship" (Williamson 1992, 120).

The majority of our fights with others stem from us wanting them to change. We think that if we explain our need for them to change well enough or often enough, they will make the change. Some of us spend our whole lives complaining, blaming and feeling victimized, hoping that one day they will change. When we do this, we are suffering from unresolved feelings and waiting for something that will likely never occur. We say to ourselves, "If only they would … I could forgive them" or "If only they would accept me for … I'd be able to get along with them."

What we don't realize is that the majority of people don't change. The only ones who do are the ones who want to change. The more we resist who they are, the more their personality traits will bother or annoy us. And if we are constantly criticizing, judging or shutting down those we love, how can we possibly expect them to appreciate us?

It is only when we accept others as they are that our relationship with them can improve. It is only when we come to truly understand another person that we can never be let down by them. It is our expectations of others that get us into trouble. Our expectations can really wreak havoc in our lives. Some would read this and say, "So I need to lower my expectations." My response would be,

"No, we only need to lower our expectations of those who do not see their own greatness." When we only love others if they conform to our expectations and needs, it is called conditional love. If we stop trying to fit others into our preconceived notions of what we like and dislike and stop judging and resisting people based on what needs to be healed within ourselves, we find that relationships really can be easy. And this is how we experience unconditional love.

I remember my daughter Paige suffering through Grade Five with two people, a girl and a boy. For months, she came home after school and poured her heart out to me about what had gone wrong between her and these two children. One day, it came to me that there was one thing that her conflicts with these two children had in common. Her expectations of them were different from their own expectations of themselves. In other words, she saw the greatness in these children but they did not see the greatness in themselves. I shared this with Paige. I told her it was time to drop her expectations of these particular children. I told her to expect that they were going to lie and bother others. Then we practised role-playing so that Paige learned a new response to the children. Paige never had another conflict with either of these children after that discussion. Her expectations had been a problem simply because they had been unrealistic. It was her unrealistic expectations of them and their inability to meet those expectations that had caused her distress; they never disappointed her again.

Sometimes, we are in relationships with others for years with everything going smoothly. Then one of us reaches a new level of awareness. We come to learn something new, such as a way to attain greater physical, emotional or spiritual health, and we are so excited to share it with others because we know it is going to become a big part of our lives. But we find that the person we have been close to for years has no interest and maybe no belief in what we have learned. This can cause great conflict. Many of us want to try to "convert" that person to believing in what we now believe in, and when they don't capitulate, we feel they don't believe in *us*. Sometimes, we find ourselves trying for years to "convert" them. It is only our expectation that is causing this conflict. What if their life experience does not open them up to wanting to learn or embrace this new passion of ours? They can carry on their way and we can carry on our way and we can both remain in a relationship together, as long as we have enough common interests. You never know, they might see us flourish in a new way and one day decide that they need our expertise. Then they might take an interest in what we have come to learn. The other option is that our awareness becomes so great that we can no longer see our old lives or relationship the same way again. Our increased awareness can make us decide to stop living our lives the way we used to and end our relationship with that person.

Interestingly, keeping our expectations high of certain people can actually do wonders for them. I remember thinking so highly of one of my employees in the corporate world because she would hand projects into me ahead of deadline. She told me that she had never done that for anyone before but she wanted to make me happy. When our belief in and expectations of certain people are high, those people want to meet our expectations and prove their worth, which is fantastic for both parties. The key is to choose the people for whom we hold the high expectations.

Increasing Our Understanding of Why Others Treat Us the Way They Do
"When others lash out at us with anger, their battle is not with us but with themselves" (Hicks and Hicks 2010).

You already learned that others can treat us badly only if they have been treated badly themselves. You also learned that we can treat another person disrespectfully only if we do not respect ourselves. And you learned the reasons why others cannot always meet our needs. We can draw upon that knowledge each time we experience being treated badly or disrespectfully by another and each time our needs are not met. We also learned that all negative emotions stem from fear. What is this person who is lashing out at us afraid of? What are they really wanting or feeling they are lacking? What are they really thinking? We can ask them any of these questions. There is another possibility as well. Sometimes when people become angry at us, they want us to react adversely to them because their negative tension can then be released. Famous author, Sonia Choquette (2010) refers to this as "toxic relief". Once we understand the realm of possibilities for why others treat us the way they do, it makes it so much easier for us to refrain from taking things personally.

Once we are adults, others are our mirrors. When we are kind and good to others, generally they will be the same to us. When we love ourselves, others sense it and treat us with love in return. Let me explain by telling you about a bus tour I went on in Maui. Normally on these tours, the various tourists are picked up early in the morning and climb onto the bus not fully awake and perhaps a little leery of spending the day with a bunch of strangers, seeing sights they may or may not view as spectacular. On this particular trip, we did board the bus very early in the morning and many of us had these apprehensive feelings. But what happened as we each boarded the bus? A wonderful, friendly driver was there to greet each of us. He spoke at length to each new person who climbed onto his bus, using their name more than once and asking questions about their hometown and their interests. Even once seated, he continued talking to the newest passenger and found ways to connect them to the others on the bus. Once everyone was on the bus, he had each of us share further details about our lives with one another, one at a time. He then told us one interesting or funny story after another, even when the sights before our eyes were nothing to write home about. How do you think the people on this tour felt? We felt safe, comfortable, happy and connected to one another. It wasn't a great tour in terms of the sights, but at the end of the day, every single person felt it was one of the best tours they had ever taken. Why? Because of that one tour guide. It turns out that he was a minister; the love he has for himself and his fellow humans is reflected back to him every single day. Simultaneously, he improves the lives of everyone with whom he comes into contact. What an example he sets for others!

Increasing Our Understanding of How We Allow Others to Affect Us

Many of us believe that others have the ability to negatively affect us and that other people's happiness depends on us. This is simply not true. It can seem that way, but each of us is responsible for our own response to another, and only the response that we choose to adopt can positively or negatively affect us.

We might become very upset when someone becomes angry with us, for example. We might be upset because we think we have done something wrong. Subconsciously or consciously, we might feel we have caused them to be angry. Or maybe we really did make a mistake and their anger at us is justified and we now need to take steps to correct our mistake or learn from it. Often though, they are angry at us because of their own fears and life experiences, which have nothing to do with us. We might be upset at their anger because we have a hard time handling any amount of conflict due to our own low self-esteem. Or we might do everything we can to avoid conflict because our pasts have had too much unresolved conflict in them. We might be upset because we have had a really rough day and cannot take on anything else right now. Or maybe we are upset at their anger because we are not being understood. Just as there are any number of reasons for someone being angry, there are any number of reasons for allowing ourselves to be negatively affected by that anger. ***When we have perspective on why we are responding the way we are to others, it makes it easier for us to let go of the way in which we are responding if we are not pleased with it or it is not having the desired effect.***

 "If our emotional stability is based on what other people do or do not do, then we have no stability" (Williamson 1999, 159).

Changing Our Response to Another

We can spend our lives seeing ourselves as victims of our unhealthy relationships and blame others for our problems or we can change our response to others and heal our relationships—it's our choice. We always have two distinct ways in which to respond to another; we can respond from a fear-based and protective place or we can respond from a loving and open place.

The more we understand the concept of not taking things personally and the more we work on loving ourselves, the happier we will be with our responses to others and with our relationships in general. For example, if we have just relaxed or meditated before beginning a discussion with another, our responses will be much more to our liking.

Once we love ourselves, we can remain ourselves and be true to who we are in each of our relationships. When we can be ourselves in our relationships, we can remain bonded to other people but feel detached from their pain and behaviour. Our ability to listen, empathize, speak our truth and respond healthily to others increases because we know that we are responsible only for our own thoughts, feelings and actions and others are responsible for theirs.

A pivotal moment in my life comes to mind when I think of this concept. Once I had my children, there were many years when I only took one weekend away annually from my family and spent it with my girlfriends. How I looked forward to those weekends, and I can tell you, they were never a disappointment! However, each time I returned, I would arrive home to find my home, children and husband a complete mess. Although I would arrive home happily, invariably I found myself being yelled at. Then I would feel bad that I had left my family, been selfish and put them into such chaos and discomfort. I didn't like conflict and, remember, I was a people pleaser. I would then proceed to do everything I could to make things right between all of us again. One year when I came home and everything was in the usual state of chaos, my husband started yelling at me and I responded differently. This time, without even planning it ahead of time, I said, "I go on one girls' weekend a year. I am a stay-at-home mother; I work hard to do right by our children every single day. I need this weekend away each year and I will continue to take it, so you'd better figure out how you are going to cope!" Well, that silenced my husband. He was shocked that I had finally stood up for myself and he knew I was right. More importantly, he now knew that I loved myself enough to say no to being treated badly and to feeling guilty. I walked away from him with my head held high and once I rounded the corner, a smile began to stretch across my face; I was filled with utter pride in myself. I then found myself asking, "Now why couldn't I have done that sooner?" And that is what we always think once we overcome a challenge we have had to contend with for years of our life. The fact is that we cannot respond differently until we love ourselves enough to do so. And when we do love ourselves, we can come up with all sorts of favourable responses.

This brings me to the point that if we do everything to please another, we are not helping them. *It is only when we expect and believe that another will succeed without the benefit of our help that they do succeed.* My husband turned every subsequent girls' weekend (and the number increased each year!) into a weekend of fun times for himself and our children. Kudos to him! Some of you will ask, "Did he start cleaning up the house on those weekends too?" And my response would be, "Come on now. What do you want, the world?"

What are other ways in which we can change our response when someone is angry at us or speaking disrespectfully to us? One of the *best* approaches is to pull ourselves out of the conflict and become a witness to it. We do this by not responding immediately when we are spoken to harshly. We can take a deep breath, silently count to three and then respond in a calm manner. The best way to respond in a calm manner is to first view the other person with new perspective. So when we are breathing deeply or counting to three, we are trying to understand the other person in a new light. If they are angry, we know they are scared, so we might calmly respond to their anger by asking, "What are you scared of?" or "What are you worried about deep inside?" or "I am so sorry that you feel that I made you so angry. It is not my intention to upset you. Can you please explain your feelings about this to me?" or "I understand why you are so angry. What can I do to make things better for you?" Eventually we might even determine what it is we are supposed to learn from this exchange.

If we are right in the middle of the conflict, we are likely to ask ourselves "Whose fault is this?" and "How can I win this or be in control again?" *But if we are witnessing the conflict, we can view it more lovingly and ask, "What part of this conflict am I responsible for? What can I learn from this? What do they need?"*

"When we are immersed in our challenges, we cannot gain perspective on them. When we become observers watching the movie of our life, we can just notice our moods and behaviours without judging them; this is what ushers in change. When we can do this, we can separate our reactions from their behaviour and make intentional choices rather than just reacting to others. When two people are fighting, for example, and one becomes the observer and can watch themselves being angry, they have the advantage because they are able to separate themselves from the anger. When they can do this, they can learn from their challenges and turn the situation around for both of them" (Berger 2000, 175).

Here are some examples of replacing usual responses with healthier, more freeing responses:

- Our parents are always criticizing us: We can see ourselves the way they do or we can focus on our strengths.
- Our partner is angry with us: We can pull back emotionally or we can take responsibility by apologizing or setting boundaries.
- Our partner cheats on us: We can fear intimacy in future relationships or we can start by trusting a friend.
- Our caregiver physically abused us: We can be afraid to express and meet our needs or we can begin speaking our minds with supportive people and begin setting goals for ourselves.

Using Compassionate Communication to Express Our Needs for Our Relationship

"With every encounter with another, there's a chance for a miracle" (Williamson 2008, 162).

Communication helps us to understand, and when we understand, conflicts fall away, strengthening our relationships and our confidence while furthering our healing.

The word "communication" shares the same root as the word "communion". There is no true communication without communion. The books *The 7 Habits of Highly Effective Families* (Covey 1997) and *Emotional Freedom* (Orliff 2009) use the term "compassionate communication" to describe the process of bringing compassion to exchanges. This "meeting of hearts" involves honestly expressing our needs and empathetically listening to others. When we do this, our bond with the other person deepens and our relationship transforms. There is a direct correlation between being able to articulate our feelings and building mutually rewarding relationships. *If we could all communicate in this way, there would be no misunderstandings, violence or wars.*

Compassionate communication involves letting another know that we are only reacting the way we are because one of our needs wasn't being met. When we are angry, instead of saying, "I am angry because she _____" we say "I am angry because my need for _____ wasn't met." We then discuss how our need might be met, as opposed to discussing the "faults" of the other person.

Emotional Freedom sets out the seven rules of compassionate communication (Orliff 2009):

1. Calmly express your feelings.
2. Be specific about why you're angry; stick to one issue.
3. Request a small, doable change that could meet your need. Clarify how it will benefit your relationship.
4. Listen non-defensively to another's position; don't interrupt.
5. Empathize with the person's feelings. Ask yourself: "What pain or shortcoming is causing this person to act so angrily, to behave in a manner that doesn't meet my needs?" Take some quiet moments to intuitively sense where the person's heart is hurting or closed. Then compassion will come more easily.
6. Work out a compromise or resolution. Don't stay attached to simply being "right."
7. If a person is unwilling to change, you can either accept the situation as is and try to emotionally detach from it or limit contact. (p 370)

When we use compassionate communication, we are letting go of the judgment and blame that sabotage our communication with others. We are taking responsibility for our own needs and hurt feelings. We are seeing and speaking to the best in people, which, in turn, brings out the best in us. We are all intelligent and have integrity, and these qualities flourish in us when we sense that others see them in us. When we use compassionate communication, it makes it easier to see ourselves and others through the lens of our heart. Many like to role play compassionate communication with a friend or enlightened witness before embarking on the real thing.

Here is a more specific example: You asked your spouse to join you at your doctor's office to receive some test results. Your spouse is late. When they arrive, you can berate them for being late. Or you can use compassionate communication and say, "I am scared. I don't know if I am really sick. I wanted you to join me here so that I could feel more comfortable. Can you please promise me that you will come on time to my next doctor's appointment?"

We can arrange regular compassionate communication sessions with each other, and couples can reward each other for successful expressing and listening sessions by going on a bike ride together, taking a bubble bath together or giving one another a massage, to give a few examples.

Setting Boundaries with Another So That Our Needs Are Met by Our Relationship

Say we take all of these steps to improve our relationship with another but they continue to mistreat us. This is when we need to think about how much energy we are giving away to our relationships. Sometimes it is helpful to make a list of the people in our lives and decide whether they are a major or minor energy draw.

When we come to love ourselves yet others continue to treat us badly, we have reached a point where we love them more than they love themselves. We might want to tell them this, to make them aware that they are being their own worst enemies. We can remind them that we do not want to change anything about them. Sometimes, as you now know, we simply need to say "goodbye" for the day or forever.

Other Exercises for Improving Our Relationships
How are you blocking love?

We can ask how we have prevented ourselves from receiving love and pleasure, thereby opening the doors to receiving love. This requires quiet time and being brutally honest with ourselves. We get out a piece of paper and record our thoughts. Examples include the following:

- I have shut down relationships as soon as the girl gets serious about me.
- I turn away each time my husband tries to hug me.
- I blame her for the problems in our relationship.
- I say things trying to get him feeling angry and insecure.
- I am scared to share my feelings with her.

When we realize how we stand in the way of receiving love, we no longer need to blame our partner, or prior partners for that matter. Once we recognize and change the patterns that keep love at bay, our relationships become far more rewarding.

How do you help your relationship meet your needs?

This exercise involves sitting down and determining the most important thing that you want from your partner. Once you determine what it is, start giving it to your partner, expecting nothing in return. The best way to receive what we want is to give what we want to another. When we do this, we make it okay for our partner to give it back to us. For example, if we want to be understood, we begin by understanding our partner.

 "Prior to the work the mere thought of my mother would make me cringe and tense up, now I felt only peace. The exercise had opened the gate, I had walked through it. The cancer stopped spreading and began to slowly recede" (Ford 1988, 83).

What Constitutes a Healthy Relationship?

What do healthy relationships look like? I did not know the answer to this for many, many years. **Our family members seem to have been slated with the task of teaching us the biggest and hardest lessons, and a poor accompaniment is often unhealthy relationships.** As I matured, my friendships became healthier before my other relationships did, which, I believe, is often the case. So when we think about our friendships, what goes on there?

We look forward to spending time together. There is usually a lot of laughter and fun times. We respect, trust and support one another. A deep sharing invariably takes place, demonstrating great trust in one another. We seem to know when to leave things well enough alone, appreciating our differences. Conversations don't often escalate into arguments. We feel safe and therefore can admit our weaknesses or our mistakes and, in turn, receive the compassion that each of us so badly needs but rarely receives. We ask and receive the exact advice we seem to need. We help one another see things positively and have faith in ourselves and our futures. We do special things for one another to express our love and appreciation, remembering the little things that are important to each other. We compliment one another easily and regularly. We see the greatness in one another, and that is the bottom line.

"Loving behaviour doesn't grind you down, keep you off balance, or create feelings of self-hatred. Love doesn't hurt, it feels good. Loving behaviour nourishes your emotional well-being. When someone is being loving to you, you feel accepted, cared for, valued, and respected. Genuine love creates feelings of warmth, pleasure, safety, stability, and inner peace" (Forward 1989, 305).

What Happens to Our Relationships the More We Come to Love Ourselves?

When our love for ourselves grows enough, we are no longer afraid of others and become comfortable with speaking our truth in a loving, gentle way. Even more amazing is that when others know we are operating from a place of peace and love, they feel our love for them and don't become offended by our words; therefore, healthy discussions regularly take place. Eventually, we take stock of our lives and realize that every active relationship we have is absolutely beautiful. Some relationships are more fulfilling than others, but they all serve a purpose and fill us with good feelings. We continually send and receive loving and supportive texts, emails, phone calls and cards. We find ourselves chatting with strangers, salespeople and people helping us over the phone, finding ourselves perpetually astonished at how fulfilling and heart-warming every encounter is.

Something to Think About

All of the information and exercises in this book are designed to help you along on your journey to becoming emotionally healthy. However, it's important that we discuss the fact that other circumstances are always taking place at the same time as our healing. For example, someone we love dies; we are raising children; we're mistreated or fired from our job; our partner breaks up with us; or we move to a new home or location. We also have all sorts of personal commitments and responsibilities to contend with simultaneously: performing our job; paying our bills; grocery shopping; making meals; doing housework. Don't forget that we also have to discover our talents and make a difference in the world. It's so easy to see why many of us live in overwhelm much of the time.

We don't need to be taking the steps discussed in this book at all times. We can pick and choose when we are going to focus on an aspect of emotional health. There is no rush. *Eventually, after years of doing the work sporadically, we find that we are doing the work at all times and living authentically. Seeing ourselves and others from the lens of our heart becomes a way of life for us.*

Also, it doesn't matter what order you begin implementing aspects of this book because even if you address one area, you will likely find yourself going back and doing more work in that area at a later time. This is because our awareness continues to expand, helping us to delve deeper and deeper, gaining greater perspective the more we age.

Seven

Parent-Child Healing

Each of us navigates through challenges in our childhood and adulthood and then chooses one of three different routes when it comes to having our own children:

1. We decide not to have any children because our childhood experience was so horrible or because we have seen others' experiences and know that parenting is not for us. Or we may personally choose to not have any children but then discover that our spouse wants children—yikes!
2. We decide to have children and end up parenting similarly to the way we were parented.
3. We decide to have children but raise them very differently from the way we were raised.

There are positives and negatives to each approach. Our society puts a lot of pressure on people to have children. I applaud the people who know themselves well enough and are strong enough to stand up for their convictions and declare, "No children for me." Some of them see the job of parenting so clearly and view it as so important that they would never attempt to take it on.

The second approach is the most commonly taken road. Most of us don't think we will parent the way were parented, but that's the way things often end up. In some cases, parenting the way we were parented is a good thing. In most cases, it is not. We pass on the pain we feel and the needs that were never met just as our parents passed theirs onto us, and their parents before them, *ad infinitum*. If many lessons are learned by both parent and child, this is a good approach. If lessons are not learned, this becomes the least desirable approach.

My goal was to parent using the third approach. I wanted to raise my children very differently from the way my brother and I were raised. I was fully aware that by raising my own children, I was also raising my grandchildren, and I was determined to do right by them. But how can we parent to our liking if we were not parented to our liking? Isn't that impossible? Certainly not. Our children will teach us how to parent if we listen to them.

Please don't think that it is ever entirely possible to parent completely differently from the way we were parented though. It *is* possible to make significant improvements, so much so that when we spend time with our children and our parents together we can find ourselves truly shocked by the ways in which our parents interact with our children, while simultaneously reliving some of the unfavourable memories of our own childhood.

As far as I am concerned, there are only two methods for parenting: one method produces children whose primary emotion is love and the other method produces children whose primary emotion is fear. My greatest wish is to show you the way to raise your child so that their primary emotion is love. But first, it is vital that I share some discoveries with you about our potential for inner growth once we become parents.

Growing Alongside Our Child

The majority of new parents have not healed from their own childhoods. Obviously, the more we parent ourselves and heal before we have our own children, the better. The more accomplishments we have under our belts, the more ready and willing we will be to make the sacrifices required of us to raise our children. As soon as we become parents ourselves, an extraordinary, one-of–a-kind opportunity is born to help us heal and grow as individuals: We are put back into the parent–child relationship but in the reverse role. The very fact that we are a parent demands that we become the most loving, caring and wise we can be. Parenting calls upon our best selves. Although our child is not responsible for healing us or helping us grow, they have great potential for doing so. The roles of parent and child provide the ultimate opportunity for reciprocity.

 "You will continue to learn as your children do and you will grow right along with them. It is one of the personal benefits of becoming a mother (or father): you emerge a better human being as a result of your experience" (Carter-Scott 2002, 161).

Giving birth immediately makes us a parent, but it is only by learning to be motherly or fatherly that we give birth to ourselves. This can only occur if we come to understand that our essence is love and if we learn to express love like never before. Then, when we can see the good and lovable child not just in our own child but in everyone, including ourselves, we have learned compassion and can see the people, the circumstances of our lives and the world through the lens of our heart.

For some of us, parenting may be our *first* opportunity to love and be loved unconditionally. When we spend time with our child, we no longer feel separate or isolated. The innocence and dependence of a child allows us to feel needed and worthy. ***When we know we are loved and needed, our healing potential is at its peak.*** Just watching a child under our care grow at the rapid pace they do, as well as sit up, crawl, walk and talk, is an immensely transformative and self-esteem–building experience.

Our Children Are Our Mirrors

Not only do children look like their parents, they often end up being like their parents. My eldest, Taylor, looks more like her dad and has many of his personality traits but has my interests and thought process. My youngest, Paige, looks more like me, has my thought process and many of my personality traits but her dad's interests. Every family can describe their children in a similar way. We can figuratively view our children as hand mirrors that reflect not only the messages and cues they receive from us but also our thoughts and actions. This mirroring helps us see ourselves more clearly, which makes raising our children an ideal time to heal our childhood wounds and truly come to know and love ourselves.

If we are still wounded (incomplete or hurt) from our childhood, we will wound our child, usually without being conscious of it. When children come to me for coaching because they have depression or anxiety, I wonder who in their family is depressed or anxious, because these emotions are often picked up from their parents. A child living in their parents' home with no way of escaping, will often take on their parents' emotions.

If we are worried about being separated from our child, bedtime might be a nightly battleground for us or our child might be worried about starting school and leaving us. If we were not accepted by our parents for who we are, we, in turn, might not accept or value our child for who they are. If we are frequently angry, we might teach our child to be angry. If we have an exaggerated sense of responsibility for our child and allow our mind to work overtime, our child might be busy, restless or unable to fall asleep quickly or sleep soundly. Unfortunately, whatever we have not dealt with from our past, we pass onto our children.

"Our children are ceaselessly nursing on our consciousness and being nourished or malnourished accordingly. ... So what is a new parent feeding the new baby? Often mostly milk and worry—also discouragement, guilt, resentment and general uptightness. ... However, when we feed him love—the true stuff of his true self—we see this translated into a physical state of peaceful well-being" (Berends 1983, 54).

I think of the many women I know who were unable to breastfeed exclusively or for long. Many of them remain racked with guilt years later. Many of them were so stressed or sleep-deprived while breastfeeding that the main food they were feeding their baby was stress. Knowing that our children feed on our consciousness, I remind those mothers of what they were feeding their child and that, in their case, it might have been better that they were unable to breastfeed for long. Then I help new mothers who are able to be breastfeed to view breastfeeding not as an unwelcome interruption in their lives but as a welcome lull, a time for nourishment for both them and their child and a time of self-fulfillment rather than self-sacrifice.

 "We may be unable to bear seeing our children unhappy because of our own unconscious hurt and so we may not be able to be with them while they cry and feel their disappointment. We may buy them things we cannot afford because of this. We are driven to see the delight on their faces in order to fend off our unconscious sorrow or anger. We are trying to give them things to fix up our unfelt deprivation. We are easing our own pain through our children" (Berger 2000, 203).

Whatever character trait we don't like in our child usually mirrors something we don't like in ourselves. For example, each time a mother sees her daughter lazing about the house, she finds herself getting really angry. Telling her daughter that she is lazy is not going to incite a work ethic in the girl; in fact, it will accomplish the exact opposite and the daughter will only resent her mother for not seeing the beauty inside her. When the mother delves into her deeper feelings about the situation, she realizes that she has a tendency to be lazy and has set this example for her daughter. The mother has a choice about whether she accepts her own laziness and thereby accepts that aspect of herself or whether she takes steps to change that aspect of herself so that her daughter doesn't adopt this trait for life. You already learned that there are positive aspects of each seemingly negative trait. The mother may come to the realization that her laziness is a good thing because relaxing in our society is underrated! As long as we are accomplishing things at other times of the day, being lazy for a few hours a day can be just what the body and mind require. *When we become less critical of ourselves, we become more supportive of our children.* But if this mother feels that her laziness is too much for her liking, she may decide to start living her life in a way in which she could never be described as lazy and will get one step closer to becoming the energetic, goal-achieving person she wants to become.

From these examples, you may be seeing that the biggest task in parenting is seeing things from a perspective that does not necessarily come easily to us. If we can look at each challenge with our child as an opportunity to understand ourselves more than ever before and as potential for further growth, this helps us ease up on our children and prevents us from seeing things as "wrong". In fact, this is how we convert our "problem child" into our teacher. As long as we view our child as a problem child, we have not learned what our child can teach us. Perceiving the parent–child relationship in this way, can provide immense relief to parents who are frequently challenged by their children. Those parents who feel they have given up their lives for their children can drop their resentment and be grateful to their children for helping them on their path toward self-realization.

In fact, parenting well is a process of becoming more ourselves. It involves becoming the whole people we truly are inside, before we were diminished through the wounding that so many of us experienced in our childhoods or later in life. *So, in fact, the job we do of parenting is not only crucial to our children's safety and happiness, it is crucial to our own self-healing and growth as individuals.* And really, what do our children truly want? They want us to believe in ourselves. They want us to know that we are good people. They want us to know we are good parents. The more we believe in ourselves and our abilities, the better parents we will be.

 "There is no generic set of lessons that all mothers learn, since each mother is different and each child is unique. However, since motherhood is a rite of passage, the very act of giving birth to another human being brings with it some universal lessons. Each developmental stage your child passes through has its gifts, its challenges and its lessons. You enter each stage of your child's development as a neophyte. As you learn about this new being —

its needs and the brand new world of the infant and child care—you gradually shift from fear to uncertainty to competence. You consequently develop more and more self-confidence and trust in yourself. As your child continues to grow, so do you. You eventually shift from competence to mastery with each developmental stage. As soon as you achieve mastery, the cycle starts all over again with a brand new stage" (Carter-Scott 2002, 136).

Our Parenting Challenges Help Us Learn Certain Lessons

Here are some of the lessons that can be learned in parenthood:

Your challenge (You are)	Your lesson
Anxious or worrying	*Trust*: Let go of the things you cannot control and learn the lessons presented to you.
Controlling	*Surrender*: Your vision of the way things should be may be in sharp contrast to how things actually are. Your child may be different from your vision of the ideal child. Your lesson will be to accept circumstances for what they are and your child for who they are.
Difficulty prioritizing	*Prioritize*: Assess what is important to you and determine more efficient ways to meet your needs, your child's needs and the needs of others.
Hurt easily, hold grudges	*Forgiveness*: Your child may let you down. Your lesson will be to find compassion for your child regardless of what they did.
Disrespectful	*Respect*: Your child may always want to do things differently from what you expect. Your lesson will be to learn to honour and respect your child.

Judgmental	*Compassion*: Your child may test the limits of your compassion.
Resistant of authority	*Abiding authority*: Your child may have similar difficulty with authority, but now you will be the authority figure.
Self-involved	*Selflessness*: the importance of putting someone else's needs before your own.
Self-neglectful	*Self-love*: Focus on spending more time caring for yourself.
Weak in setting boundaries	*Strong in setting boundaries*: Your child may push the limits until you find the strength to say no.

Rigid individuals need to learn to be more flexible. Impatient individuals need to learn to be more patient. I think you get the idea. Certainly, some of those lessons are universal to all parents. When a group of parents was asked what changed about their lives when they had their children, almost everyone mentioned the loss of control over how they allocated their time and energy. All the chaos in parenthood definitely provides us with the ideal opportunity to learn how to surrender. The more set in our ways we are, the harder it will be for us to learn that lesson.

Parenting involves unmistakable confusion. Once we recognize and embrace the confusion, we open ourselves up to the possibility of better understanding. When we can accept our child's invitation to slow down and appreciate the beauty that life offers each day, the joy of being a parent returns again and again. As adults, we forget that it's miraculous that a caterpillar turns into a butterfly. Children can also give us back our astonishment at life.

Wisdom only comes about from loving. All children have the strong potential to teach their parents unconditional love. Many parents come to love their own children unconditionally but stop there; the lesson could be extended to others, as well.

It is the learning rather than the accomplishing that is so important in parenthood. **Often, it is when we are most discouraged, ashamed or filled with despair that we discover that the turning point is right around the corner; the wisdom that has eluded us for so long finally takes over.** Whenever we learn the lesson we are to learn, we are liberated, and then it's time to learn another lesson.

"Mothers who have children with physical or emotional disabilities are given special and unique growth opportunities. ... It is these mothers who reach the upper echelons of growth as they find ways to shape the life of a child who is different or difficult" (Carter-Scott 2002, 148).

Taking Responsibility with Our Child

We learned in Chapter Three how to take responsibility for ourselves. Now we are going to discuss how to take responsibility for ourselves with our children. When we say to ourselves, "I can't believe how these kids are behaving! They're driving me crazy!" there is an opportunity for us to take responsibility and put an end to the unhealthy patterns in our family. We do this by becoming aware of our own unhealthy patterns or areas in need of healing. If we are not aware of our patterns and that we have choices for how we respond to or behave with our children, we cannot choose to end our unhealthy patterns and learn the lessons we are meant to learn.

When we take responsibility, we believe that when conflicts occur between us and our child, we need to look at our own part in the difficulties; the conflicts are not because our child is doing something wrong. Often what looks like misbehaviour in our young child may be something else; our child may be tired, hungry, thirsty, sick, angry or sad, just to give a few examples. When a wife is doting and affectionate with her children, a husband can re-experience anger with his mother for the attention that he did not receive from her. When a man feels that his siblings were always stealing his mother's attention away from him, he can resent the competition for his wife's attention. If a woman was always in trouble from her mother for her messy room as a child, she may find herself giving her children a hard time about their messy rooms. In each of these cases, the parent has the opportunity to stand back, see themselves more clearly and take responsibility for their feelings and behaviours, rather than repeating the unhealthy patterns stemming from their childhood.

Here are some specific examples of taking responsibility:
- If we were emotionally abused as children, we might find ourselves belittling or criticizing our children or withholding our affection. When we can talk openly about our anger about being victimized, stop displacing our anger on our children and follow the healing steps outlined in Chapter Four, we can break the cycle for our own children.

We can then be considerate and model the kind of loving interaction we would like to see in our relationships.

- If we broke our dad's tool when we were a child and went directly to him to admit what we did and apologize to him and he hit us and called us stupid, that incident might have changed our perception and behaviours for the rest of our lives. We might have decided to never admit to our mistakes or allow ourselves to be vulnerable again, and this might be what we are teaching our children. It's never too late to share our story with our children and teach them that it is right for them to admit their mistakes and allow themselves to be vulnerable, for that is how we learn and grow.

- If our mom always told us as children, "You are too young to know about that," or when we asked the meaning behind a certain rule and were told "Just do it because I said so," our importance was diminished and our curiosity stifled. We might decide to be more open and communicative with our own children.

- When a mother is continually frustrated and angry at her children, she needs to know that by not taking some time to meet her own needs, she is not acting with integrity toward herself and is therefore taking her own frustrations out on her children. In order to bring balance to her family, she might make new friends in a parenting group or exercise class, start getting regular massages, listen to her own breath for ten minutes while sitting on a toilet or start saying no to some of the activities that are taking her time away from nurturing herself. Taking these steps and others in Chapter Five will make her less vulnerable to her old patterns and more worthy of nurturing herself. It is only when she meets her own needs that she can meet the needs of others. She might also create rules in her family that enable her children to learn about the consequences of their behaviour and look for opportunities to teach and reinforce positive behaviour.

 "When you put yourself last, when you chronically sacrifice for your kids, you teach them that a person is only worthy insofar as he or she is of service to others. You teach them to use you and make it likely that later on they will be used. Setting consistent, supportive limits and protecting yourself from overbearing demands sends a message to your child that both of you are important and both of you have legitimate needs" (McKay and Fanning 2000, 312).

"Selfless, self-denying mothers are exhausted and resentful. Self-nurturing mothers are energetic, aware, and open-hearted" (Domar 2000, 14).

Taking responsibility means being vulnerable with our children, at times. Some parents feel that it's not right to be vulnerable in their children's presence. They feel they need to be someone that their child looks up to and wants to emulate. What these parents don't know is that sometimes by acting strong, they distance themselves from their child. Their child does not feel they are on the same team as their parents. They might not feel understood or empowered. We are all scared and vulnerable at times—it is part of the human condition. If Dad says he is never afraid, he teaches his child that it's not okay to feel afraid sometimes. And if it's not okay to be afraid, a child feels there is something wrong with themselves when they do feel afraid. If Dad says he is never wrong and his child feels they have been wrongly treated by their Dad, Dad teaches his child that they are wrong. A child who feels there is something wrong with themselves cannot grow up feeling strong in this world.

How many of us have felt sadness not knowing what our fathers or mothers were going through when we were young because they didn't open up to us or share their fears? *If we can be vulnerable by admitting our weaknesses, our confusion, our sadness, our needs—that is true strength. Humility is true strength. Conversely, if we show only our vulnerabilities, we become our vulnerabilities, and that is true weakness.* None of us are simply our vulnerabilities. We each have strengths *and* weaknesses. It is our job to get to know ourselves and capitalize on our strengths while recognizing and working on or accepting our weaknesses. When a parent knows their strengths and weaknesses and shares them with their child, as the need arises, they show their child that it's okay for their child, too, to have strengths and weaknesses that need to be discovered and utilized.

What would be an example of a vulnerability that would be appropriate for a parent to share with their child? A father continuously criticized and yelled at his daughter in her formative years. Morning and night, he told her what she was doing wrong and what she needed to improve upon. She grew up feeling unloved and unappreciated by her father, and her self-esteem suffered greatly. Because her father did not see her value and because he hurt her (his parents had not seen his value and had hurt him), she no longer trusts him. Years later, relations continue to be strained between the father and daughter, even though the father has changed his ways and is trying to be good to his daughter. It is suggested to the father that he apologize to his daughter for hurting her. He doesn't feel that completely opening up his heart to his daughter puts him in a position of strength; he doesn't want to look weak in his daughter's eyes. Yet all she needs is to know that he is truly sorry and that he wants to do right by her; she desperately wants to be on the same team as him. She doesn't need him to be perfect, just on a team where each player has their strengths to contribute toward winning. Her father doesn't know that his ability to be completely vulnerable will be his strength in gaining the relationship he has always wanted with his daughter. Admitting and communicating our vulnerabilities is actually our strength in every relationship rife with challenge, as you already learned.

If this father apologized specifically for the ways in which he hurt his daughter, opened his heart and told her that he was hurting too (from his childhood and from not being able to spend time with her), if he explained to her that he wanted to become closer to her and that he was sorry he pushed her away, do you think his child would reject his apology? Not likely.

Becoming a more nurturing parent involves learning new emotional skills, which can be mastered in the same way we learn a new skill at work or train for a sport. At first, it might feel awkward practising a new emotional skill. Old habits might reappear, which makes it important to coach ourselves or hire a life coach to help us through the transition. With practise, we find that we lose our awkwardness and our new behaviour becomes completely natural.

Exercise for determining inherited unhealthy patterns when it comes to raising our children

Describe in great detail the things your parents did that ended up making you feel rejected, belittled or unloved. Recall incidents when they didn't meet your needs. Which examples of being a parent did you find harmful or ineffective? To help you remember, you can look at a picture of your parents from when you were a child. Next, examine the times in which you felt most loved, appreciated, encouraged and special. What specific parental qualities did you admire in your mother and father? Remember a time when your parents taught you something valuable.

 "Becoming your own best parent is not a final destination but a new beginning. You can live your life with more inner peace instead of being controlled by unresolved conflicts from your upbringing. Taking charge of your life will give you more energy and vitality to express your own special talents more effectively" (Bloomfield 1983, 214).

Our Response to Our Child Is Our Starting Point for Taking Responsibility and Healing

When it comes to the raising of our child, one of the major ways in which we take responsibility for ourselves and our emotional healing is by noticing, processing and choosing our response to our child's words or actions. Each response is triggered by our interpretation of each situation. The key to overcoming conflicts with our child lies in changing our responses or reactions to them. Once we start responding to them positively and with self-composure, we can literally turn our interactions around with our children.

 "Suppose that we become aware that we are regularly losing our temper and treating our children in a disrespectful, disparaging way. We can begin examining our intentions, opening with acceptance to the thoughts and feelings that arise as we do so. Perhaps we realize that we want to push our children away because we feel too stressed to handle their needs: 'I'm sinking and trying to save my own life.' Along with this thought, we might feel a tightness in our belly that spreads like a wave and grips at our throat. We might also look and see the actual effect of our behaviour on our children. Have they withdrawn from us? As we notice that our children are becoming secretive and fearful around us, we might feel in our chest a rising sense of sorrow" (Brach 2003, 29–30).

Each time we have a challenge with our child and we react with major intensity, usually negatively, we discover an aspect of parenting that is difficult for us, and invaluable information is provided about the parts of ourselves that need healing. When we react adversely, we are protecting a vulnerable part of ourselves; it is *that* aspect of ourselves that needs to be uncovered and healed. Many of us are triggered most by our children when they are at the age in which we suffered the most. When our child misbehaves and we become really upset, subconsciously we come face to face with our past and are reminded of how we once felt in similar circumstances. When we become conscious of those memories and work with them, we heal. If we don't do this work, our memories will trigger us, causing us to continually over or under-react, both of which damage our child's well-being.

Over-reacting involves turning a small challenge into a much bigger challenge or turning one occurrence into a habit or character flaw. When we over-react to our child misbehaving, we are acting from our perception of what our child is doing without understanding our child's specific needs or interpretation of things. I remember my daughter eating the soil from a plant one day and her father's reaction when he saw her do it. He was appalled, and most parents would respond the same way. Parenting in this way stems from a belief that the conflicts with our child exist because the child is doing something wrong; we often do not see our own contribution or take responsibility for their difficulties. When we become angry in instances like this, the bond between our child and us tarnishes; our child's view of the world becomes tainted; our child comes to believe that there are parts of themselves that are unacceptable and their love for themselves decreases. I happened to witness this exchange between my daughter and her father, so I asked her father when he had fed her last, and he admitted that it had been many hours. Aha! We had uncovered our daughter's unmet need and therefore had a whole new understanding of why she did what she did. (And no, she did not have an iron deficiency, as some of you nutritionists might be thinking! If she was regularly wanting to eat soil or sand, that would be a different matter.) We apologized to our daughter for not feeding her and said that we understood exactly what made her eat the soil. I could feel my daughter's relief at being vindicated and I thoroughly enjoyed the trust and closeness that instantly grew between us.

 "Children are labelled as misbehaving in our culture when what they are doing is totally reacting instinctively, trying to get their needs met" (Berger 2000, 58).

I would like to share another example with you of this concept in hope of encouraging you to think outside the box when something goes wrong. I remember taking my girls to a cranial osteopath for an appointment for each of us. My girls were uncharacteristically poorly behaved, even downright rude. I became angry with them but said very little as we were in the presence of another. As I lay on the table for my treatment, it occurred to me that we had just gone raspberry picking prior to the appointment and they had eaten way too many of the insecticide-laden berries. My girls were extremely sensitive to chemicals at that age, so when I realized what had made them behave the way they did, I was overflowing with compassion for them. I then thought of the level of anger I had felt for them and tried to look into my past to determine what had got me so worked up. I realized that it was my perfectionist tendencies that were rearing their ugly head once again. My attempts to try to be perfect as a result of my childhood did not mean that I could or would expect that of my children. When we left the practitioner's office, I had a conversation with my girls. This is how it went: "Girls, it was really unlike you to behave the way you did during that appointment. Do you know why you behaved that way?" They had no idea. I proceeded to explain my theory about the raspberry picking and their resulting behaviour, based on the same behaviour occurring after we went apple picking the previous fall. My girls looked at me with gratitude and apologized for behaving the way they did. I apologized to them for being angry with them for something that was not their fault. I did not explain my perception of my reaction to them because of their young ages, but I can assure you that when they matured, I easily and often shared those perceptions with them.

We do not need to parent from the limited, judgmental, wounded or unhappy aspects of ourselves, a way of parenting that many of us inherited. We can choose to respond to our children from our open, accepting, loving and happy selves. As you now know, it is entirely possible to recognize our subconscious unhappiness and begin to love the hurt aspects of ourselves back to health. Each of us has a child inside us. If we honour that child, we reclaim the love we owe ourselves. **It is only by loving the child within us that we ensure that the legacy we pass down to our own children is love.** It is important to take responsibility for our actions, but it is equally important not to blame ourselves for not knowing better; for having wrong beliefs and teaching them to our children; for failing to act in an idealized manner; or for not being further along in our own growth. It is far more helpful to be appreciative of our observations of ourselves and newfound awareness and to know that our efforts will pay off eventually.

 "A child who sees his parent in the process of becoming a more conscious person will be equipped to do the same in his own life and will contribute to the increasing consciousness of our species" (Hendrix and Hunt 1997, 36).

Special note: Some of you may have noticed that the two examples I just gave you both ended up showing you the impact that diet has on our children's behaviour. As a pediatric nutritionist, I can't help but explain that it is crucial for a child of any age to be fed a protein source the size of their palm every two to three hours to maintain blood-sugar balance, which, in turn, stabilizes a child's mood, behaviour, concentration level and energy. Remembering this will make your job a whole lot easier.

Exercise to arrive at a compassionate response

The next time you see your child act inappropriately, become still, watch and breathe, if only for a moment. A moment is all it takes to acquire the perspective to turn a situation around. Each time we become the observer, we find it easier to calm ourselves, and we usually find ourselves feeling more proud of our response. To understand your child's problematic behaviour and arrive at a compassionate response, you can ask yourself three questions:

1. What need are they trying to meet with that behaviour?
2. What beliefs influenced their behaviour?
3. What feelings (e.g., pain) influenced their behaviour?

Exercises for ending unhealthy patterns with our children

1. Write down a positive statement about yourself and a new behaviour that you will try the next time your child pushes your buttons. For example: "I am a positive role model for my child. It is my job to successfully resolve the conflicts I have with others. I am going to stay calm the next time my child pushes my buttons, look beyond our conflict and discuss the needs that are not being met on both our parts."
2. If you realize that certain situations always trigger the same reaction in you and you can't seem to change that reaction, ask yourself "What lesson do I need to learn in order for my reaction to change?"
3. If you catch yourself responding negatively to your child's words or actions, say, out loud or in your head, a firm no to your programming. Then respond in a way that makes you feel good about yourself. That no can change everything.

Our Response Teaches Our Child about Themselves and the World They Live in

Just as our response teaches us about ourselves, our response teaches our child about themselves and the world they live in. A child can learn that the world encourages wholeness, health, balance and love or they can experience the world as cold, unfeeling and unloving. However they experience it, their life will be shaped by this awareness.

When a little boy accidentally drops and smashes his glass of water on the floor and is yelled at, he is taught that the universe doesn't care if he has hurt himself. When a little girl is told to finish everything on her plate, even though she knows she has had enough, she is taught that the universe doesn't honour her bodily needs. The young child who is punished because they accidentally ride their bike into the street while learning to ride is taught that the universe is not tolerant of mistakes.

If we are unhappy, fearful, guilty or angry, our children are bound to receive a negative view of themselves and the world they live in. If we blame them and others for our challenges, how can our children learn to take responsibility for themselves? If we don't respect ourselves, our children won't respect us. If we break our commitments to ourselves, our children will also learn to break commitments to themselves. If we don't believe in our children, how can they possibly believe in themselves? When we teach our children this negative way of being, our children cannot help but treat themselves and others the same way we treat them. ***Our children learn what they live, they learn more by what we do than what we say, and they learn better by witnessing our learnings than by any other means.***

This verse entitled "Children Learn What They Live" was on the wall of my childhood home. I read it over and over for the first ten years of my life. I never knew when I read these words that they would be part of my purpose on earth or that I would be sharing their importance with others one day.

Children learn what they live

If children live with criticism, they learn to condemn.
If children live with hostility, they learn to fight.
If children live with fear, they learn to be apprehensive.
If children live with pity, they learn to feel sorry for themselves.
If children live with ridicule, they learn to feel shy.
If children live with jealousy, they learn to feel envy.
If children live with shame, they learn to feel guilty.
If children live with encouragement, they learn confidence.
If children live with tolerance, they learn patience.
If children live with praise, they learn appreciation.
If children live with acceptance, they learn to love.
If children live with approval, they learn to like themselves.
If children live with recognition, they learn it is good to have a goal.

If children live with sharing, they learn generosity.

If children live with honesty, they learn truthfulness.

If children live with fairness, they learn justice.

If children live with kindness and consideration, they learn respect.

If children live with security, they learn to have faith in themselves and in those about them.

If children live with friendliness, they learn the world is a nice place in which to live.   (Nolte 1972)

Our Response Can Strengthen Our Relationship with Our Child

How we respond to our child's negative behaviour can strengthen or weaken our relationship with them. If our child comes home from school and is irritable and difficult, we can think of our own need for harmony within our home and respond angrily by telling them we are sick and tired of taking on the brunt of their challenges in life. I can assure you that this response will only serve to elongate their bad mood! Or we could think about what might have occurred that day to make them feel unhappy. We might decide to talk with them about the cause of their irritability and discuss their feelings with them. Once we let them know that we understand their feelings and the circumstances, we can remind them that they don't need to take their anger out on us the next time they have a bad day.

When our child is young, we can tell them the story of their day at bedtime. By doing this, we help our child remember and integrate the events of their life and augment their understanding of themselves and those around them. I have always found bedtime to be the best time to have a good conversation with my girls and review the day's activities. They can release any negative energy and fall into a peaceful sleep for the night. Here is an example of how to carry out this conversation. We can describe the things about the day that went well. Then we can remind our child that they became angry with us because we were gardening and didn't play with them, so they threw dirt. We can then discuss the fact that we became angry with them and used a loud voice and told them to stop it immediately. We can ask them if we scared them. We can remind them that they cried and that we then made up. Then we can discuss other aspects of the day that went well. Next we might create a plan together to avoid the negative occurrences from happening again. We might suggest setting the kitchen timer so that when it goes off, that is when we are going to play.

By reflecting on the day, our child begins to make sense of their world. And if we also come up with a plan to avoid future challenges, our child gains some control in knowing that they are going to have their needs met. We can reframe the events of the day to bring about insight and healing on the very day the event occurred. When we respond with understanding and compassion in this way, we show an appreciation of our differences and mutual respect for one another. ***Each time we are compassionate, we teach that sharing our emotions and being able to feel one another's pain is infinitely valuable.*** And we can't help but deepen our relationship with our child.

Eight

Parenting Our Own Children

Our Child's Emotional Health: The Most Important Component

"There is no unimportant day in a child's life; every moment, every conversation, every activity is important. ... We often mistakenly believe that the big orchestrated occasions like the trip to Disneyland are the landmarks in a child's life. What children carry in their hearts is not events but relationships. It is the giving of ourselves that matters" (Gordon 2005, 209–10).

The most important component of our child's emotional health is having a good relationship with us, their parents. The structure of our families is far less important to children than the relationships they have with each family member. Many believe that divorce or the death of a family member will ruin a child; that is unequivocally false. As long as a child has a minimum of one loving adult meeting their emotional needs, they will be emotionally healthy and have the belief system of "I am loved". That adult is a witness to the child's essence and their life. As a child undergoes challenge after challenge in the process of growing up, having that one stable adult who truly knows them and can help them make sense of it all is absolutely essential. When a child can make sense of it all, they are emotionally healthy and become a self-directed, responsible adult who knows and loves themselves. If they don't have this one adult in their life, they need to learn to become emotionally healthy on their own, a much more difficult task.

Having a healthy relationship with our child begins with having a healthy relationship with ourselves and ends with our child having a healthy relationship with themselves as an adult. The more we experience who we really are, the more freedom we give our children to be who they really are. The more our needs are met, the better equipped we are to meet the needs of our child.

Ironically, each time we meet our child's needs, we give ourselves the love and care that we need to heal our own wounds, thereby completing a circle of love that reaches far beyond us and our child. If our childhood left us feeling insecure and anxious, we can heal many of the ways that we felt hurt and misunderstood by being the kind of parent that our parents never were to us. No one had a perfect childhood, and some of us had more challenging experiences than others. Yet even those of us with overwhelmingly difficult past experiences can come to resolve our issues and have meaningful and rewarding relationships with our own children. If we remain open to our own growth, our relationship with our children has no choice but to flourish.

Coming to Understand Our Child

"The deepest hunger of the human heart is to be understood"
(Covey 1997, 213).

In my first book, I explained the importance of coming to understand our child's body in order to meet their physical needs (proper nutrition, identifying their particular problematic foods, adequate sleep and exercise). In this book, I explain the importance of coming to understand our child emotionally. None of us intends to hurt our child in the parenting process. It is simply that we don't understand our child; we don't see clearly into their hearts. **Our paramount task in raising an emotionally happy child is to come to honour what it is that our particular child needs in order to feel loved and appreciated. And the more we understand our child, the easier our relationship with them will be.**

The place we start in understanding our child emotionally is in the womb. If mother is calm and feeling well in her pregnancy, baby will be feeling similarly. If mother is fearful of being pregnant, of her pending labour or of bringing her child into the world or is experiencing pain or stress in her life, baby will be fearful. Our baby's birth also determines whether they come into the world with love-based feelings or fear-based feelings.

 "Suffice it to say, whatever feeling baby is experiencing at birth, with the first breath the baby takes, this feeling is sealed in the flesh; encoded in every cell of the body!" (Truman 2003, 35)

When a baby is negatively affected during birth, there is nothing a mother can do to help this situation at the time. If she is able to hold her baby skin-to-skin for at least forty-five minutes following birth, the baby has a much better chance of embracing love-based feelings rather than fear-based feelings. But even if this didn't happen or if pregnancy caused fear-based feelings in a child, there are many ways to help a child increase their love-based feelings as they grow.

My daughter, Taylor was the product of a forty-two-hour labour, wherein two sets of forceps were used to yank her out because the umbilical cord was wrapped around her in three places. One of the forceps cut the cornea of her eye and caused permanent damage to her sight. For the first twenty-four hours after birth, she experienced countless heel pricks in the hospital as nurses drew blood for various tests, causing Taylor to scream out repeatedly in pain. To add insult to injury, she was fed formula by a nurse because her glucose level initially appeared low, and even though she had only one ounce of the formula, she reacted badly to it, with more screaming, as well as gas and vomiting that lasted for many hours. Then, I wasn't able to supply her with enough breast milk, and she became so dehydrated that her skin became loose. I still feel sad for Taylor when I write about her start on this earth. Nonetheless, I'm telling you about it so that you understand what is possible. Taylor's start in life did not dictate the way the rest of her life went. Yes, fear *was* her predominant feeling for many years, but because of the methods I describe in this book (which I learned *because* of her start in life), she is one of the most confident teenagers you could ever meet.

We Are Our Children's Mirrors

We are our children's whole world—the source of all safety and contentment, the eradicator of their fears and pain. Every moment, our child learns about themselves from us by the way in which we communicate with them. We are the mirror that shows this new person who they are.

 "When parents are genuinely present and loving, they offer their child a mirror for his or her goodness. Through this clear mirroring, a child develops a sense of security and trust early in life, as well as the capacity for spontaneity and intimacy with others. When my clients examine their wounds, they recognize how, as children, they did not receive the love and understanding they yearned for. Furthermore, they are able to see in their relationships with their own children the ways they too fall short of the ideal—how they can be inattentive, judgmental, angry and self-centered" (Brach 2003, 13).

Following our baby's birth, it is our baby's cries that help us the most in coming to understand our baby. Imagine if each time we heard our baby cry, we thought to ourselves, "Thank you, little one, for helping me to understand your needs." What a positive way to view crying! Each time we hear our baby cry, the majority of us are naturally inclined to try to comfort them. Each time we are able to comfort our baby, we honour them; we teach them that the world will respond to them and that their needs are valid and will be met, that they are important and that they are effective at letting us know their needs. Each time we smile at our baby, our baby learns that they are enjoyable. Each time we hold our baby close, they learn they are safe. It is a powerful feeling for a baby to be in a family where they feel physically and emotionally safe. Each time we respond in these ways, we teach our child their first lessons about their worth and provide them with the building blocks of their self-esteem.

 "It is this first relationship that affirms the power and efficacy of human connection: Baby is hungry and starts to cry, Mommy listens and cues into baby's hunger, Mommy picks baby up, comforts him and feeds him. Daddy smiles, sings baby's name, lifts her in the air; baby has an answering smile, gurgles, spreads out her fingers to touch daddy's face. Circles of communication, understanding and connection are completed. These and similar circles are repeated throughout the first years of life. ... Reading cues and responding lays the foundation for the emotional learning that allows empathy to take root and flourish" (Gordon 2005, 33).

The way we respond to our child and our small, repeated exchanges form the most fundamental lessons of our child's emotional life. Some parents pick up their child and tell them to stop crying or stop being bad. Parents who subscribe to this "tough love" approach with young children sometimes believe that it will help their child cope better with the harshness of life later on. In fact, the opposite is true. Early nurturing and responsive care enhance a child's resilience and ability to cope with all adversity. For example, if each time our older child falls and hurts themselves, we respond calmly and lovingly, our child's ability to stay calm each time they have a challenge will grow, as will their knowledge of their resilience.

More than any other time period, a child's first six years have the most important influence on that child's whole lifetime. In those years, the majority of brain development takes place. ***The fact that the brain matures in the world, rather than in the womb, means that young children are deeply affected by their early experiences.*** Their relationships, feelings, experiences and challenges actually affect the way their brains become "wired", subsequently shaping the way they learn, think and behave for the rest of their lives. These are also the years when their values and attitudes are formed and when the bulk of their empathetic skills are learned. All of these aspects form the foundation for a strong sense of self, which helps children build strong relationships in the world at large.

Our Children Are Not Ourselves

As our babies grow into children and then into adults, their uniqueness becomes more and more apparent. Every individual is one of a kind. In Chapter One, I discussed the importance of every family member needing the freedom to express themselves as individuals. Our children are not ourselves. It is exceedingly important that we see our child as separate from ourselves, particularly if they are very different from us or they are not the being we envisioned. The more we understand and accept our differences, the better understudy to our child we will be—the better able we will be at understanding, valuing and protecting who they truly are. When we can do that, we can support and encourage them to come to know and love themselves. Trusting who our child is and nurturing our child's uniqueness is the secret to building self-esteem. People who are cherished for who they are usually feel good about themselves. Building our child's self-esteem is one of our greatest responsibilities in the healthy parenting of our children.

"Look at your child. It is not easy to really see your child. Your vision is clouded by your hopes and fears. Your son might remind you of yourself or your mate or another child. You have opinions about how your daughter ought to be, and how you hope she will be. It's a challenge, but when you are able to see your child accurately, you will be rewarded with a relationship that is more enjoyable, with more reasonable expectations and less conflict. And you will be contributing to your child developing good self-esteem" (McKay and Fanning 2000, 281).

It is crucial that we distinguish our needs from our child's needs. If we transfer our needs to our child in order to make our lives more meaningful, we avoid taking responsibility for our own needs and only let ourselves down. Every time we have our own agenda for our child or use our child to fulfill our dreams, it makes it very hard for us to see and appreciate our child for who they are. It also makes it next to impossible for our child to come to know and love themselves in order to deal effectively with the world. This is why taking credit or blame for our child is essentially "taking the life" of our children.

When our child scores a goal, we did not score that goal ourselves. When our child falters in her dance competition, we did not falter. A mother whose athletic potential was not realized might be more likely to care too much about her daughter's athletic abilities. If she were to see that she was indeed caring too much, she might begin her own healing process. When our child is freaking out, we are not freaking out; we can remain calm. Each of us can use times of unhappiness with our child as an opportunity to see ourselves differently.

Steven Covey describes some of the ways in which he saw himself differently while raising his children. "I was trying to win social approval for myself through my children's behaviour. I wanted to get other people to like me because of their good behaviour. I constantly feared that instead of winning approval, my children's behaviour would embarrass me. Because of that lack of faith in them, I instructed, threatened, bribed, and manipulated my kids into behaving the way I wanted them to behave. I began to see that my own hunger for approval was keeping my children from growth and responsibility. My actions were actually helping to create the very thing I feared: irresponsible behaviour" (Covey 1997, 30).

It is imperative that we each come to know ourselves, as Covey did, in order to understand our real motives in each situation. We do this by becoming aware of the thought that precedes the thought that we need to be a certain way or do something for our child to meet our own need. For example, when we give our child what they want yet again, are we doing it so that they feel loved and love us in return? **Often our motive is our subconscious desire for love or acceptance. When this is the case, we are not really loving our child but are using our child to help us to love ourselves.** If our child feels or looks good or behaves well, we feel good. When we feel good, we feel that we are being loved. If we were to follow the advice in Chapter Five instead, we would come to authentically love ourselves and allow our child to do the same.

Every child has their own rhythms. For those of you who have more than one child, you will invariably see that each of your children tends to have their own rhythm, likes and dislikes that differ from their sibling's—just to make sure you learn all there is to know about parenting! Your one child might like to get up an hour before it's time to leave for school so that they can leisurely prepare for the day. Your other child might like to get out of bed as late as possible and even want to eat their breakfast en route to school. The idea is to come to understand and respect each child's rhythm and teach them to do the same. This is what brings our children great inner peace.

Every child has their own likes and dislikes. One of the ways we get to know our child's preferences and encourage them to find their own voice is by giving them choices. When we enrol our children in sports or activities that we want them in and they end up not liking them or not excelling at them, we need to honour their needs and refrain from signing them up for that sport or activity again. If we do not honour their needs, we could be hurting them the exact way in which we were hurt. We all know what it felt like when our needs were denied; why would we do that to our child? Even more importantly, when we honour their needs to spend time doing the things they love doing, we help our children connect with their own gifts, which connects them with their con-science, and this is how their love for themselves blooms.

 "Make a pact with yourself to never consciously stifle your child's essence, and you will be amazed at how clearly it becomes apparent to you. If you commit to keeping the light in their eyes alive, you will automatically seek out ways to keep it aglow. Focus on and nurture who she is and her seeds will grow abundantly" (Carter-Scott 2002, 85).

Every parent intrinsically knows their child better than anyone else. However, there are varying degrees of the depth of knowledge that each of us has for our child. Our two main methods for coming to know our child are to watch and listen to them. The more we watch and the more we listen, the greater our depth of knowledge of them will be and the more our child will share their lives with us.

Understanding and Meeting the Needs of Our Child
"If we could bring up one generation of children whose needs were more fully met we could change the world" (Berger 2000, 200).

All children have the same basic needs; these needs are behind their motivation and the choices they make. Every child is unique in how they choose to satisfy their needs. Children's needs include:

- physical survival
- mental stimulation
- being loved by and loving others
- having the freedom to be themselves
- feeling competent
- experiencing joy

Our society provides the least amount of support to families in the history of humankind; children and parents are forced together under the same roof like never before because of the dwindling of large extended families, the more frequent relocation of individual family members and the advances in technology changing the way we socialize. As a result, it is absolutely impossible for us to be able to meet the needs of our child at every moment. ***Regardless of who is involved, mistakes will be made in the parenting of every child; the question is whether they are truly mistakes or whether the "mistakes" go into the creation of another person who has challenges they need to overcome, as is the case with each of us?***

If we want our child to grow up emotionally healthy, it is crucial that we truly understand their needs and that we put their needs first most of the time. When both parents understand the importance of putting their child's needs first and allow them to own their feelings, they can help each other meet the needs of their child, as well as their own. When we understand and value our child's feelings and needs, our child comes to know that their feelings and needs are acceptable. More importantly, they come to know that *they* are acceptable and that it's okay to be themselves.

"In today's world, society is not on the sidelines giving praise and affirmation in your role as a father or mother. You're not paid to do it. You don't get prestige out of doing it. No one cheers you on in the role. As a parent, your compensation is the satisfaction that comes from playing a significant role in influencing a life for good that no one else can fill. It's a proactive choice that can only come out of your own heart" (Covey 1997, 122).

I have noticed that some adults think that just because they are the adult, their needs are more important than their child's. Why would an adult think this—because they have lived longer? Because they have responsibilities that their child does not? Our needs are no more important than those of our child's. If you have to go to work and your child is dawdling or playing with his soldiers in his room instead of getting ready to get out the door, you might say to me, "But of course what I need to do is more important than what my son is doing!" And my response would be "Not in the eyes of your son."

The bottom line to ensuring our child feels important is making them feel loved and appreciated, and we do that by letting them know that we recognize their needs to be just as important as ours. Do you know how many times I see a child playing nicely, minding their own business, happy as a lark, without a care in the world, and then see their mother come up to them, frantic and rushing, saying, "We have to go!" The child has no idea where they are going or what the rush is. This is exactly what initiates anxiety in a child. It is also what incites lack of cooperation. There is no need. ***Planning and communication put both parent and child on the same team, and that is where peace and happiness can thrive.*** When we tell our child what is on the agenda for the next few days, go over each day's schedule on the actual day, give them time frames for when things are going to happen shortly before they take place and give our child some choices about the timing of certain events, we are encouraging our child's cooperation while promoting teamwork. When we ensure that our child knows that one or more of their less important needs are going to be met each day, in addition to their more important needs, they are far more willing to go along with our plans. It's all about negotiation with a child, starting when they are only one year old. It is all about negotiation with all of our relationships.

Determining Our Child's Love Language

"By speaking your child's own love language, you can fill his 'emotional tank' with love. When your child feels loved, he is much easier to discipline and train then when his 'emotional tank' is running near empty" (Campbell and Chapman 1997, 17).

Ross Campbell and Gary Chapman wrote a bestseller called *The Five Love Languages for Children.* I believe it is essential that every parent know their child's primary love language in order to meet their needs. Understanding one another's love languages also gives insight into ways of relating more effectively to one another and helps to develop stronger, more trusting connections. Adults have love languages too, so please determine your primary love language and use this information to help meet your own needs as well. Campbell and Chapman describe the love languages as follows:

1. **Words of affirmation:** These children feel appreciated and loved when they hear or read positive messages from others. Examples include "I love you" and "You did an incredible job playing defence today. Did you see how many times you prevented the other team from scoring?"

2. **Quality time:** These children feel appreciated and loved when they are given undivided attention. Examples of quality time include playing a game together, snuggling on the couch and having a conversation on a car ride.

3. **Receiving gifts:** These children feel appreciated and loved when they are given presents. Examples include coming home from school and finding a new set of markers in their bedroom, being taken shopping and receiving a CD filled with their favourite tunes or an iTunes gift card.

4. **Acts of service:** These children feel appreciated and loved when things are done for them. Examples include making their bed for them or cleaning up their room (if they don't mind you entering their lair!) or fixing their broken bike for them.

5. **Physical touch:** These children feel appreciated and loved when they are cuddled or touched in a loving manner. Examples include hugging them when you see them first thing in the morning or before they go to sleep at night, touching them on the arm when you are speaking to them or playing wrestling games with them.

Do you know to which of the five love languages your child responds the most? Even a child as young as two knows their love language when asked. You may have one child who needs words of affirmation and one who needs quality time, as I do. Or maybe you have four children, each having a different love language—that will keep you on your toes!

It is certainly sad when a parent has assumed for years that their child wanted to receive gifts when all they really wanted was physical touch. Or if our child's love language is physical touch and we were never hugged or kissed as a child, this language will be more challenging for us to learn. In either case, all we need to do is explain this to our child and ask them for their help in reminding us to use their love language. It may have been many years that our child has not received their love language and we may have struggled in our relationship, but it is never too late to start filling our child's love tank.

"In raising children, everything depends on the love relationship between the parent and child. Nothing works well if a child's love needs are not met. Only the child who feels genuinely loved and cared for can do her best. You may truly love your child, but unless she feels it—unless you speak the love language that communicates to her your love—she will not feel loved" (Campbell and Chapman 1997, 17).

A friend of mine is a wonderful parent to her children. She listens and watches them and has always been very close to her daughters. There came a time when one of her daughters stopped thriving; there had been signs along the way that something was awry but things finally came to a head. The little girl began pulling her hair out, was racked with anxiety, wore dark colours all of the time and was easily troubled. My friend couldn't understand these behaviours given everything she had done to make a good life for her daughter. I suggested that she determine and provide her daughter with her love language. My friend identified that her daughter's love language was quality time. She explained to me that she was always taking her to her sports and watching her games but that they were not sitting down and doing something together without interruption. My friend began giving her daughter her love language, and everything turned around. Every single challenge her daughter was experiencing literally disappeared. Seeing her daughter wear bright clothes and her eyes shine brightly again was the most incredible sight in the world for my friend.

Teaching and Encouraging Our Child to Express Their Feelings, Needs and Wants

Each of us is born with the capacity for empathy—the ability to experience what others experience. Babies respond immediately to the sadness or happiness of significant people in their lives and will even try to reassure a distressed parent or other children. They know whether there is harmony or discord. Their capacity for empathy grows even more as they develop a sense of who they are. The more aware a child becomes of their own emotions and their effect on them, the more they can recognize the emotions in those around them.

Every child starts out being very honest and direct in expressing their feelings, needs and wants, but many of those feelings, needs and wants are brushed aside by adults. ***Many children are taught to eliminate discomfort at all costs rather than allow discomfort to run its course.*** Because they are taught to turn away from their emotions by the time they are five or so, their understanding of emotions tends to stay at the same level of development. Unfortunately, we know that this makes children doubt themselves, bury their feelings and, eventually, develop inauthentic behaviour or negative patterns.

"We catch on very quickly (starting at age 4/5) to the fact that most people are inauthentic with one another—that they lie about their feelings, leave important words unsaid, and trample unheedingly over each other's obvious emotional cues. Learning to speak is often a process of learning not to speak the truth and attaining an uncanny level of pretence in most relationships. Every culture and subculture has a different set of unspoken rules about emotions, but all of them require that specific emotions be camouflaged, overused, or ignored. Most children—empaths one and all—eventually learn to shut down their empathic abilities in order to pilot their way through the social world" (McLaren 2010, 5).

Earlier, I described how the first step in taking responsibility for ourselves and coming to know and love ourselves is identifying, understanding, feeling and expressing our emotions. Self-esteem is based on the acceptance of all thoughts and feelings as one's own. If we want our child to take responsibility for themselves and come to know and love themselves, we need to help them identify, understand, feel and express their emotions in the same way that we accomplish this task. In this way, they will learn to see feelings as information. As we learn to balance our own emotions, we are better able to show our child how to balance their emotions. ***It is through the sharing of emotions that we build our connection with our child and genuinely come to know them.***

 "Kids with high levels of intrapersonal and emotional intelligence are able to identify what they are feeling and can regulate their emotions in order to think through a problem or issue. They are also better able to recognize the emotions of other people and situations and can handle relationships more effectively. Self-awareness of their feelings helps kids react to situations in their lives in a more proactive manner, helps to identify what they value and what fulfills them" (Howson 2010,4) .

When our child is just one year old, if we are able to see things through their eyes, we can help them identify their feelings by labelling them. We can say, "You look sad right now," which helps our child realize that there are words to describe what's going on inside them. Children act out their feelings in their behaviour. If every time our child throws something in frustration we say, "Oh, you seem really angry," over time our child will learn to associate each particular feeling with a word. Then, when our child nears three years old, they begin to understand words like "angry" and "sad" and they will actually be able to talk about how they are feeling. By allowing our children to feel and label negative emotions, as opposed to shutting them down, we teach them that negative feelings and emotions are a normal part of life and we provide them with the most valuable tools to maintain emotional health for their rest of their lives. It is through the expression and exploration of our feelings that we obtain greater awareness and new perspective on each situation. Then we can more competently choose the next best steps for ourselves.

Some children are frightened by their negative emotions and act out when they have them unless we talk to them about their fears and explain that these are natural feelings to have in certain circumstances. Some children are introverts and don't want to talk about their feelings when they are experiencing them; they like to share their feelings only after they have had some time and space to think about them. We can let our introverts know that we are available to talk whenever they are ready. Some might prefer to talk to us about their feelings through puppets or dolls, and that's okay, too.

Children who are allowed to fully release their anger, sadness or other negative emotions in healthy ways automatically express these emotions appropriately as adults, too. For example, if a child throws things in anger, this is not a healthy way to express their emotions. When we see them throw things, in addition to saying, "Oh, you seem really angry," we could say "I know it's hard when you can't do what you want, but we don't throw things when we're angry." Then we could share healthy ways of releasing negative emotions (as described in Chapter Four).

In *Self-Esteem* (2000), authors McKay and Fanning suggest the following ways for helping children specifically with expressing their strong, negative feelings in a healthy manner:

- Encourage little children to growl, hit a pillow, or stamp their feet to express angry feelings. Older children might draw a pic or write a letter or telephone a sympathetic friend to tell them what happened.

Sports and strenuous physical activities can provide another outlet for strong feelings.

- Encourage your children to use their imagination to express their feelings. Do you want her to disappear? Be invisible?
- Share a story about yourself in a similar predicament, feeling similar things. Your child can feel that she is not alone in her feelings and take comfort that you understand.
- Be a good role model in how you deal with your own strong feelings. Share some of your own coping skills.
- Help your children feel good about themselves even in the face of defeat or disappointment. 'Even though you were lost and confused, you had the good sense to ask the saleslady for help. How did you think of that?' (pp 292–93)

When we teach our child healthy ways and unhealthy ways to express their negative feelings, we can also teach them about other people's feelings. We might say, "We don't hit because hitting hurts and makes others feel bad." or "Wouldn't you feel sad if that happened to you?" When we read to our child, we can talk about what the characters might be thinking and feeling. ***These kinds of discussions help develop our child's empathetic imagination and, also, provide them with a new level of meaning for each interaction they have with others.***

 "Acknowledged feelings go away sooner and more completely than feelings that are denied. Our 'whining' child will stop whining sooner if he or she gets the attention needed. ... Most often when our (young) children are allowed to cry all they need to cry, they finish and become sunny for the rest of the day" (Berger 2000, 214).

Just prior to my mother-in-law's funeral, I read about the need for a child to "own" and express their feelings fully, without judgment or curtailment. I came to understand that when we tell our child that their feelings are wrong or inappropriate, our child doesn't feel safe. When my mother-in-law's funeral service ended, our family and friends began filing out of the church, while Paige, at the age of six, sat on my lap crying. She cried and cried and cried, long after everyone had left the church. I held her, gently telling her to let it all out. When she finished crying, we left the church and climbed into the limousine to attend her grandmother's burial. Years later, Paige had the same full release of sadness and pain when her dog was attacked by another dog and killed instantly. In both cases, I noticed that she never cried about either death again; she didn't have the need because she had fully released her tears instead of burying her feelings. Did she still experience sadness months and years later? Yes, of course, but the intensity of that sadness was entirely gone, which meant that no emotional blocks had been created. This means that she will not be triggered by similar events again later in life. This also means that she will not develop negative behaviours or patterns in order to be heard, because she is at peace with those painful events in her life.

"We want our children to be alert, aware and open to learning. When unacceptable feelings must be repressed then the ability to experience excitement, interest and curiosity is also shut down. ... If they are full of conflict and pain and no one is helping them, they may become hyperactive, unable to concentrate and to learn" (Berger 2000, 214).

We Love and Support Our Child Best by Validating How They Feel and Who They Are

Far too large of a percentage of parents report not enjoying the job of parenting. *It is very difficult to find pleasure in parenting when our focus is on controlling our child and forcing them to obey the rules all the time.* When we are rigid and tense, our children feel unloved and become loaded with self-blame. Their need to be accepted as they are goes unmet. When our children live under the threat of criticism or punishment, their need to feel safe is not met. When we open ourselves up to the possibilities of our relationship, trust our child and talk *with* our child not *at* them, our parenting experience blooms. Cooperation from our child is full proof, and everyone's needs are met.

We are told not to be friends with our child; however, when we can describe our relationship as one of communication and cooperation, we can't help but become friends. Friendship grows out of mutual respect. Yet just because there is a friendship does not mean that we cannot still parent our child. When our child is younger, we need to teach them morals, values and what is and is not acceptable in our society. However, as our child grows, they look for more of our understanding, gentle guidance and friendship. A big part of a friendship is feeling safe with one another to express ourselves fully. This involves talking to our child about what they find to be important, whether they feel something is "good" or "bad" and what they feel like doing. We can also ask our child how they feel in their bodies in various circumstances. We can ask them if their stomach feels relaxed or as though it is in knots. We can ask them if their heart is racing or if their neck feels tight. We can ask them what they think their body is trying to tell them. If a child feels safe and truly heard, they feel understood. The more open we are and the better listener we are, the more our children will be willing to be vulnerable and authentic with us and the more control they will feel they have in their lives.

Some girlfriends and I met one night and started talking about the fact that Grades Three and Four seem to be the years that children's emotions really come into play. It is in these grades when more fights using words break out and children's hurt feelings can take a little longer to mend. My friend told me that when she was a child, she had a teacher who distributed circles made of white cardboard to her Grade Four students each morning. One side of the circle was a happy face and the other was a sad face. Each morning, the children were instructed to turn their card up to show the face that most accurately depicted how they were feeling. If the child turned the sad face up and placed it on their desk, the others knew to tread lightly with that child and be extra kind that day. We all have good and bad days. What this teacher taught her students is that it is okay to have good and bad days and that we should respect and honour what we are each going through at any particular time. What a valuable lesson to learn!

We learn something else by this example. We don't need to "fix" or "rescue" our child. The teacher in this classroom wasn't trying to fix her students. When our child is having a bad day, they need us to support them in feeling what they need to feel, listen to them and maybe discuss possible courses of action for them to take. Each time we offer our child this type of support, we allow our child to feel safe and loved. ***If we constantly fix our children, they will not gain the confidence to fix things themselves.*** Instead they will think of themselves as needing to be fixed or in need of a fix. Knowing this is what our child needs from us, we can help them no matter what trauma they may suffer.

Here are some ways to help our child express who they are and feel in control of their own lives:

- We regularly let our child make choices for themselves. When our child is given the freedom to make choices, their experience and ability in making good decisions increases and their belief in themselves augments. Making choices is also necessary for the life of the mind.

- We say yes to our child as often as possible. Saying yes is a way for parents to honour their child and also encourage them. To this day, Taylor thanks me for the number of times I responded to her requests with "Maybe" or "Let's see what happens" as opposed to saying no to her.

- We look our child in the eye and tell our child, "You are in control," providing them with options to choose from for their best course of action in any particular circumstance.

- When we share our opinion with our child, we state that it is only our opinion, not "the way", thereby encouraging our child to develop and share their own opinions.

- We allow our child to question authority and standards. We want our child to be an independent thinker, while showing appropriate respect in a world where there are rules and values.

- We discuss with our child the challenges that come from making inappropriate decisions, as opposed to becoming upset or punishing them, when they reveal things to us that they are not proud of. We want to encourage them to open up to us, not discourage them. They, like adults, also need to understand the relationship between their feelings, beliefs and behaviours and potential consequences. This awareness helps children come to know and love themselves at a young age.

- We assure them that it is okay to be different and encourage them to do so. I remember buying Taylor a nightie that said "Stand out from the crowd", explaining to her that we are all unique and it is wrong to try to make ourselves fit any kind of mould. She wore the nightie for years, telling me much later that it was that nightie that gave her the confidence to regularly show her uniqueness. She has never worn the latest brand names or dressed the way the majority of children dress. She has felt very comfortable with her own personal style. She values her uniqueness and has no interest in "fitting in", yet she has many friends and still feels connected to the world.

- We avoid shaming or devaluing our child. This means that we do not call attention to what we believe to be our child's faults. We don't tease them or make jokes at their expense. We don't compare them to others.

- We learn to communicate well with our children. Conversations between us and our child can build our child up and bring us closer *or* make our child feel unimportant. Conversations that encourage our child to express themselves include asking more open-ended questions, on our part, as opposed to closed-ended questions. One of the famous questions asked of children is "Did you have a good day at school?" Well, it is too easy for a child to respond with a simple yes or no to that question. Instead, we can ask, "What did you like about your day today?" or "Did anything funny happen today that you can tell me about? I love it when you make me laugh!"
- We help our child experience joy, doing the things they love to do and laughing deeply when we are with them, showing our enjoyment of who they are.

Honesty, Trust and Respect Form the Foundation of Our Relationship with Our Child

Trust comes from honesty. It is only when we are honest that we can take responsibility for our mistakes, learn from them, and grow as people. Trust is also the foundation of any successful relationship. Children always seem to know when we are telling the truth and when we are not. If we always speak the truth to our child and others, our child will do the same. When we don't know the answer to our child's questions, we just need to tell them that we don't know the answer. Our child's trust in us grows when they know they can count on us to support and understand them. Our child doesn't need to trust everyone; they just need one individual who will never let them down. If we always convey trust in our child and respect them through our words, gestures and facial expressions, our child will feel good about themselves. In turn, they will feel more in control of their lives and won't need to bully or put others down because they respect themselves too much to engage in that type of behaviour. When love, honesty, trust and respect form the basis of our parent–child relationship, the peace in our homes is indescribable.

 "Respect means to hold in high regard; to honour yourself or another. Respecting children means elevating them to the same status you reserve for yourself and for other adults. It can be hard for a kid feeling powerless and diminutive. When you offer children respect, you demonstrate to them that they are worthy and you teach them to respect themselves." (Carter-Scott 2002, 153).

Taylor wrote an essay about respect in Grade Eight, and these were her words: "Respect is a very difficult subject—almost like a riddle. It cannot be given, forced or stolen. It can only be earned. … The teachers who really know how to handle their students are the ones who have earned their respect." I like how she describes respect and I like her understanding of the role it plays in relationships. It is the same for parents as it is for teachers—if we want to have a healthy relationship with our child, it is paramount that they trust and respect us.

One day when Paige was ten, I asked her how I had taught her to respect others. At first, she didn't know, but when I was putting her to bed that night she said, "I know what you did. You taught us to treat others the way we wanted to be treated and you explained this to us many times. When we did this, we felt even better about ourselves. By respecting others, our respect for ourselves grew."

As always, it starts when our child is a baby. When we speak baby talk to a baby or a child, it is not respectful. Do you remember being a child and being spoken to that way and how it made you feel? Or do you remember wanting to be treated as though you were older than you were because you felt older than you were? The majority of children feel this way. We can be playful and use playful language, but baby talk is usually not welcomed by babies or children. **When we teach our child the names for things, they want to know the proper names, so that when they use them they are understood.** I remember going grocery shopping with my girls when they were babies and telling them the correct name for each item that I added to our cart. Not only was this educational for them; these discussions also helped them understand that they were part of things and that they mattered. I could literally feel their pride in being spoken to as though they were little adults.

Each time we make a promise, we need to be prepared to deliver; this reinforces to our child that they are a priority. If we tell our child that we are going to leave the store if they misbehave, we must ensure we do just that and leave as soon as they misbehave, not after numerous warnings. This not only shows our child that we tell the truth and stick to our word but it also teaches our child to respect us. **Many parents think their child will be happy if they do not take them out of the store immediately after misbehaving. In fact, our child wants to have boundaries and they want to be able to depend on our word.**

A child needs to know that truth is valued above all else. When they tell us the truth and admit to a wrongdoing and we punish them, we are literally teaching them that they need to lie in order to escape punishment. They learn that they need to lie when they are too afraid to tell the truth. When they tell us the truth and our first response is, "Thank you for telling me the truth and admitting what you did wrong," we show our child tremendous respect and that we love them regardless of what they did. This allows us to have an open and honest discussion about the consequences of their wrongdoing and what can be done to rectify matters.

It is also important that we tell our child the truth about what is going on with the people in their lives, as it pertains to them. If we don't tell our child the truth about a relative's serious illness, a parent's job loss or other matters that affect them, we are not protecting them—we are isolating them. They end up not trusting the adults in their world. We want to protect our child from sadness, pain or the things we ourselves don't understand. But by protecting them, we are not teaching our children that pain, sickness, separation and death are part of living nor are we helping them make sense of or deal with the ups and downs that are part of life. When my father-in-law had cancer, I discussed each step of the process with our children, either before it happened or after it took place. When their grandpa began chemo, I explained to the girls what chemo was and that Grandpa was going to lose his hair, so that when they saw it happening they were not alarmed. I also prepared them for his eventual death. Sometimes, parents are unable to prepare their child for what is to come because they are in their own pain or in denial of what is to come. In such cases, it is helpful if someone else in the family who is very close to and trusted by the children can take over that preparatory role enabling the children's understanding and acceptance of the loss of their loved one. It is only uncertainty that breeds fear; truth and understanding eliminate fear. You already know that if a child develops a lot of fear in their childhood, they will carry that fear into adulthood.

Each time we tell our child what is going to happen in any given day and the day unfolds as we said it would, our child's trust in us and their stability in the world grows. When we know how something is going to unfold ahead of time, how much more confident are we as we prepare for that event or meeting with another? What if the day does not unfold as we predicted it would? We simply need to explain to our child why things happened the way they did.

When we learn to speak our truth from the deepest core of our being, our communication becomes all the more powerful. Three years into my separation I was noticing that, every once in a while, my youngest, Paige, treated me disrespectfully. One day I had to sit for two hours in the car and wait for her on a stiflingly hot, summer day. At first, I sat in anger. Then I sat in thought. At last, I had an awakening. The time alone that was forced upon me by Paige ended up being vital to our relationship. When she got to the car, she was actually very sorry for keeping me waiting so long. I told her what I did with the time and asked her if she knew why she was disrespecting me. She told me that she didn't mean to disrespect me. I suggested that she was still angry at me, subconsciously, for not being with her all the time, the way I used to be before her dad and I separated. Hearing this, she cried, and I knew that the truth had touched her soul. She said that she was not aware that she had felt that way but that she had. I then apologized to her and spoke my truth from the deepest core of my being. I told Paige, with tears falling down my face, that because of his work I had not expected her dad to ask to be with her half the time. I explained that I left her dad, not her. I told her how important she was to me. I described how I thought she must have felt all this time. I assured her that I wanted to be with her every chance I was given. I had always shown her that, but there were many opportunities to prove it to her again after our discussion. Paige and I forged a new bond, deeper than ever before.

We all need to take the time to be alone, dig deep and look for the truth that melts our children's defences and opens their hearts. We owe it to ourselves and we owe it to our children.

How to Further Build Our Child's Self-Esteem

Children are extremely sensitive, far more sensitive than adults. Why is this? It is only through seeing or experiencing something over and over again that we become desensitized to it. As a young child, if we hear our parents yelling and fighting, we are usually horrified because it is new to us. Jump ahead fifteen years, and if our parents are still fighting we find ourselves simply leaving the house, knowing some things will never change. It's not that their fighting doesn't still affect us; it just doesn't leave us feeling terrified or outraged anymore.

Because children are so sensitive and haven't had experiences before, it is easy for them to take things personally and feel unimportant. Do we, their parents, feel they are unimportant? Of course not! But many of us behave in certain ways that make our children feel unimportant and therefore we don't meet their needs. Look at the child who is being left with someone other than us on a regular basis. Look at the child who is chastised because they are not moving fast enough. Look at the child who is criticized more than complimented. Look at the child who only wants someone to play with them but is plopped on the couch and given a bowl of crackers to eat instead.

Here are some other ways in which we make our children feel unimportant and disrespected:

- When we are driving and we end up on our phone while our child sits in the back seat alone, our child feels unimportant, unless we explain who we are talking to and why the conversation needs to take place at that very moment. Time in the car is not just time spent picking up or dropping off our child. It is an opportunity to have our child to ourselves without distractions, to communicate with one another about things that are important to us. Or it might be a time to listen or sing songs together or discuss them. Or it might be a time to play simple games, such as seeing who can find the first construction vehicle along our route or asking and answering trivia questions.

- When our child is talking to us (when we are not driving) and we do not look them in the eye or we walk away or continue doing something else instead of stopping to listen to them, we are making our child feel unimportant. When our child is speaking and we interrupt them, we are saying that they are unimportant. If we need to point something out while they are speaking, we can say "Excuse me" and tell them why we felt it necessary to interrupt them at that moment.

- When we forget the names of our child's friends or teachers or when we ask them to repeat something that they told us before, we are making our child feel unimportant, because we are showing them that what is important to them is not important to us.

- When we are regularly late picking our child up from school or from their activities, we are telling our child that they are unimportant; it is simply how our child feels when we are not there when they need us.

- When we regularly make appointments or visit with people we could have seen when our children were in school or at their activities, we are telling our children they are not important.

- Did you know that young children actually want their parents to snuggle beside them on the couch and watch television together? When we sit our young child in front of the television by themselves for hours on end, we are telling them that they are not important.
- Any criticism makes our child feel unimportant.
- When we don't give our child choices and act as though we are the authority, we are teaching our child that they are unimportant.
- Telling our child that they have to follow through on a commitment, even though they have decided it's not right for them, is telling our child they are unimportant. If we teach our child that the commitment they made to their coach or to their teammates is more important than their own feelings or following what is right for them, our child cannot come to understand their own importance or come to love themselves.
- Taking our child to an event where they are not going to enjoy themselves makes our child feel unimportant. I attended Paige's dance recital; all the parents knew ahead of time that it was going to be three hours long. In the row behind me, parents had brought a baby and a toddler to watch the show. You can imagine the noise, the crying and the complete frustration that my row had to endure before those parents finally realized they had to leave. Their children were made to feel as though they were wrong because their parents were constantly telling them to be quiet or getting angry at them for not behaving. It doesn't make sense to put children into circumstances where they will surely "fail" in the eyes of those around them.
- Always rushing our child is not going to make them feel important. Usually our child is not the one responsible for making us late. It is up to us to plan accordingly, knowing that our child never goes at the same pace we do. Over-scheduling also doesn't make our child feel important. Some parents unfortunately use extracurricular activities to take the place of parenting. Our child can be accomplished in so many areas of life, but are they getting the time they need with their parents to feel loved and appreciated? Are they getting time on their own to just be? And I don't mean that they need a couple of hours here and there on their own; I mean that they need significant time to just *be*. When a child has time on their own, they have to determine how to

fill that time. In order to do that, they need to learn the ways in which they like to spend their time. This becomes another way in which a child comes to feel good inside. When a child learns to be completely comfortable with themselves they will be more comfortable with others.

- Abruptly interrupting our child at play is like interrupting an adult at work and makes our child feel unimportant. The time investment to discuss transitions (e.g., putting away toys, getting ready for bed, etc.) before they occur is well worth it.
- Not respecting their privacy as much as we would respect the privacy of a complete stranger makes our child feel unimportant. This means we should knock on our child's door and wait for their permission to enter. This means giving them the privacy to be on their own within our home.

Every moment spent with our child is a privilege. As long as we keep this in mind, we increase the chances of always treating our child with importance and meeting their needs.

"In fact, self-esteem is the mainspring that slates every child for success or failure as a human being" (Briggs 1970, 3).

If our child has high self-esteem, they know their value. Our child's feelings of self-worth form the core of their personality and determine how they live all parts of their life. There are many ideas throughout this book for helping our children believe in themselves and become confident in who they are. Here are a few more ideas:

- Be present with your child, meaning focus only on your child and the present moment, your heart connecting to their heart. You can never spend too much time with your child, but it is vital that you spend a minimum of ten minutes a day having a discussion with them, playing with them or doing an activity with them; this is also how they learn the most. When they speak to you, you look them right in the eye, and when you respond, you respond with love.
- When your child wants to you to be with them and you cannot, make an exact plan to spend time with them, letting them know they are important to you. If your child asks you to swim with them and you are not ready to take the plunge, simply tell them why you can't join

them yet. Even if you are simply tired, tell them so. Then let them know what time you *will* swim with them and stick to it.

- Offer your child plenty of love and support. Tell your child every single day that you love them. And explain to your child that you love them regardless of how they behave or the mistakes they make; you can even tell your child that there is a name for what you share and it is "unconditional love".

- Consistently show your child that you value what they have to say and respect their opinion. By asking your child for their opinion, you are saying that their opinion matters. But if you then follow through and go with their opinion, you are strengthening their belief in themselves. If you ask them which outfit looks better, be prepared to wear the outfit they choose!

- Use manners with your child. If you run into one of your friends while out with your child and you end up talking to the friend for a few minutes, thank your child for waiting patiently for you. Thank your child for anything they do to make your life easier, for being thoughtful or for any behaviour you want to continue. Apologize to them for taking longer on the phone than you had planned during their lunch time.

- Ask your child for permission for certain things. When you are spending time together and someone calls, you answer the phone and then ask your child for their permission to take the call, telling them how long you expect to be. You might say, "I know we were playing together, but my friend is calling and she needs some help right now. Would it be okay with you if I spoke to her for about twenty minutes?" At the end of the call, remember to thank your child.

- Organize fun places to go and unique things to do. You can even have a picnic in your family room.

- Clearly define reasonable expectations and limits on your child's behaviour. A child wants limits; rules help your child know that they matter and feel safe and supported. When we bend a rule for our child, we are not believing in them; we are saying that we don't think they can handle it.

- Keep a routine. Structure helps children predict and understand what is to come, makes transitions easier, helps a child feel safe and normalizes things for a child. Without structure, our child ends up confused about what they are supposed to do.

- Nothing beats loving touch, and children are particularly sensitive to it. Holding your child's hand or hugging your child, even after a disagreement, goes a long way to helping your child feel loved.

- Allow your child to do something they can and want to do on their own whenever possible. Before they can even walk, it is better to let them explore freely and safely by blocking off stairs and childproofing the house rather than restricting them to a playpen. Sometimes we are worried for our child's safety or that they will do something wrong, but we don't want to squash their natural desire to take initiative. They need to learn, error by error, and we need to have faith in them. The more they can learn on their own, the more they come to know their capabilities. Real happiness grows from self-sufficiency.

- Reading with your child has a huge impact on their confidence and love of learning. It is extremely important that we read with our children and have them read to us while cuddling them. Encourage them to read on their own, too, and model your own love of reading. Reading nourishes us, increases our self-respect and teaches us about morals.

- Choose responses that show your child how valuable they are to you. Following up on the challenge that your child had the day before really shows your child how much you care, and the follow-through might be needed in solving their challenge once and for all. We can ask them questions such as "Can you describe the way you felt when the teacher said that to you?" or "Was basketball practice better for you today since we came up with those strategies for you to try?"

- Give your child responsibilities. Doing jobs around the house brings order and security to our lives. When we explain to our child that we each need to contribute to the happiness of our family by performing jobs, we reframe housework. The earlier we do this, the better; our child can help out starting as young as two years old. When a child uses the cordless vacuum to clean up from their lunch, they feel good about themselves. When we point out what we are able to do because they are cleaning up after themselves, our child feels needed and appreciated. When we make our individual requests few and far between, give our child choices within timeframes in which to complete jobs and enlist their help rather than command their obedience, we maintain a good relationship with them. When they listen to music while doing the dishes or dance while cleaning up, they are far more apt to enjoy and complete their housework.

- Refrain from fault-finding or correcting your child and certainly avoid reprimanding them in public. It is not what is or isn't allowed but what needs to be understood that is critical. Instead of saying "No! Bad boy! I told you not to touch the knife!" try "Knives are not a toy. They are for cutting. Here is something better to play with." You can always ask your child questions to help them to discover better alternatives for themselves.
- Keep track of your child's history. Remind them of how much more capable or perceptive they are compared to last year. In this way, your child learns to recognize and trust their developing abilities.
- Have your child write "I am important because ..." and encourage them to take as long as they want to finish the sentence over and over again.

Self-Esteem (McKay and Fanning 2000) has been used as a bible for decades in helping parents build self-esteem in their children. The authors suggest consistently following three steps in order to build our child's self-esteem:

1. Notice examples of your child's ability (talents, skills, interests) in many circumstances. Point their skills out to them; your child is likely unaware of their abilities without us pointing them out. We might point out that they are very talented at taking pictures from the most interesting angle to end up with the best picture.
2. Find many occasions to praise your child to themselves and to others. Display your child's work, trophies, ribbons or writings. Tell the story of how your child patiently and cleverly solved a problem.
3. Give your child many opportunities to show their ability. To develop any ability, a child needs a lot of practice, whether it be reading, swimming or analytical thinking.

These three steps will reinforce positive behaviour. Your child will learn to value their talents and see themselves as capable and unique. *Even when your child is struggling in other areas of their lives, they will still feel alright because they know their strengths.* In time, you will become accustomed to finding the special, positive qualities in your child. Since you can see your child in a positive way, your child will start to see themselves in that way too. Parental voices can nurture or destroy self-esteem; let your voice provide your child with the emotional nurturance they crave and deserve. In turn, your child will develop the ability to nurture their own self-esteem.

Our approval is what shapes our child's behaviour. Pleasing us is what motivates our child to learn absolutely everything. There are effective ways to praise our child and ineffective ways. When we praise our child too much, we actually make them uncomfortable. If we tell our child that he is "the best little boy in the world", he knows this isn't true. When we provide backhanded praise by saying, "That outfit looks much better than the one you had on earlier today," we are simultaneously providing criticism. Effectively praising our child involves sharing our feelings. We say, "I appreciate that you cleaned your room today. I like that feeling of orderliness when I pass by." This form of praise teaches our child something about us and themselves.

It won't surprise you to read that the very best way to teach our children self-esteem is to model self-esteem. When we have the self-esteem to forgive ourselves, they forgive themselves. When we accept or like our behaviour and appearance, they learn to do the same. When we have the self-esteem to set boundaries and protect ourselves, our children follow suit.

Believing in Our Child

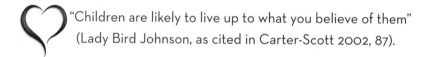 "Children are likely to live up to what you believe of them" (Lady Bird Johnson, as cited in Carter-Scott 2002, 87).

It is when we open our hearts and see the innocence and goodness in our child and others, no matter what happens, that we help them reach their full potential. When we accomplish this, our job of parenting becomes the most rewarding. I remember doing a nutrition seminar for a group of Grade Five students. There was a boy in the class who was not allowed to sit with the rest of the children because he had misbehaved too many times. I wanted to share samples of healthy chocolate bars with the class. The boy asked me if he could distribute the chocolates to his classmates. Out of the corner of my eye, I could see his teacher start walking toward him as if to prevent this from happening. The boy knew she was coming and looked at me with fear in his eyes. Before she could arrive at the boy's desk, I held out the tray of chocolates to him, looked him right in the eye and said, "I trust that you will take this around to each of your fellow students carefully and quietly, ensuring that every child takes only one sample and that you will return the tray to me. Thank you." He did exactly that. I could feel his gratitude for my trust in him and his pleasure at being given this responsibility. And because I believed in him, he believed in himself. Imagine if this boy had been parented in this way each and every day. How different would his life be? How much would he come to love himself? You might say "But I trust *my* child, and he keeps getting into trouble at school!" There is only one reason that this could be the case; your child's needs are not being met. It is up to us, the parents, to determine which needs are not being met. ***It is when we blame our children for the mistakes they are making, rather than taking responsibility for not meeting their needs, that our jobs as parents become infinitely harder.***

Some parents not only don't believe in their children, they pity them. If we pity our child, they think they have the right to pity themselves. Instead of taking responsibility for themselves by facing and overcoming their challenges, they rely more and more on the pity of others, wanting them to console them. Pity belittles us and weakens our self-reliance. Some parents are continually watching over their children for signs of bad habits, questioning them to see if they have bad thoughts, or incessantly worrying about their morals or their health. What we focus on persists. Some parents frequently interfere or pressure their children when it comes to their school work or music practice; they can turn the anticipated enjoyment of a school subject or music into a detested chore. Some parents expect too much of their child, which is a form of imposing our demands on them rather than simply having confidence in their abilities and respecting them.

I know of a father who saw only the problems in his son, not the promise. This infuriated his son, who ended up quitting school, leaving home and causing a lot of trouble. Eventually, his grandmother asked him to live with her. She loved and respected him and saw only the best in him. She encouraged and inspired him, believing he would turn his life around. He returned to school and, with her love and guidance, graduated and began putting his life together. I have seen a parent focus on the potential of their mentally challenged child and cross over one barrier after another. I have seen devoted parents of children with attention deficit disorder tirelessly and successfully eliminate all signs of the condition.

The Greatest Gift We Can Give Our Child

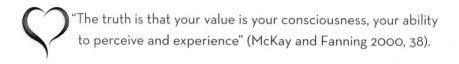 "The truth is that your value is your consciousness, your ability to perceive and experience" (McKay and Fanning 2000, 38).

Every parent has a brief span of time in which to shape a life. The greatest gift we can give our child in helping them to shape their life is to help them see the beauty in themselves and their circumstances. Our lives can be entirely transformed by our perspective. I touched on this in Chapter Three when I described the need to reframe things for our children. The only obstacle to obtaining peace is our limited way of looking at things. Every difficult circumstance or seemingly problematic personality can be seen with new eyes. We can teach our children to honour their experiences. By this, I mean acknowledging their purpose and seeing all experiences as opportunities to learn and grow.

We know we cannot change the world for our children. We know we cannot keep them from the world. But if we teach them to see beyond, they learn to make our unpredictable and confusing universe more orderly and understandable, they learn to keep custody over their thoughts and their world remains filled with treasure. The child who finds fulfillment in their relationships or in music, reading, cooking, performing a sport, writing, drawing or some other craft does not need recognition or power or some "high" to feel worthwhile and good.

The best thing in life is life. The child who sees the beauty in life, well, that child has been given the greatest gift of all. How do we help our children see the beauty? We help our child see how they contribute to their poor relationships and that they are not a victim. What did the Grade Three student learn by being bullied so often? Maybe that it was time that she minded her own business and not care so much when others were breaking the rules. Bullies want to get a rise out of us, but they have respect for those of us who can't be bullied. Maybe it was time she ignored or stood up to the bully, possibly even using humour, showing the bully that she was no longer intimidated. What did the Grade Seven student learn when he was the only student in the class to be excluded from the Halloween house party? He didn't really want to be friends with those kids anyway, which is why he had chosen to go to the library to read each lunch hour instead of hanging out with the others. What did the boy learn when his parents split up this past year? That sometimes two people don't grow at the same pace, so they reach a point where they each find greater happiness apart. Nothing needs to be fixed; we just need to understand.

In each of these cases, it is finding out what is really going on and facing the truth that is key. Too often the truth is not vocalized. And it is the truth that is so beautiful. ***They say that beauty is in the eye of the beholder. But often the eye must be trained to see the beauty or to see beyond.*** Each of us is inherently good at our core and every apparent problem can teach the involved parties a lesson. Our task is to feel the sadness, anger or disappointment in particular circumstances and then to climb out of the darkness into the light. If you think about it, many of us do this time and time again. The key is to be okay with being in the darkness *and* in the light while being grateful for both. For without one, we cannot appreciate the other.

 "Seeing everything in terms of what is and isn't rather than what should or shouldn't be or what we want or don't want makes us evener, surer, firmer, more reassuring and understanding. Our whole being demonstrates to [our] child that life can be counted on" (Berends 1983, 198-99).

How else can we bestow this important gift to our children? We talk to them; we find the good in the bad and explain it to them. We go on a walk with our child and suggest they look for beauty. We discuss a scenario and ask them to find the lesson. We give them examples. It might go like this: "Why do you think Gregory was mean to you on the last day of school before the Christmas holidays?" Your child might answer, "I don't know." You might say, "Did anything happen to get him worked up?" And your child might say, "No, he just snapped." Your response might be any of the following: "Well, you know how you told me that you were exhausted from school and that you were really looking forward to the break? Gregory might have been feeling the same way. Or maybe Gregory's body doesn't do well with all the treats you were eating at your school party that day." The key is to put a few scenarios into your child's head so that he or she looks at Gregory with compassion, as opposed to disdain.

The more often we do this in our own life, the better equipped we will be to offer this assistance in the life of our child. The more often we train our eye to view people and situations this way, the more often we will see beyond. It takes effort to do this. "Why must I always be the bigger person?" some of you might ask. Because when we see each person and circumstance as beautiful, we experience a beautiful moment. And one beautiful moment leads to another. Before we know it, we find ourselves living a beautiful life. I don't know if you have noticed but our eyes take on a look that conforms to our outlook. Others will see the same look in your eyes that is in their eyes and recognize that you, too, are seeing the beauty. It is in this way that we become surrounded by others who see the world with different eyes. When we are surrounded by others with trained eyes and we are all seeing beyond and helping one another to do the same, eventually we will find that we are expending very little effort at all to live an infinitely rewarding and joyous life.

Nine

Parenting Our Children by Helping Them Love Themselves

❝I can think of no more sacred, pressing, essential and relevant expression of our humanity than what we have come to call 'parenting'. As living beings that rely on their offspring to ensure a future, this is our single, most powerful act. This day-to-day, often mindless and habituated process is the overriding force in all cultures, in all religions and all economic levels that determines our future from one generation to the next" (Allen and Lebrun 2009, 2).

Helping Children Love Themselves

Babies come into this world loving themselves. They understand their importance. They have the freedom to express themselves fully when they are happy, are unhappy or need something. They cry, smile and laugh easily and speak their truth when they get older. Unburdened by judgment or shame, they have access to every part of themselves. They know only *love*. They are not prejudiced or judgmental of race, sexual preference, appearance, financial status or any other differences amongst humans. They don't criticize themselves or others or take things personally. They know what they love to do and they do it. They love to play and explore the world. They don't engage in doing things that they don't enjoy. Babies have full trust in themselves and others. They think positively. They are loaded with creativity. They readily accept help and have faith that they will receive it whenever they need it and that life will go smoothly for them. They don't worry about the past or the future; they live in the present moment. Babies accept every part of themselves. If each of us were to remain this way, we would experience emotionally healthy and happy lives. Our innate tendency is to enjoy life—to play, to learn and explore, to be happy and to love.

Unfortunately, the majority of children remain this free until the age of three to five years old. What happens then? Most lose their inner peace and therefore their freedom. They learn from the people around them. They are taught when to eat and when to sleep. They are taught which behaviours will bring them acceptance and which will bring them rejection. They are taught which needs are acceptable and which ones are not. They are taught which feelings they can express and which ones they cannot. In some cases, they are exposed to severe negativity, abused, neglected or given adult-type responsibility at too young of an age. To summarize, they are taught how to please others in order to be accepted by them. They are not taught how to live their lives to meet their own needs and please themselves. Therefore, they are not able to come to know and love themselves. If they were taught this, they would remain free—imaginative, creative, inspired—for their whole lives, and the world would be an entirely different place.

I once heard a parent ask his four-year-old son, "What do you want to be when you grow up?" The child proudly responded, "David!" which was his own name—a fantastic answer! His father replied by saying, "That's not good enough." When we love our child unconditionally, our child knows that just being the person they are is all that is required of them. So many of us wanted acceptance, forgiveness, recognition or appreciation from our parents and we never received it. We learned in Chapter Five how to give these presents to ourselves. We can give these presents to our children. ***When we give them acceptance—when we really see and appreciate them—we provide our children with the psychological armour that will protect them for their whole lives.***

 "The value of a human life is that it exists. You are a complex miracle of creation. You are a person who is trying to live, and that makes you worthwhile as is every other person who is doing the very same thing. Achievement has nothing to do with it. Whatever you do, whatever you contribute should come not from the need to prove your value, but from the natural flow of your aliveness"
(McKay and Fanning 2000, 38).

You already learned about the importance of taking responsibility when it comes to our child, as well as how to come to understand our child, meet their needs and help them to identify and express their emotions and express their very essence. All of these help our child come to know and love themselves. In a nutshell, we want our child to truly *live*—to be free and at peace. We want to encourage them to speak their truth, act with integrity and be who they are. And we want our child to see life through the lens of their heart. This chapter contains many more ideas for helping us truly nourish our child emotionally and build harmony within our families. The importance of most of the headings in this chapter was discussed in detail in Chapter Five, so it might be helpful for you to look at them again there.

Understand and Implement the Concept of "What Would Love Do?"

 "Parenthood is just the world's most intensive course in love" (Berends 1983, 20).

Young children know exactly what love would do because they are pure love. You might be saying to yourself, "My child is not pure love. He is a devil. And he is out to get me." And I would tell you that you don't understand your child. Yes, I am brazen enough to tell you that.

It bears repeating, every child is pure love.

Some of you might be saying, "But my son told his teacher that he hates her." Or you might say, "But my child is always up to no good. He purposely does the wrong thing all the time." My response would be "His needs are not being met." Yes, I am telling you that this is my response each and every time a parent is not pleased with his or her child's behaviour.

When interacting with our child, all that is required is love, and out of love comes truth. Let's imagine our child misbehaved at school today and hit another child. We learn of this and may be appalled because our child is a reflection of us. We may be embarrassed that a child of ours committed such an act. We know we need to teach our child that what they did was very wrong and completely unacceptable. Most of us would speak sternly, yell at them or punish them in some way; we would make them ashamed of themselves and scared of the repercussions for their action, so that they never do it again.

But say, instead, we ask ourselves, "What would love do?" What would that entail? We know that our child has been reprimanded by school authorities already and probably faced a whole other slew of problems with the child he hit. The last thing we would want to do is hug our misbehaving child. But isn't that what love would do? Or maybe our child is now a teen, who finds hugging to be completely uncool, and the last thing we would want to do is look at them with compassion in our eyes? ***If we are not our child's ally, no matter what happens in their life, who is?*** Potentially, no one. Love would give that child of ours a hug. Love would have us look at that teen of ours with all the compassion we could muster. Then, when our child is enveloped in our love and feels they have our trust, we ask them what made them hit the other child. For if we don't know their trigger, how can we prevent it from happening again? Nine times out of ten, our child will know why they hit the other child. Once we hear their reasoning, we need to determine our thoughts on our child hitting the other child and decide what we would have done differently. Maybe nothing at all. Maybe we would have wanted to do the same thing. Imagine that! Now imagine saying to our child, "I would have wanted to hit them too." How is that for honesty? You are shocked I would propose this possibility? Why not? Our thoughts do not need to dictate our actions and our child needs to know this. The solution is to suggest another way to have handled the situation or ask our child how else they could have handled the situation. One of us will arrive at a better alternative or maybe even a few. Then the two of us can strategize how to make amends now that the damage has been done.

Now imagine if we took things one step further? Maybe we think about our child's misdemeanour, review the last few days, weeks or months and determine that we haven't made them feel important enough recently or allowed them to get enough sleep. What would be wrong with us sharing in some of the responsibility for our child's unhappiness leading to this misdemeanour? Once they know they have done wrong and we have helped them determine how they could have handled things differently and decide on how to make amends, we can then accept some of the responsibility for how they were feeling at the time and verbalize our responsibility to our child, if warranted. You might ask, "But my son made the mistake. If I accept responsibility for any part of that mistake, aren't I taking the responsibility away from him for the mistake he made?" When we take some of the responsibility for what went wrong, when warranted, we help our child gain compassion for themselves, which hastens their forgiveness of their actions. And we are teaching our child by example how to take responsibility for their part in things. These results are of utmost importance. Maybe our parenting had nothing to do with our child's error, but we point out that our child didn't listen to us over the past two weeks when we repeatedly told them to go to bed at a better time.

Teaching our child how to take responsibility for their actions, using either approach, helps our child understand themselves better. The process of working out answers together increases their knowledge and confidence in thinking things through for themselves. By having this discussion, our child feels our love and a team is born. When our child feels they are loved and on a team, the world is their oyster. But remember, how we respond to one incident does not build a team. *It's when we respond with love to one incident after another, over the course of many years, that the strongest team is built.*

To summarize: There is the approach that employs fear and makes our child fearful of making mistakes, fearful of others or, worse, fearful of us. But then there is this whole other approach—the approach that employs love. Which approach raises a stronger, happier child? Which approach provides a child with tools to draw from? Which approach brings us and our child closer? The approach that employs love. Reading this example, do we need to instil fear in our child? No, that is a choice we make. A fearful child does not believe in themselves. A child who does not believe in themselves has a hard time getting through any aspect of life.

Set Limits with Your Child

 "Every action your children make is an attempt to meet their needs. ... A son who is defiant might need you to set consistent limits on his behaviour or he might need to make more choices in his life. A daughter who nags or whines might need your exclusive attention for a moment so that she can express what she really wants and feel that you are hearing her. In many cases, if you can determine what need is being expressed, you can help your child meet the need in a more appropriate way" (McKay and Fanning 2000, 284).

If our child perpetually asks for dessert before dinner, wants something every time they enter a store or acts out, there is a need to set limits. Some parents believe that the best way to build our child's self-esteem is to never set limits on our child. This is not true. *A child raised without boundaries tends to be more anxious because they never know what their limits are and are always wondering when they will be chastised.* This child often feels unloved because they are missing the physical and emotional protection of limits and rules. They often think that their parents must not care for them because it doesn't matter to Mom or Dad what their child does or doesn't do. Children of overly permissive parents have a hard time developing self-control and setting their own boundaries based on what is safe or appropriate for them. This then makes it more difficult for them to adjust to society, starting with school.

It is vital that we set limits in order to reinforce our child's feeling of safety and support, as well as their respect for us. Amazingly, when a child finally perceives that their teacher is in charge, their challenges with them come to an end. Children need adults who demonstrate an ability to handle them.

Discipline Rather Than Punish

When we do set and enforce limits, we have two choices if our child disobeys those limits: we can punish them or discipline them. When we punish our child, we make them *suffer*. **Punishing teaches them humiliation, rebellion and to live in fear; it rarely corrects their behaviour.** It teaches them that those who love them will purposely hurt them. Punishing does *not* help our child come to love themselves or strengthen our relationship with them.

In contrast, when we discipline our child, we can truly *teach* them. (Discipline is derived from the Latin word *disciplina*, which means teaching.) We can help them change their behaviour by being firm about what we expect and allow them to discover the natural consequences of their misdemeanours. The idea is to use our child's behaviour as an opportunity to teach them rather than make them suffer. When our child experiences the consequences of their actions, they learn to distinguish right from wrong and take responsibility for their actions. Taking responsibility builds self-esteem because it puts our child in control. When our child gets older, they can actually choose their own consequences; this further increases their aptitude for solving problems. We don't want our child to behave only when we are around. When others are trying to pressure them into making wrong choices, our child will have the strength to resist because they will have learned to set limits for themselves; this is called internal discipline. For all of these reasons, experts say that the disciplinary approach that parents use during the first three years of their child's life is critical.

I would like to give you an example to explain the difference between punishing and disciplining a child. Punishing involves putting a child into a time-out and telling them that they need to remain there for half an hour. Disciplining involves putting a child in a time-out and telling them they need to remain there until they are ready to live by what we agreed to or until peace fills their body and mind. The amount of time a child spends in a time-out is irrelevant, as long as they are ready to make the right choice by the end of it.

 "So discipline is certainly an act of love. And the more a child feels love, the easier it is to discipline the child. The reason is that a child must identify with her parents in order to accept their guidance without resentment, hostility, and obstructiveness (passive-aggressive behaviour)" (Campbell and Chapman 1997, 114).

When disciplining, which we should start when our child is at the ripe age of one year, we need to determine the natural and logical consequences for each misdemeanour. To do this, we just need to think about what would happen if we didn't interfere. Ruined toys are gone, not replaced. Clothes that are not put into the laundry basket are not washed. Poor behaviour in the car means we immediately pull over to the side of the road and go nowhere until our child decides they are ready to behave. Incomplete homework results in an angry teacher. Sometimes we need to arrange consequences. If our child is not behaving at the table, we can refuse to eat with them until they remember their manners. Sometimes we need to let the natural consequences happen. Natural consequences may temporarily hurt our child, but this is how they learn. If our child eats too much junk food at a party, they probably won't feel well afterward. If they refuse to wear the proper footwear, their feet will be cold, but they will know to listen to our footwear suggestion the next time. It is the experience of the natural consequence that does the teaching.

When we introduce consequences, very few words are necessary. Certainly, lecturing can be completely avoided. If consequences are delivered in anger or used as a threat, they cease being consequences and become punishment, and children can easily tell the difference. *The more we fuss, scorn, criticize or punish our child for bad habits or behaviours, the worse their habits or behaviours become. In contrast, when we downgrade the seriousness of their misdemeanours, speak quietly but firmly and enforce the consequences, our child learns which behaviours are acceptable and which are not.* Most importantly, they know that their relationship with us is not on the line and that we still love them, despite their mistake.

Consequences need to be decided and agreed upon in advance, which allows our child to make choices with full knowledge of what is to come. When we can anticipate problems before they occur, we translate more experiences into successes. Consequences need to be enforced consistently, so that our child learns that the world is predictable and safe. Our brains respond to repetitive patterning. If we agree on a consequence for misbehaving in a restaurant, we cannot fail to follow through the next time our child misbehaves in a restaurant just because we are involved in a good conversation with our spouse at that moment. When children receive mixed messages, they need to spend more time thinking, and this can result in difficulty learning.

There is something else we can do each time we discipline our child in order to build empathy, help them learn healthier behaviour and enhance their self-esteem. It is a five-step process:

1. Point out the behaviour we find unacceptable, without judging our child.
2. Communicate our reasons for wanting a different behaviour from them.
3. Ask our child how they would feel if someone talked to them or treated them that way.
4. Acknowledge our child's feelings, discussing their predicament and potential motives.
5. Replace their actions with a better choice.

Each time our child misbehaves, we can ask ourselves what need is being expressed by their behaviour and then determine how to help our child meet their needs in a more positive way. Our teen has a party when we are out of town without our permission. Their need might have been to have more fun, gain the love and admiration of their friends or rebel against us. We can explain to them that next time they want to have a party, we would like to be home but elsewhere in the house. This way our teen meets their needs and the attendees know that we are not far away if they plan to cause trouble. Or we might agree to our teen hosting a party elsewhere. If they are rebelling against us, then more is involved.

When there is misbehaviour, we want to focus on the misbehaviour rather than questioning our child's character and motivation. A child needs to know that we are unhappy with what they have done but that we are not questioning their value as a person. It is our responsibility to offer love and support to our child without conditions. We cannot love our child more or less because they perform in a certain way. When they misbehave or we fight, it is paramount that we still tell them afterward that we love them and don't hold a grudge. Holding a grudge is an adult form of having a tantrum. Repairing our relationship in a timely and caring manner ensures that our child becomes resilient and emotionally strong. Our child also learns that although things can be tough at times, reconnection can be achieved, along with a new sense of closeness with their parent. Children usually cannot recover unless we take the initiative and reconnect with them.

 "Trust comes when a child feels able to rely on his caregivers. The child comes to trust when he senses that his structure can be counted on and that it will exist, come rain or shine. The structure is trustworthy when it is an anchor, when the child can count on being noticed, enjoyed and recognized for the good things he is doing, and when he can count on being held accountable in a predictable and neutral manner for any rules he breaks. If the basic structure is not consistent, the child remains guarded" (Glasser and Easley 1998, 225).

Refrain from Rewarding Your Child

"The system of rewarding children for good behaviour is as detrimental to their outlook as the system of punishment. The same lack of respect is shown. We 'reward' our inferiors for favours or for good deeds. In a system of mutual respect among equals, a job is done because it needs doing, and the satisfaction comes from the harmony of two people doing a job together" (Dreikurs 1964, 72).

A child who is always rewarded for good behaviour feels they only belong when they get something in return for their actions. Why do we pay our child to do chores? Our child shares all the benefits of living in our home: they eat the food, have clean clothes and enjoy all of the entertainment our home has to offer. Therefore, doesn't it make sense that they share in the upkeep of our home and contribute to the well-being of our family? We want our child to feel part of the team that is our family and motivated to want to help our team. When we are always rewarded or paid, we learn that we don't have to do anything unless there is something in it for us. It is impossible to develop a sense of responsibility or genuine satisfaction under these circumstances, because the whole emphasis has been placed on "What's in it for me?"

Parents who offer rewards are attempting to gain cooperation from their child because they are unaware of their own capabilities for gaining cooperation. Children don't need to be bribed to be good. They actually want to be good. They want to belong, contribute and co-operate. When we bribe our child in order to elicit good behaviour from them, we are demonstrating our lack of trust in them, which is a form of discouragement.

Help Your Child to Do More of What They Love

Earlier on, I described how children are controlled in unbelievable amounts owing to their age and lack of knowledge of the world. You also learned the importance of allowing children to express themselves and be who they are. There are always places that our child goes and things that they do where they do *not* need to be controlled.

My girls went into countless sports and activities before finding what it is they loved doing. This involved many years of watching, listening and honouring on my part. Some people criticized me and told me that I was teaching my girls to be quitters, but I remembered what it had felt like when I was a child spending time doing things I disliked, and there was no way I was going to put my girls through that. My girls always completed the sessions they had signed up for and then they would start a new sport or activity. I remember the pleasure I felt when I witnessed my girls finding the sports and activities that "filled them up". I remember when Taylor discovered that she loved sewing. The more she came to love it, the more her skills multiplied until she excelled at it. I remember the many dresses and skirts Taylor made me and the look of pride in her eyes when she saw that her creations fit and suited me so perfectly. I remember Paige telling me that dancing was her happy place. I remember her pleasure learning how to play baseball with her father, one of the greatest experts on playing and teaching the sport. I revel in watching her dance and play ball year after year.

If every step our child takes and every decision our child is allowed to make, is made on the basis of whether it will make them feel good inside, it will always be right for them; the same goes for us. Each time we let our feelings guide us, we make the best choices for ourselves, gain trust in ourselves and experience greater love for ourselves. Paige was on the school track and field team in Grade Five. She was an incredible runner who often came in first. The trouble was that she felt such intense pressure to perform that she sometimes hyperventilated or suffered from anxiety before the races. When she reached

Grade Six, Paige asked me if I thought she should be on the track and field team again. In response, I asked, "Would it make you feel good inside to be on the team again?" "No," she said, "it would not."

It does not matter how good an athlete or performer your child is, any amount of pressure to perform is a risk for a child who is developing their self-esteem. Interestingly enough, Paige chose to remain on her competitive dance team—many of you can attest to the pressure involved in that sport! But for her, that was a pressure she enjoyed and delighted in. The key is helping our child find the activities they look forward to doing.

There are some children who feel good inside when they do certain activities for a while, but if they are pushed to do those activities for longer periods, at a higher level or with greater agility, they may no longer feel as good about them. If we offer our child a reward to obtain a certain number of goals at their soccer game and they don't complete the mission, they feel bad about themselves. *Each time a parent becomes heavily involved in how well their child is doing at a particular sport, that parent is actually fighting their own demons.* A competitive parent is an insecure parent, and an insecure parent hasn't had their needs met over an extended period of time. A parent can invest all the time, money and frustration they desire into *their* want and run the risk of ruining their relationship with their child, or they can choose another way. The child's goal, pardon the pun, is to enjoy the game and always do their best. It is a parent's job to know when their child is no longer feeling good in their activities and to make the necessary changes. I applaud the parents who move their child from recreational to competitive sports and then back to recreational sports.

Now you might say, "Well, there are certain things a child *needs* to do that don't make them feel good inside. What happens then?" Examples of this might be attending school, participating in a family function or going to the dentist. The answer in each of these cases is to find ways to ensure that our child experiences some kind of enjoyment while there, even if it is not coursing through their veins the whole time. Sometimes it is a matter of helping our child to see the silver lining or finding things to be grateful for, so that they appreciate their current circumstances more. Our child may not like school too much, but their best friend is there; we might need to remind them of the importance of this. Our child may dread attending family functions and being told, once again, how much they have grown, but maybe the food is always delicious. There may be no way to make the dental appointment okay in our child's mind, but we could tell them that we will go for a bike ride with them after it is over or suggest doing something else that they love to do with us. They do need to understand that not everything is joyous, but as long as they surround the unpleasant tasks with moments of joy, balance reigns.

Encourage Your Child to Say No to the Things They Don't Love

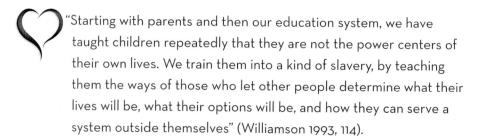 "Starting with parents and then our education system, we have taught children repeatedly that they are not the power centers of their own lives. We train them into a kind of slavery, by teaching them the ways of those who let other people determine what their lives will be, what their options will be, and how they can serve a system outside themselves" (Williamson 1993, 114).

The example I am about to share with you is a tricky one. I am about to discuss when a child is not happy with their school experience. If this is the case, first and foremost, everything about our child needs to be examined. Are they happy when they are outside school? Do they obtain good marks despite being unhappy at school? Do they generally get along with other children? If our answer is no to any of these questions, we need to focus on meeting our child's needs and helping our child become happier within; they would likely have the same challenges in another school as they are having at this school. There are many ideas within these pages to help accomplish that task.

If our answer is yes to these questions then we need to evaluate things differently. The school experience, from a child's perspective, includes four important aspects: having friends, enjoying what is being taught, liking and being respected by the teachers and feeling good overall in the school environment. It may be okay if one, two or even three aspects of the school experience are not what our generally happy child would want, but if none of these aspects is meeting our child's needs, it may be time to say no to this school and look into other alternatives. Certainly, if a generally happy child is unhappy at school for any longer than two years, I recommend looking into other school options, if possible. I know of a mother who put her depressed son into an institution before exploring other school options. She told me that her son had been so unhappy in school the prior year and that he had particular challenges with his main teacher. She must not have been aware that he might have been a different child in another school; it does happen. She must not have known that a "problem" child is only a child whose needs are not being met.

There will usually be a year in which our child is not happy at school. One year, Taylor had a main teacher whom she simply could not understand nor learn from. This teacher did not understand Taylor either nor did he respect her. And a child knows when a teacher does not respect them—trust me! Taylor became very depressed in this teacher's classroom. I told her that how she does in school determines how she feels inside and that she cannot let anyone else take away the opportunity for her to feel good inside. I also explained that it was her responsibility to do the best she could in Math, despite her teacher. That was the only year I was heavily involved with teaching Taylor any subject. She did not excel in Math that year but she ended up with an average in the seventies, an average with which we were both thrilled. But when we learned that Taylor was going to have the same teacher the following year, we began looking at other options for her.

Teach Your Children Not to Criticize or Judge Themselves or Others

If we criticize or judge ourselves or others, our children will do the same. When my children learned that someone they knew had a breast augmentation, they were terribly bothered; criticism and judgment were flying off their tongues. I let them express all of their thoughts and feelings, never saying they were wrong. When they were done, I asked them if they knew one of the main reasons why someone might have plastic surgery. They didn't have the answer. I explained that people often have plastic surgery when they don't love themselves. The expression in my girls' eyes changed from indignation to compassion and under-standing. *If children are taught that one of the reasons why others act in ways we don't understand or treat others badly is that they don't love themselves, our children can go all the way through their lives truly understanding why things happen the way they do.*

We do need to teach our children what is appropriate and what is not, but there is no need to include criticism and judgment in our words. A good way to teach what is appropriate and what is not is to watch television shows or movies together. Walking out of movies with my girls when they were younger sure taught them what I felt was inappropriate in a hurry (we only did this with two movies, just so you know!). I remember explaining to them that I wanted to protect their innocence (describing what that was) for as long as possible and that they did not need to sit through anything that made them feel uncomfortable or bad inside.

I talked earlier about how we each have strengths and weaknesses and that it is helpful to find the benefits of some of our so-called negative traits. I also talked about the damage that is caused if we criticize our child for such traits. I would like to help you reframe your child's traits in a more positive way. Here are some examples:

Negative traits	Positive traits
Picky	Selective
Anxious	Cautious
Stubborn	Assertive (they keep going despite challenges), decisive (they know what they want)
Loud	Enthusiastic, passionate
Demanding	Has high standards
Bossy	Has leadership potential
Nosy	Curious

 "If fighting with your child, make a list of what you value and appreciate in your child. You may dislike your child's aggressiveness but also admire her fearlessness. You may feel overburdened by their oversensitivity but admire the way that this sensitivity reveals insights about the world that you might not have seen. You might like his seeming lack of ambition but admire her ability to remain relaxed and calm" (Coleman 2008, 120).

Teach Your Child Not to Take Things Personally

If we tell our child they are smart, kind and important and that we love them, then smart, kind, important and loved they are. In the movie and book "*The Help*," it was the hired help, Aibilene who told the little girl she was caring for, "You is kind. You is smart. You is important." Aibilene repeated this mantra to her little charge every morning, as well as when things went wrong in the girl's life. She even made the girl say the words back to her. The little girl's mother had no idea how to raise her daughter, and the little girl surely would have taken every bad thing that happened to her personally had it not been for the hired help loving her and teaching her the truth about herself.

Once we understand how to prevent ourselves from taking things personally, we can teach our child how to do it. When a child can view life events as brief, temporary or specific to a situation rather than personal, they remain open to seeing things in a variety of ways. When others mistreat our child, it is time for us to have a discussion with our child about what might be going on in the life of the perpetrator, as well as help our child take responsibility for their potential role in what happened. Once we determine these factors, we increase our child's understanding of the world and themselves and they learn not to take things personally.

I am not a big fan of telling a child that others are envious of them. Sometimes this is the case, but often it is not. I encourage parents to dig deeper and find other reasons for their child to consider. I prefer to say that the perpetrator is in their own pain or that their needs are not being met; we all know that a happy child won't say or do hurtful things very often.

Teach Your Child to Speak Their Truth and Communicate from Their Heart

A child's way of being tells us how they feel deep inside, but our job is to teach our child to examine what they are feeling and express those feelings truthfully, which we already discussed in great detail. There are rarely problems with truth and communication; the problems come about when there is falseness and communication.

A home that values the truth above all else is not judgmental but open and welcoming. It offers a loving and nurturing environment—an environment where it is safe to be vulnerable. Space and time are allocated for listening to one another. Privacy and quiet time are allotted and encouraged. Books, CDs and healing cards are available for all to use. Conversation is seen as shared participation in the discovery of the truth. There is no preaching because that is a sure way to close the mind of a child. Events and interactions are looked at for meaning and infinite value.

A child who speaks their truth says, "I didn't have fun skiing today." A child who speaks their truth and communicates from their heart says, "I didn't have fun skiing today because you were skiing too far ahead of me and I felt lonely." If a child learns how to speak this way, they will be adept at communicating their needs in all of their relationships.

Show Your Child How to Operate with Integrity

When we operate with integrity, our child learns to operate with integrity. I credit a special book for helping many children learn moral strength, honour, loyalty, sincerity and honesty: *The Book of Virtues* (Bennett 1996). Fortunately, most children's movies teach these important concepts as well.

I recall instances when each of my daughters, and I myself, stole something— yes, we each tried this when we were young children. ***How parents handle our child's first transgression is one of the most impactful and lasting ways in which we teach our child integrity.*** The way to handle a transgression is to correct our child as soon as we find out about it. Both of my girls had to immediately return the items they stole and apologize to the store employee or owner, just as I had to do. Confessing and apologizing to the owner feels extremely shameful to a child but it is a very effective consequence.

Recently, I happened to be a witness when a father realized after the fact that his son had stolen something from a store. I heard the father tell his son, "Well, it's done now. There is no point in returning this, but don't do that again." The boy got to keep the item he stole. In other words, the boy learned that if he steals and no one notices until the item is out of the store, he gets to keep what he stole. This is not how we teach integrity.

Help Your Child to Set Boundaries

We teach our child about setting personal boundaries by modeling them. Personal space, our time and the right to privacy are three examples.

We also need to teach our child about setting boundaries with others. My children used to come home from school and tell me about their challenges with others. Invariably they would bring up that their school policy didn't allow them to exclude other children. This meant that if another child was teasing our child, our child needed to continue to be nice to that child by sitting with them at lunch and never telling the child to leave them alone. Why was that the school's policy? Because it made things easier for them. If kids had to be good to one another, no matter what went on behind the scenes, it was not the school's problem. I understand why this policy came to be, and in an ideal world the policy would be wonderful. However, my children were asking for my help to handle situations with other children, even though I wasn't seeing what was going on at the school the way the teachers were.

What this school policy does not recognize is that it teaches children that no matter how badly they are treated by another child, they cannot tell that child to leave them alone. What does that teach a child about setting boundaries? Absolutely nothing. Here is where our job comes in. We need to teach our child that there are always going to be people with whom they will not get along. It's just a fact of life. Then we need to discuss the options for what they can do, despite school or other policies. Our child can tell the other child to treat them better. They can ignore the other child. They can ask the other child if there is anything they can do to help the two of them get along better. We can take our child to play therapy. There are many options. The bottom line is that our child needs to be able to stand up and take responsibility for their unhappiness and do something about it. Too often, our children are taught simply to live with being treated poorly. That is not acceptable.

Paige had a problem with a girl in her class. She discussed it with me and we came up with a few options. Paige decided to tell the girl the ways in which she felt the girl had been mistreating her and her other friends. She then gave the girl the choice of correcting her ways or simply not hanging out with the group anymore. The girl chose to leave the group and hang out with other girls. Thus, Paige hadn't excluded the other girl. I congratulated Paige for choosing the option that felt right to her and for having the courage to speak to the other girl. *The real reward for setting boundaries and taking action is always when the problem that pervades our lives finally comes to an end.* This example also shows you how to teach your child to let go of those who don't appreciate them.

I have talked about children setting boundaries with their peers, but sometimes children have to set boundaries with their own parents. And some of you are reading this thinking, "I am the parent. I set the boundaries." Yes, you do set some of the boundaries, but if you truly respect your child, you know that your child has needs that may not mirror yours. Our seven-year-old might tell us that he does not want us to pick out his clothes for him all the time. How we respond determines the future of our child setting boundaries for themselves. If we respond by telling him we are happy he shared his feelings and is setting boundaries with us, he will share more of his feelings as time goes on. If we respond by telling him that we set the rules, then he will be far more reticent to share his feelings with us the next time.

Some parents let their kids choose whatever they want to wear, and sometimes the clothing their child chooses doesn't match or isn't appropriate for the venue for which they are dressing. The key is to be able to listen to your child but still ensure they dress appropriately for each venue. You can say, "How about each Saturday, you get to choose what you wear?" or "How about I put out two or three options for what you could wear each day and you decide which one you want to put on?" It is perfectly fine for our child to set boundaries with us and for us to comply, while simultaneously setting a boundary of our own as well. Whatever options you present, make sure you have the time to bring those options to fruition.

Let's face it. If children are allowed to be who they are, everyone is happier. And a child who sets boundaries becomes an adult who sets boundaries. We all know adults who are dying inside because they are not setting boundaries and, subsequently, are not spending enough time on nurturing and loving themselves.

Encourage Your Child to Surround Themselves with People of Integrity, Who Love and Appreciate Them

What if we were all taught as children that we are fully deserving of loads of love? How different would our lives have been? How many relationships would we have walked away from, knowing we deserved more? How many more days, months or years might we have spent feeling appreciated instead of unappreciated?

The best way to teach our child this concept is to carefully choose the people that we want to participate in their lives, whether it be their babysitter, playmates or family members. The more we love ourselves, the better job we will do of this for our children.

With all the birthday parties that children are invited to these days, sooner or later a child will likely tell us that they do not want to attend a certain party. Many parents would feel it is right to encourage their child to attend, regardless. Unfortunately, that is teaching a child to put the needs of others before their own—the exact teaching most of us had, which we now know to be wrong. Instead, when our child tells us they don't want to go, we need to ask why and discuss it with them. If they don't want to go because of a fear they have, we might still encourage them to go and help them cope with their fear. But if they don't want to go because the birthday child doesn't operate with integrity or our child provides us with other valid reasons, then we can tell our child how much we respect them for being true to themselves and show our support for their decision. When we call to RSVP for the party, we simply need to state that our child is unable to attend. We do not need to give an explanation. Certainly, there is no need to lie.

Teach Your Child to Let Go of the Aspects of Their Life That Are Not Working for Them

Many of us, as parents, think we need to push our children to do certain things or ensure they stick to the commitments they have made to others. For example, our son had a very emotionally taxing day and then slept little that night. The next morning, he doesn't really feel up to going to school. How would many of us deal with this situation? We would push him to get to school, because we were taught that we have to be on our death bed to miss it. At the end of the year, we pride ourselves on the "no absences" section of our son's report card. How much happier and stronger would our son have been if he had spent a day at home with us, being loved and enjoyed? By sending our son to school, isn't that teaching our child the very thing we, ourselves, are so often grappling with? *When we don't put our needs first, we are teaching our child to do the same.*

How about when we start the day rushing around, trying to get our daughter to school on time? She is trying to wolf down her breakfast while we are yelling at her to hurry up. We end up angry with one another. Then, just before she climbs out of the car in front of her school, the dog bites her. But she makes it on time. "It was all worth it," we might say as our daughter heads through the school doors. But was it? We are so conditioned to do certain things that we don't even see the harm those things are doing to our families and to future generations.

When we really think about it, how bad is it to show up late to school but drop off a happy child? Isn't that more important than making it somewhere on time? If we are perpetually late, then that is another issue and not acceptable either. The goal is to maintain moderation and the sanity of our family, above all else.

Help Your Child to Face Their Fears

When she was in Grade One, Taylor was sent to the principal's office one day. The principal told her that if she didn't behave, there would be big repercussions and her parents would be called. We all know that this technique is designed to scare our child into behaving, but if a child is perpetually scared, how can they come to love themselves? When Taylor shared this with me, I immediately assured her that even though her school's opinion mattered to me, helping her and being on a team with her was my top priority. I will never forget the look of relief on her face. I explained that I will always be her advocate and have her back and all I asked is that she be honest with me and willing to take responsibility for her mistakes. Without an advocate, it is next to impossible for a child to grow up strong in this world, as previously discussed.

When our child is afraid of the dark or monsters or spirits and we tell our child there is no such thing, we do not eliminate their fears. In fact, we do the opposite; we increase their fears. Neither do we help them cope with their fears. It is paramount that we put ourselves in their shoes, come to understand what they are afraid of and recognize how their fears must feel to them. Once our child knows we understand how they feel, we can offer some suggestions about how to deal with their fears. This also gives our child an opportunity to weigh their options.

When Taylor was in Grade Two, she had a nightmare about a man kidnapping her that truly terrified her. She couldn't stop worrying about being kidnapped by this man. I suggested that she draw a picture of the man and that we burn it. This is exactly what she chose to do, and I never heard about the dream again. To this day, she remembers her sense of relief when she faced her fear in this way.

Often, children have fears of completing a project or doing public speaking. The less they think about their fear and the more they focus on researching and completing the project or practising the speech, the more their fears dissipate. Taking deep breaths, envisioning things going well, saying positive affirmations and having faith are methods that are just as effective for our child as they are for us. Each time we support our child in facing a fear, they conquer another challenge; the more challenges they conquer, the better they feel about themselves.

Help Your Child to Trust Themselves and Their Intuition

It is vital that we trust our child has their own inner guidance and that they will find their way. When we do this, our trust that our child will be safe in this world increases and so does our child's belief in themselves. Most children are more in touch with themselves and their intuition than adults. When this is not the case, we guide them best by showing them how we make decisions for ourselves by trusting our emotional monitor.

We can teach our child how to meditate by playing a child's meditation on an iPod, by suggesting they sit quietly for ten minutes listening to their own breath or by teaching them to imagine they are flying on a magic carpet through the night's sky. They can usually get to that quiet place in their mind very quickly. The more they do this, the more in touch with their intuition they will be. Then when they share their intuition with us, the more favourably we respond, the more they will believe in their intuition and share their intuitive thoughts with us in the future.

Help Your Child to Be Grateful

The amount of gratitude a parent feels and shares determines the amount of gratitude their child will feel and share. *When we regularly tell our children what we appreciate about them—verbally or in writing—or when we share our feelings of gratitude for all the good things our family gets to experience or talk about what we are personally grateful for, we set the example for our child to do the same. When our child focuses on appreciating themselves, others and various aspects of their lives, they feel good inside. When they feel good, they will be a magnet for attracting pleasant situations and people and feel fulfilled.*

When our child feels and shows gratitude, they are demonstrating empathy—the ability to share in another person's thoughts and feelings. Not only is empathy critical to a child's healthy and happy development and their sense of connection to others but it also helps them feel more connected to their parents. Even a four-year-old, if they have learned over time to appreciate what their parents do for them, can call on their emotional memory to get through the friction with their parents that we know is bound to happen from time to time.

There are many ideas in Chapter Five that would be helpful in raising our child to be grateful. Here are some more ideas for fostering gratitude:

- If we don't expect gratitude from our child, we are unlikely to receive it. When our child is as young as eighteen months old, we can teach them to say please and thank-you. It's not just about teaching manners; it's also about teaching empathy. We can help them to make the connection between acts of kindness and appropriate words. Teaching a child good manners also teaches a child respect for themselves.
- After we ask our child how their day went, we can say, "Aren't you going to ask me about my day?" If one day, out of the blue, our child asks us how our day was, we can respond with incredible surprise and pleasure by saying, "Thank you for asking me!" or when our child spontaneously thanks us for going to all their practices and games, we can respond by saying, "You're welcome. And thanks for saying that. It means a lot to me."

- We demonstrate gratitude in front of our child by thanking the waitress and cashier. Should the opportunity arise, we tell our child how grateful we are for what the employee did to make our lives better.
- We say to our child, "Thank you for being so cooperative" or "I appreciate that you and your brother are getting along so well in the car." Taking notice of good behaviour is a time-honoured way to increase it. It's also important to express gratitude to our child for something they are not even aware of by saying, "You were really fun to be with at the zoo today. Thank you for helping to make this a great day for me."
- Many parents go all out for their children on special occasions, but it is also important that children be taught to reciprocate sometimes. It helps teach them that life is a two-way street. For example, Dad can help our three-year-old make up a tray so that Mom can have breakfast in bed on her birthday.
- We teach our older children to have appreciation for the smallest details in life, understanding that every single thing is meaningful and worthwhile. Younger children know that this is the secret to happiness.
- We suggest to our child that they write about or draw at least five things they are grateful for in a special book each night before going to bed.

Help Your Child to Think Positively

What if were taught as children that what we thought and said determined the course of our lives? How different would our lives have been? How much faster would we have come to love ourselves?

You read throughout this book about the importance of remaining positive. It won't surprise you to read that one of the biggest ways in which we teach our child to be positive is by being positive ourselves. This means being positive about what we have, about our interactions with others and about the incidents that occur in our lives. I remember being amazed by the negativity of a four-year-old boy when his mom brought him during a visit. I knew that the only way that he could be so negative at such a young age was if an adult had set that example for him. When the little boy was out of earshot, I asked his mother if she knew why her son didn't see the possibilities in the world. His mother started to cry and said that her ex-husband had taught their little boy to think negatively. From that day on, the little boy's mother consciously began to show her son the positive way of looking at things each time the opportunity presented itself.

Being positive involves reframing things for our children. If every time our child tells us of something bad that happened to them we empathize and then help them see the lesson or the positive in what happened, then we teach our children how to be positive. Each time we expect something to go well for ourselves and it does, it is important to point it out to our child. This reminds them of what is possible for themselves. Sometimes an older child needs to be convinced of the power of positive thinking. We can suggest that they think positively for the next month and then witness the ways in which their world improves.

Being positive involves recognizing and appreciating our child's good behaviour and ignoring their difficult behaviours. When we see them being thoughtful of another, we need to let our child know that we see what they are doing and explain the importance of what they are doing. We will then find that they become even more thoughtful of others. In contrast, when we expect the worst for our child, the worst is what we will receive. If we dwell on their poor marks, their marks will only get worse. If we react strongly each time they act inappropriately, we are rewarding their poor behaviour, lack of respect and bad attitude by giving more energy and attention to the problem than the solution.

Help Your Child to Treat Their Body with Love and Respect

Again, if we set this example, our children will follow suit. If we live our lives in balance, meaning that we leave time each day for work, exercise, play, rest and sleep, then our children will also live their lives in balance. If we eat natural, alive and good-quality foods the majority of time and exercise regularly, our children will usually do the same. If we do not, we will invariably end up with physical symptoms or a health condition and so will our children.

The easiest way to help our child begin to treat their body with love and respect is to link their symptom or condition to something they need to improve with their nutrition or exercise regime. If their symptom or condition bothers them enough, they will want to start treating their body with love and respect.

My first book explains all of this in great detail, but I would like to give you one example. A child has eczema all over their back and they don't even want to go to gym class because they don't want the other children to see it. The eczema is also causing them constant pain and itchiness. They are bothered enough by all of this that they want to start doing things differently. Dairy is the biggest dietary culprit for eczema. Their mother had been telling them that they had to cut down on the pizza for nutritional reasons, but now she can explain that the pizza is also greatly contributing to her child's eczema. As soon as a child experiences any improvement in their health as a result of a change that they have made to their diet or exercise regime, they are likely to make more and more improvements to their lifestyle. However, if something is bothering a child emotionally, many subconsciously feel they deserve to suffer and are likely to carry on by not treating their body with love and respect.

Assist Your Child in Finding Their Talents, Skills and Passions

 "Parents need to help their children develop their special gifts and talents so that the children will feel the inner satisfaction and sense of accomplishment that comes from using one's innate abilities" (Campbell and Chapman 1997, 23).

If our child is going to be happy and emotionally strong in this world, they need to be seen as their own individual with their own unique set of talents and skills. They need an identity based on their talents and skills rather than their appearance, popularity or sexuality. They need to be aware of what their natural abilities are. As parents, we need to look at our child's talents, skills, habits, creativity, favourite activities and characteristics. What do they love to do? What are they best at? When are they most energetic? What makes their heart sing? What is their happy place? When kids are able to tap into what is important to them, they are more committed to doing and excelling in those areas and they develop personal leadership and responsibility. They also develop the ability to stand in the truth of who they are—their unique magnificence—regardless of their circumstances. There is an excellent and heart-warming children's book by Max Lucado called *The Oak Inside the Acorn* (2011) that explains that we all have a purpose. Children feel very important when they know they have a specific purpose here on earth.

I remember complaining to my dad, when I was around fifteen years old, that I didn't have a talent. I looked around at the other children and saw them excel in music, sports and dance, to give a few examples. I didn't excel in anything, as far as I could see, certainly nothing obvious. My dad told me that I excelled in communicating. I responded with "What am I going to do with that?" and walked away from him, filled with disgust for myself. While I was walking away, my dad described all the areas in which I could use communication skills.

I didn't feel a lot better at the time, but it did help that my dad believed I had a talent and thought it was significant. It took me many years but I have now embraced my talent and use it to help others understand what I am most passionate about—raising healthy and happy children.

I recall teaching a pediatric nutrition class to a roomful of adults a few years ago. A young woman approached me after class and asked for my help in eliminating her facial acne. We discussed her diet, nutrient levels, possible food sensitivities and stress levels and came up empty in terms of the root cause. I asked her if she was doing something that brought her joy. Her response was "No, I just study nutrition. I used to be a dancer. My face was clear when I danced." Our eyes met and our thoughts connected. I never saw that young lady again. I wasn't surprised to learn that she had returned to dance. She had been interested in nutrition but it wasn't making her feel good inside or, in this case, outside either.

Encourage Your Child to Spend Time Being Creative

All children are born creative. If we allow them to remain creative and encourage their abilities, without fear of correction, their creativity will always remain a large part of their lives. Creativity provides us with a sense of pride that is unparalleled. Whenever we remain in the present moment, doing something creative for an extended period of time, we experience joy.

When we participate in anything creative with our child, such as painting, colouring, dancing, singing, moving or anything where we remain in the present moment with them, we will have a relationship with our child unlike anything else. It's the feeling that we experience while we are engaged in the activity with them that is so remarkable, not the activity itself. It's a sense of connection; connecting to our senses and connecting to our child. Interestingly enough, the people who truly enjoy being with their child are the ones who are generally happy in their own lives and have a good outlook on life; they are the ones who are most effective in raising an emotionally healthy child.

Encourage Your Child to Help Others and Receive Help

Children are usually pretty good at accepting help, having needed help since they were babies. But at those times when they want to be independent, our help can be swiftly rejected. And I already talked about the importance of encouraging children to do what they are capable of doing and allowing them to learn from their mistakes.

Teaching our child how to help others begins in our own homes. How we respond to the way in which our child performs a job determines whether our child hates the failure connected with their efforts and becomes uncooperative or loves the success connected with their efforts and becomes helpful regularly. All things need to be learned; sometimes we don't realize how many times our child might need to be shown how to perform certain tasks before mastering them. **Each time we find an aspect of their work to compliment them on, we encourage our child to feel good about themselves, and they, in turn, want to help more.** Saying things such as "Can't you do anything properly?" may be what some of us think, but we don't need to say it.

We also need to teach our children to help others on a larger scale. It is becoming more difficult in North America to find ways to help the poor when our poor are nowhere near as poverty stricken as the people in other countries. Ever since Taylor and Paige were four and two years old, whenever we have travelled outside North America to vacation destinations (e.g., Cuba, Mexico, Dominican Republic) we have packed an extra suitcase for the poor. We always dedicate half a day to visiting a poor village and distributing items to the children there. My girls have seen children living on mud floors in homes that are missing a wall or portion of the roof. They have seen children wearing only underwear, playing on hills made of dirt. They have seen children who sleep on hay each night without a mattress in sight. Taylor and Paige have handed these children clothes, toys, shoes, crayons, paper and dolls and seen the looks on their faces. They have touched one another's souls. As much as Taylor's and Paige's hearts went out to these children, their ability to help them made them feel absolutely incredible inside. It also made them grateful for what they had in comparison.

Help Your Child to Set Goals and Intentions

When we help our children establish and meet goals, even small ones, we help them determine what is important to them and what their dreams are. We also help them perform an honest evaluation of themselves and augment their self-motivation by helping them devise strategies for success. While they work on and accomplish their goals, they feel good about themselves, and eventually this mobilizes them to accomplish bigger things and come to love themselves even more.

We can teach our child to write their goals down, knowing this is a very effective way to help ourselves accomplish our goals. Recording in a calendar the various steps that our child is going to take to reach their goal is also very effective, because time frames are set for taking each step.

Now that our world is so focused on instant gratification, credit cards are used excessively, and children often receive items that technically could not previously have been afforded by their parents. Helping our child save up for items that they want and purchase them with their own money is an excellent way to help our child set and meet a goal.

The whole process of setting and meeting goals teaches a child that they deserve the good things in life and can achieve what they set out to accomplish. Seeing their parents meet goals often gives children all the encouragement they need to do the same.

 "The greatest gift you can give your child is the example of a [parent] who is living [their] dreams" (Carter-Scott 2002, 195).

Teach Your Child to Have Faith

Even if we don't have faith in a higher power, I strongly encourage parents to teach their children there is a higher power. A child who believes that they can accomplish what they want to in life with the help of something or someone beyond them never feels alone (particularly when we are not with them) and knows they always have help. These children are more likely to succeed in meeting their goals.

I remember explaining a higher power to my girls by sharing the age-old concept "When one door closes, another opens." A few weeks after this explanation, their teacher and owner of their Montessori school was told that she could no longer operate her school out of the location she had been in over the past twenty years. She tried and tried to find another location for her school but to no avail. We were all asked to sign a petition for her landlord, asking that she be allowed to keep the school where it was. I didn't sign it. Instead, I believed that it was perfect timing for her to close her school. She didn't have anywhere near full enrolment for the following year for the first time ever; both her children were now through university and independent; the new man in her life wanted to spend more time with her; her first newly born grandchild would certainly want her attention. I couldn't get over how perfect it all was. Interestingly enough, the directress never found another location for her school and has been travelling the world ever since, spending more time with her family than she ever imagined, and I hear that she is blissfully happy. What an example she set for my girls to see that there is always a higher power working behind the scenes. ***Once we surrender and allow the help to enter our lives, we will receive it, often in a way that is beyond our wildest imagination.***

How Do We Know If Our Child Is Emotionally Healthy?

To summarize, we know our children are emotionally healthy by:
- the glow we see on their faces
- the happiness and laughter they exude
- the clarity in their eyes
- the comfort they have in their own skin
- their willingness to be cooperative, participatory and help others
- their ability to give themselves attention and enjoy being independent
- their ability to speak their mind
- their desire and ability to take in new circumstances, information and places
- their healthy ambition and accomplishing of goals
- their favorable relationships with others
- their love for themselves and for life itself

You may also find it helpful to read the description of how we know we have come to love ourselves in Chapter Five and use it to visualize what we want for our child.

What Do We Do If Our Child Is Not Emotionally Healthy?

The first question we need to ask ourselves when our child is not emotionally healthy is "Which of my child's needs are not being met?" We might have already determined the answer to that from reading this book. The second question we need to ask ourselves is "Why have my child's needs not been met?" Of course, there are hundreds of reasons why a child's needs may not have been met. But the bottom line is that we are either modeling the way we were parented or we are suffering ourselves or both. Many of us are suffering from our own childhoods. We may be tired from working so hard or long. We may be physically unwell. We may not be getting any time to ourselves. We may be worried about paying the bills. The reasons are endless. *But there is only ever one root cause for our suffering—we haven't come to love ourselves by parenting ourselves.*

We usually want to protect our child from it all, so we don't tell them what is wrong or why we are suffering. But our child knows we are suffering. On some level, they always know this. Unfortunately, because we don't communicate the cause of our suffering, our child usually comes to believe that things are going wrong because of them or something they did. A child who blames themselves has needs that are not being met and they, in turn, begin to suffer. *There is only ever one root cause for our child's suffering—they haven't come to love themselves through our parenting.*

Some of you may be saying, "But my son knows the challenges I face. I do tell him what's wrong. And he still is suffering." There are two reasons for this. Number one: Your challenges have gone on too long and your child feels that you will always be a victim. If you are setting the example of remaining a victim, your child might wonder how there could ever be hope for them. You already read that a child's worst nightmare is having a parent who is unhappy. Nothing torments a child's soul more than seeing his parent unhappy. Nothing. And how common a problem is this? Unfortunately, in the majority of families, one or both parents are unhappy or suffering in some way. Number two: You didn't apologize to your child for how your suffering has or is impacting them. Just as many of us wanted our parents to apologize to us, our child wants us to apologize to them.

Having a Healthy Confrontation with Our Child

Every parent needs to accept that even though we make countless sacrifices for our child, at some point we cause problems for them. It can be painful when we look back into our past and clearly see our mistakes. We may need to connect with and feel compassion for ourselves, knowing we did the best that we could with what we were going through and our level of awareness at the time. We may need to feel compassion for our child's belief that we caused them suffering.

One of the most powerful acts in the world is an apology from a parent to a child. An apology from a parent is rare, unexpected, beautiful and healing.

By apologizing to our child, we:
- show our child how much they matter
- teach them to trust their feelings; they probably thought we were treating them unfairly and our apology shows them that they were right to feel that way
- teach our child that even though we make mistakes, we are willing to take responsibility for the challenges we cause in our relationship and this, in turn, teaches our child to do the same
- show our child our strength, which then helps them rely on us more, something they should feel comfortable doing (to an extent)
- are operating from our heart and showing our child what loving behaviour is
- strengthen our own healing by taking responsibility, making amends and forgiving ourselves and our child

A lot of parents think that their children will not respect them if they are anything less than perfect. Many parents desperately want their children's lives to be perfect and want to shield them from everything about our world that is imperfect. In fact, we are all perfect in our imperfection. The key is to apologize when our imperfections hurt another. Here is an example of the different ways in which we can choose to behave when we are stressed, the various ways in which our child thinks and how to apologize if we choose the wrong behaviour.

Mom comes home from work after having a bad day and berates her son. What if, instead, Mom comes home and says, "I had a bad day today, so I am not in a very good mood." That lets her son know that it is not his fault if she acts differently than she normally does. It also lets him know that he might have a bad day too; it happens, and it's okay when it does. When the son sees his mother in a good mood the next day, he knows that he, too, will recover from a bad day. So many lessons can be learned from one incident or even one statement made by a parent to their child.

Now let's go back to Mom berating her son. He is presumably feeling badly about himself after having been criticized. Many parents simply let time heal mistakes. What if Mom decided to apologize to her son once she feels better? By apologizing, she is admitting that she is not perfect; that she has bad days; that she makes mistakes—all valuable things for a son to come to understand.

When Mom apologizes to her son, something even greater occurs. Her son knows he is seen and heard and that he matters enough that Mom would actually make herself vulnerable. A greater bond between mother and son is formed as a result of the incident. Isn't that an amazing part of life? Mistakes or challenges can actually make relationships or situations better than they ever were before, if only we allow them to work their magic. When a child learns that their parent is not perfect, the child's expectations lower. This is a good thing. The expectations lower for us and they lower for our child. When expectations lower, everyone has an easier time relaxing. Life throws us curve balls; all we can do is our best at catching and returning those balls.

We apologize to our child when we become aware that we have hurt them in specific instances or in general. Some of us may have acquired that awareness simply by reading this book. *We apologize by remembering or imagining the words we longed to hear from our own parents or someone else that hurt us.* We might tell our child that we are ashamed of how we treated them; that they didn't do anything to deserve our poor treatment; that they are wonderful and it was our challenge to contend with, not theirs. We might explain to them how we were treated as children or what part of us was hurting to make us treat them the way we did, ensuring we mention that the way we were treated is no excuse for how we treated them. We might tell them we have learned a healthy way to deal with our challenge and explain how we plan to behave in future. We might come up with a solution or game plan together for handling future scenarios, taking the control back. We might explain we are obtaining outside help and what that involves. (Please refer to Chapter Ten for an explanation of the various therapies that assist with emotional healing.) We always allow them to share their feelings about the way we treated them and we empathize with them. *It is paramount that we actually say the words "I'm sorry" and tell them we love them. And then when we have done all of that, we thank our child for listening to us.*

No matter how we choose to handle it, it is vital to remember that our relationship with our child is the most important and powerful external relationship of all and it is up to us to show them the way. It is up to us to help our children come to love themselves, while we simultaneously do the same for ourselves.

What Is Peace in Our Relationship with Our Child?

Experiencing peace with our child is not the absence of frustration, anger or conflict. Peace does not mean that we always believe the same things or approach things in the same way. Peace does not mean that we will never disagree or that our feelings won't get hurt. Peace does not mean that we won't get triggered as a parent. Peace is allowing ourselves and our child to see the beauty in the craziness of life, in the back-and-forth process of learning, and in the sometimes painful process of growing.

 "You have within you the power to change your children's destiny. When you free yourself from the legacy of guilt, self-hatred, and anger, you also free your children. When you interrupt family patterns and break the cycle, you give a priceless gift to your children, and to their children, and to the children who will follow. You are molding the future" (Forward 1989, 300).

Ten

Help Is Out There! How Alternative Therapies Can Help Families Heal

Often we seek outside help when we feel ill or out of balance. When we seek outside help, many of us expect the "expert" to "fix us" or solve our challenge. Practitioners can help us only at the stage we are at in our healing journey. In other words, they can assist us only in bringing certain aspects of ourselves into balance at the time that is right for each of us. We need to do our own work, growing internally and mastering the concepts within the pages of this book. *However, the healing modalities discussed in this chapter have great potential for hastening your journey to the greatest emotional health you have experienced up to this point in your life.* They can also provide you with great relief from the pain you carry with you each and every day. My life has been forever improved because of my sessions with alternative healing practitioners.

The greatest success in emotional healing sessions arises when the facilitator possesses certain qualities. When a practitioner has come to love themselves, they can easily and always see the good in their clients and therefore help their clients see the good in themselves. A practitioner who is honest with themselves encourages their clients to be honest with themselves. A practitioner who has compassion for their clients, no matter what their plight, helps their clients view themselves and others with compassion.

Healing Therapies Involving Remedies

Homeopathy

In 1810, a medical doctor by the name of Dr. Samuel Hahnemann introduced homeopathy to the world. By 1900, almost twenty-five percent of medical doctors practised homeopathy. When the American Medical Association (AMA) was formed, medical doctors were dictated to replace homeopathy with drugs. I am happy to report that in recent years homeopathy has experienced a resurgence in popularity. The fact that homeopathic pellets are offered in the health aisle at The Superstore or Loblaws demonstrates this point.

I discuss homeopathy first in this chapter because it is the alternative therapy that helped my family the most on our path to wellness. In homeopathic terms, symptoms are the language of illness. There are over two thousand remedies, each addressing specific physical, mental and emotional symptoms and life patterns. Remedies can treat acute and chronic conditions as well as cleanse, strengthen and balance the body, mind and spirit. ***They move our bodies in the direction they need to go; they stimulate us to heal from the inside out, healing the deepest part of who we are.*** If we are on our conscious journey of coming to love ourselves, the right remedy can be the catalyst for helping us see aspects of our lives more clearly, take responsibility, stand up for ourselves, set boundaries and live the lives we want to live.

The process of finding the right remedy starts with making an appointment with a recommended classical homeopath for ourselves or our child. We spend up to two hours describing our symptoms, when they occur, if there is an emotion behind the symptoms and what helps or worsens the symptoms. We also answer questions about our sleep, dreams, energy levels, eating patterns, temperature, food and environmental sensitivities. The homeopath always looks for the scenario or incident that has led to the current imbalance—that moment described as "never been well since". At the end of the appointment or shortly thereafter, a homeopathic remedy is prescribed. A single dose of the remedy consists of two tiny pellets that taste great. The remedies are made from natural materials (plants, minerals, insects, reptiles, mammals and elements). There are no contra-indicative interactions between homeopathic remedies and prescribed drugs.

Homeopathy stimulates the body to heal itself when there is fear, grief, disappointment, severe anger, stage fright, anxiety, depression, prolonged stress from caring for a loved one or living in a domineering relationship, trauma or sadness, just to give you some examples. Natrium muriaticum has a strong affinity for ailments resulting from the loss of a loved one or a break-up. Homeopaths have witnessed countless positive reactions during the course of treatment. Fears become much less overwhelming because patients can face them and deal with them better or they are eliminated. Panic attacks occur less frequently, with less intensity and duration, until they are finally gone. The voicing of unexpressed feelings and suppressed emotions often occurs. People in situations of prolonged stress find they are stronger and can deal better with life. *Individuals who are emotionally stuck begin to make changes in their lives that allow them to move forward.* A new awareness of unhealthy patterns of thought and behaviour arise so that change is possible. Suicidal thoughts disappear and the weight of depression gradually lifts so that the patient engages in living once more. Obsessive thoughts and compulsions are slowly put aside and no longer consume the individual. People on medication start to get better and begin weaning off their medications (under medical supervision), happy to no longer have to contend with the side effects.

Here is a case study that illustrates the power of homeopathy: A nine-year-old girl, diagnosed with severe anxiety and panic disorder, was brought to a homeopathic doctor for treatment. Physically, she was very tall for her age and thin, almost looking emaciated. She had already begun puberty. She would not touch her brother for fear of contagion, could not go outside for fear something would happen, could not eat normally or go to the bathroom without anxiety and during the initial appointment was constantly getting anxious and needed to be calmed so that her breathing normalized. She was also very impressionable; she could not be told that something was bad for her because it became an obsession. There had been two very traumatic episodes in her life that contributed to this state. The first was living through a very emotional period with her parents who were dealing with infidelity, and the second was witnessing her brother having febrile seizures and being rushed to the hospital. The remedy prescribed for her was Phosphorus 200c. After approximately three to four weeks, her parents reported that she was ninety-five percent improved in every way. She began playing outside again, hugged her brother without fear, had no more anxiety attacks and began eating and eliminating normally. There was still some anxiety but it no longer inhibited her from trying new things and truly living. She had experienced a banner year at school, going from Cs and Ds to As and Bs, and participated in field trips, which was impossible before treatment. Her teachers could not believe that this was the same girl. Her fear of lightning storms had also gone away since treatment. No further treatment was required.

This is just one example of the healing power of homeopathy. There are countless others. Certainly, homeopathic remedies helped Taylor immensely in letting go of her fear that stemmed from her traumatic birth (see Coming to

Understand Our Child in Chapter Eight). Paige became less sensitive to others and stronger in herself as a result of homeopathic remedies. Homeopathic remedies helped me overcome my grief from all the deaths of loved ones that I have experienced. They helped me feel nurtured when I had not been growing up. The remedies helped me overcome my physical challenges. They helped me speak my truth, find my inner strength, and set boundaries with certain people in my life.

Flower Remedies

In the 1930s, Dr. Edward Bach began investigating the healing potential of flowers and trees and discovered that thirty-eight kinds of wildflowers improved underlying psychological and emotional states that influence physical illness. These thirty-eight Bach flower remedies form the basis of all flower remedies today. He said, "Treat people for their emotional unhappiness, allow them to be happy, and they will become well."

Flower remedies or essences are liquid elixirs that contain a blend of flowers that help to address physical, mental and emotional challenges. They capture the flower's energetic imprint and, when taken internally, help to bring harmony, balance and healing. Unlike pharmaceuticals, which suppress symptoms, but like homeopathic remedies, essences are catalysts for emotional change and work by stimulating awareness.

Flower remedies can be used with adults, children and animals and have no fragrance or flavour. A common way to take a flower remedy is to place a few drops under the tongue in the morning and at night. Drops can also be added to water and sipped throughout the day. Aromatherapy oils extracted from plants are similar in terms of their use and results.

Walnut flower essence is the universal remedy for "letting go" or releasing the emotions that do not serve us. Larch helps the individual who feels a lack of confidence. Chicory could be used for the individual who seeks attention through negative behaviour patterns. There is a remedy or a blend of remedies to assist in the conversion of every negative emotion into a positive one.

Body Work

SomatoEmotional Release

Our bodies contain our subconscious. Various types of body work such as craniosacral therapy, massage and therapeutic touch are necessary to release and heal emotions that are stuck inside us and creating blockages.

 "Almost every other culture but ours recognizes the role played by some kind of emotional catharsis or energy release in healing" (Pert 2012, 41).

SomatoEmotional Release (SER) was discovered by Dr. John Upledger, a well-known osteopathic physician who developed craniosacral therapy, and Dr. Zvi Karni, a biophysicist and bioengineer. The technique was developed when they worked together at Michigan State University from 1977 to 1980 and is now utilized in over one hundred countries.

SER is a therapeutic process that uses and expands on the principles of craniosacral therapy. SER releases emotions that have manifested within the body and its tissues from past physical and emotional traumas. The belief is that, during a trauma, the body often retains rather than releases the energy generated from the trauma and its accompanying negative emotions (e.g., fear, anger, resentment, pain, anguish). They called this retained energy an "energy cyst". Energy cysts send out interference waves and obstruct the electricity in the body. When the negative emotions causing the cyst are discovered and released through SER, the accompanying symptoms can leave the body and it can return to normal functioning.

When a trained practitioner identifies a trigger point in the body and uses craniosacral therapy, massage or therapeutic touch, they can release energy cysts. SER can release subconscious or forgotten memories.

Here is an example of this type of work. A massage therapist trained in SER was doing some intra-oral work on a client, meaning that their gloved fingers were inside the client's mouth. The client had a flash of memories of being sexually abused by their father. Their body was twitching as the memories flooded their conscious mind. This particular practitioner was trained in SER dialogue, which allowed for a deeper healing for this individual. The combination of body work and dialogue helped the client to get in touch with their emotions and release them from the tissues in their body.

BodyTalk System

The BodyTalk System was created in 1995 by Dr. John Veltheim, an Australian chiropractor and acupuncturist, and is now used in more than fifty-five countries. **The BodyTalk System views symptoms as the means by which our bodies try to communicate with us and believes in the body's innate ability to heal itself.** Practitioners ask the body a series of closed-ended questions based on a comprehensive protocol and procedure chart that incorporates Western, Eastern and Ayurvedic medicine. The body's neuromuscular biofeedback system indicates its specific health needs by alternating between tensing (body is saying no) and relaxing (body is saying yes) the muscles of the arm. In this way, the body shows what its priorities are for balancing itself.

BodyTalk sessions are easy, safe and comfortable. Adults and children lie on a table while the BodyTalk practitioner, positioned at their side, detects the weakened or broken energy circuits. The practitioner then uses a gentle tapping technique on the head and heart to release the stored charges and resynchronize and balance the body.

BodyTalk helps to mitigate physical and emotional stress, traumas and negative emotions that we are unable to process and release effectively. It is also highly effective in dispelling unhealthy or false belief systems and empowering individuals.

My girls and I were fortunate enough to be worked on by a BodyTalk master a number of times. He detected a minor hearing loss in Paige's right ear and corrected it! He discovered some fascinating emotional blocks and false belief systems in both Taylor and myself and released them. The results have been equally miraculous with clients that I have recommended to him.

Polarity Therapy

Polarity therapy was discovered by Austrian born chiropractor and naturopath Dr. Randolph Stone in the 1950s. Rooted in Indian sciences, it is based on the principle that symptoms arise from blockages in energy flow. It works with the electromagnetic field and the five elements of fire, earth, air, ether and water. Polarity hands-on techniques include manipulation of pressure points and joints, massage, breathing techniques, exercise and reflexology. The approach releases energy blockages and restores the natural flow in the body.

Polarity Therapy was the form of body work that assisted my emotional healing the most (I did this prior to learning about the other body work techniques). I remember the day that we worked on my deep and subconscious fear.

While the practitioner went through an intense process of mental focusing and performed hands-on healing, I was asked to visualize the cause of my pain. I visualized my pain as a huge boulder and imagined it being lifted off of me by a crane. At the end of the appointment, I stood up, feeling taller than I ever had before. I walked out of the office with the most amount of inner strength I ever remember feeling. For the next week, all I could notice was the fear in those with whom I interacted. After that, the work had integrated in my body and the fear in others no longer stood out to me. The way I conducted my life from that point on was in sharp contrast to how I had conducted my life up to that point. Our fear has a purpose and therefore never entirely goes away, but the courage with which I began to face life and my ability to set strong boundaries remains with me to this day, many years later.

Light and Sound Therapy

Light Therapy

Full-spectrum, ultraviolet, coloured and laser light are being used more and more to restore the body's natural rhythms physically, mentally and emotionally. **Light therapy is said to be the medicine of the future.** Light therapy stimulates the cerebral cortex in the brain, which controls our motivation, learning, thinking, creativity and emotional impressions of the world, amongst other areas. Light therapy helps to convert negative emotional states to positive states; resolves emotional blocks; reduces stress, fear, anxiety, depression and obsessive thinking; heightens mental clarity; brings about new insight and intuition; improves mood; and increases inner strength. There are many different machines, small and large, stationary and handheld, that are used to deliver light therapy to our bodies.

I experienced the amazing effects of the technology as I went through the end of my marriage. The energy it provided me with, the clarity of thought and the self-confidence astounded me and those who witnessed it in me.

Biophoton Light Therapy

In the 1970s, German biophysicist Fritz-Albert Popp confirmed the existence of biophotons. It was he who discovered that light emanates from every living cell at a rate of 100,000 impulses of light per second. These impulses are called biophotons. With the use of a Chiren instrument, co-engineered by Johan

Boswinkel and Dr. Schwab in 1982, a trained therapist can determine where biophotons in the body are disturbed based on the electrical response at acupuncture points on the hands and feet. The therapist then uses the instrument to ask the body what it needs to bring balance or coherence back. It is a communication device used to tune into the language of the body. This is so valuable today because many of us are disconnected from our bodies and do not pay attention to the messages that are constantly being given to us until they develop into a symptom that we cannot ignore.

The first step with biophoton light therapy is to reconnect the head and heart, bringing back one's ability to discern what is good and what is not good for the body. Then, using the Chiren instrument, one hundred twenty acupuncture points on the fingers and toes can be investigated to reveal any imbalances (incoherent light). As each organ is also linked with emotions, a trained therapist can assist in discovering where the client is out of balance in processing their emotions. Lastly, the instrument is used to correct the areas of imbalance using homeopathy and flower remedies. This is a brilliant, non-intrusive method of bringing the body back into balance and discovering the source of the symptoms that have presented in the body.

This healing modality brings balance to my body and mind each and every time I go for a session. It has helped children and adults alike overcome the worst forms of anxiety and depression in just one session. I have seen it clear up the worst effects of parasitic, candidiasis and other infections in just one session. Biophoton light therapy is likely the fastest and easiest healing modality that I have seen to date.

Sound Therapy

Sound and music have a very powerful effect on our emotional health. Sound therapy comes in many different forms. Toning is a form of sound therapy that balances us physically, mentally and emotionally. It has even more benefits than singing or speaking because they are faster, making it harder for the body to have enough time to balance itself. Toning involves making elongated vowel sounds and allowing them to resonate throughout the body. Toning causes the brain waves to come into balance incredibly fast, within three to five minutes, which in turn brings about great physical and emotional well-being. It does this by oxygenating the body and increasing energy flow and pulsation. Toning is akin to giving ourselves a massage internally. *It lessens pain, anxiety and depression, increases our positive feelings, taps into the subconscious and brings about strong emotional releases.* Chanting is a form of toning that monks have used for centuries for well-being.

Behavioural Therapies

Neuro-Linguistic Programming

Neuro-linguistic programming (NLP) was founded by Richard Bandler and John Grinder in California in the 1970s. It is a collection of techniques that helps people detect and reprogram subconscious patterns of thought and behaviour. It puts us in control of our minds, helps us heal emotionally and achieve success. It is an effective form of psychological therapy that helps us:

- transform our past: It teaches how to reframe past events in a more positive way.
- transform our inner voice: It helps convert our negative inner voice into a positive inner voice, focusing on what we want as opposed to what we fear.
- transform our dreams into accomplishments: It teaches us how to set realistic goals and visualize positive outcomes so that we increase the chances of those outcomes taking place.
- transform our relationships: It teaches us how to mirror other people's body language and way of speaking to increase our understanding of and rapport with others.

Some of NLP's basic assumptions are that we, as human beings, never know reality; we only know our perceptions of reality. It is those perceptions that shape our behaviour. There is good intent behind every behaviour or action (e.g., violent behaviour happens when we don't love ourselves or when we are fearful). Our thoughts and bodies are intricately linked. We always make the best choices based on our unique life experiences.

NLP practitioners ask their clients questions to determine if there are any identity issues or limiting beliefs and to understand their life goals. By reading the client's body—skin colour changes, moisture changes on the lips or eyes, eye movements, muscle tension, posture, gestures, breathing patterns and speaking patterns—*the practitioner can determine what is going on at a conscious and subconscious level and then use various techniques to help the client adopt healthier belief and behaviour patterns.*

Cognitive Behavioural Therapy

Two of the earliest forms of cognitive behavioural therapy (CBT) were rational emotive behaviour therapy (REBT), developed by Albert Ellis in the 1950s and cognitive therapy developed by Aaron Beck in the 1960s. CBT is a type of psychotherapeutic treatment that recognizes how thoughts affect behaviour and that teaches us how to change our thought and belief processes to achieve positive outcomes. CBT is based on the premise that our feelings determine our thoughts (cognition) and our behaviours. CBT teaches us to have more compassion for our limitations and to become the best people we can be through self-awareness. CBT teaches us coping skills for anxiety and negative thoughts, managing anger and stress, reducing the urge for alcohol or drugs and communicating effectively with others.

A cognitive behavioural therapist starts by helping a client identify problematic beliefs. Next, they identify the actual behaviours stemming from those beliefs that are contributing to the current challenges in the client's life. Then the client begins to learn and practise new skills to eventually use in their actual lives. CBT is the gradual process of converting unhealthy behavioural patterns to healthier ones. A wide range of strategies are used throughout the process, such as journaling, role-playing, relaxation techniques, and mental distraction.

Emotional Freedom Technique

Emotional freedom technique (EFT), also known as tapping, was developed gradually from the 1960s to the 1980s with various practitioners building on one another's discoveries. EFT is an emotional healing technique that is based on the same energy meridians used in traditional acupuncture, which has treated physical and emotional ailments for the past five thousand years, but it doesn't involve needles. Instead, simple tapping with the fingertips is used to input kinetic energy onto specific meridians on the head and chest while thinking about a specific challenge, and positive affirmations are voiced at the same time. The combination of tapping and saying the positive affirmations clears emotional blocks and restores balance to the body and mind. EFT transforms negative emotions, reduces or eliminates pain and helps us implement goals. This technique is becoming widely used due to its high rate of success and its simplicity. It is easy to do on ourselves, and we can do it whenever and wherever we so desire.

Nutrition, Life Coaching and Journey Work (What I Do)

I combine a number of healing modalities to assist each individual, depending on what they need. The majority of individuals can be helped emotionally, to a degree, by making improvements nutritionally. Over two hundred physical, mental and emotional symptoms are caused or worsened by food. As a registered nutritional consulting practitioner (RNCP), trained at the Canadian School of Natural Nutrition, I help individuals detect, manage and sometimes eliminate adverse food reactions. By looking at the symptoms or through obtaining lab work, I also help clients detect health imbalances, including vitamin and mineral deficiencies or heavy metal toxicity. I ensure that the amount of water consumption and timing and balance of meals are appropriate for each individual, all of which play a large role in emotional well-being.

Endorsed by the International Coach Federation, Kids Coaching Connection was created by Susan Howson. It provided me with my training as a kid's life coach. ***One of the most important tools for helping anyone to heal emotionally is knowing what questions to ask them and when***. Each of us knows the answers that we seek, if only we could be with someone with whom we feel safe and who can ask us the right questions to help us uncover our truths. Many of us have inner "trolls" that sabotage our efforts, and there are methods for understanding and destroying them so that we can lead the lives we want. There are also many tools for accessing and healing subconscious feelings and beliefs. My training allows me to help others in these areas.

The Journey work that I do was created by Brandon Bays. She refers to The Journey as "a road map to the soul" and it truly is. I have used her work to help many children and adults see their lives with new perspective and heal within. The Journey helps individuals go on a journey in their mind, back to a conscious or subconscious memory that created certain feelings and beliefs that may or may not have been healthy for them. It helps them release emotional blocks and unhealthy patterns. I spend much of my time helping individuals forgive others and themselves using this process. The Journey is one of my most important tools for teaching individuals how to come to know and love themselves.

Conclusion

As I continue to spread the word of how to shine from the inside out, there will be people who find fault with my words, whether they be written or spoken. They will find fault with me. They will question my motives. That's the way it goes when people stop hiding and put themselves out there. Yet, if you have read and understood my message, you will know that all I aim to do is help you remember that we are all love at our core. *My biggest desire is that I help you to see yourselves and the world through the lens of your heart and remember it always.*

As you read about everything involved in attaining emotional health for yourself and your child, you might feel overwhelmed, confused, impatient or even angry. I ask you to stop being so hard on yourself. Take stock of the person you have become. Take stock of your accomplishments. All challenges and regrets are learning ground. Take stock of what you have learned. Take stock of all the aspects of your life that are not as you want them to be. Be thankful that it's those aspects of your life that are not as you want them to be, as opposed to others. Be grateful for where you are right now, in this very moment. I ask you to be grateful for it all until feelings of acceptance and understanding engulf you.

Then, when you are ready, be grateful for taking the steps to further improve aspects of your life. Envision everything the way you want it to be. Envision feeling overwhelmed with love for yourself and others. Envision feeling more love, peace and absolute wonder than ever before.

I am imagining you experiencing these feelings and your smile as it spreads across your face. I am imagining your eyes shining brightly. I am feeling the love within you come alive. Thank you for sharing your love with me by reading my book to this very last page. I love you. You don't believe me? Start loving yourself more and you will know what I mean. I love you. I wish you the *very* best on your journey.

Bibliography

Books

Adams, Marilee. *Change Your Questions, Change Your Life*. San Francisco. Berrett-Koehler Publishers, Inc, 2009.

Allen, Anita, and Lebrun, Louise, with 9 contributing authors. *Guardians of the Vision*. Ottawa. WEL-Systems Institute, 2009.

Allen, James. "As a Man Thinketh" [essay in the public domain]. Project Gutenberg. 2003 (original essay, 1902).

Bennett, William J. *The Book of Virtues*. New York. Simon & Schuster, 1996.

Berends, Polly Berrien. *Whole Child/Whole Parent*. New York. Harper & Row, Publishers, 1983 and reissued 1987.

Berger, Janice. *Emotional Fitness*. Toronto. Prentice Hall Canada, 2000.

Bloomfield, Harold. *Making Peace with Your Parents*. New York. Random House Inc, 1983.

Boynton, Marilyn Irwin, Boynton, Marilyn Ruth, and Dell, Mary. *Goodbye Mother, Hello Woman*. Oakland, CA. Harbinger Publications, 1995.

Brach, Tara. *Radical Acceptance*. New York. Bantam Dell, 2003.

Breathnach, Sarah Ban. *Something More*. New York. Grand Central Publishing, 1998.

Briggs, Dorothy Corkille. *Your Child's Self-Esteem*. New York. Doubleday, 1970.

Burton Goldberg Group. *Alternative Medicine: The Definitive Guide*. Washington. Future Medicine Publishing, Inc, 1995.

Campbell, Ross, and Chapman, Gary. *The Five Love Languages of Children*. Chicago. Northfield Publishers, 1997.

Carter- Scott, Cherie. *The Gift of Motherhood*. New York. Random House, Inc, 2002.

Carter-Scott, Cherie. *If Life is a Game, These are the Rules*. New York. Broadway Books, 1998.

Chopra, Deepak. *The Path to Love*. New York. Three Rivers Press, 1997.

Chopra, Deepak, Ford, Debbie, and Williamson, Marianne. *The Shadow Effect*. New York. HarperCollins Publishers, 2010.

Chopra, Deepak, Simon, David, and Abrams, Vicki. *Magical Beginnings, Enchanted Lives: A Holistic Guide to Pregnancy and Childbirth*. New York. Three Rivers Press, 2005.

Choquette, Sonia. *Travelling at the Speed of Love*. Carlsbad, CA. Hay House, Inc, 2010.

Coleman, Joshua. *When Parents Hurt*. New York. HarperCollins Publishers, 2008.

Covey, Stephen. *The 7 Habits of Highly Effective Families*. New York. Golden Books Publishing Co., Inc, 1997.

Crawford, Catherine. *The Highly Intuitive Child*. Berkeley. Hunter House Publishers, 2009.

Deak, Joanne, and Barker, Teresa. *Girls Will Be Girls*. New York. Hyperion, 2002.

Domar, Alice. *Self-Nurture*. New York. Penguin Group, 2000.

Dreikurs, Rudolf. *Children: The Challenge*. New York. Penguin Group, 1964.

Dyer, Wayne. *Change Your Thoughts—Change Your Life*. Carlsbad, CA. Hay House, Inc, 2007.

Dyer, Wayne. *Inspiration*. Carlsbad, CA. Hay House, Inc, 2006.

Dyer, Wayne. *Manifest Your Destiny*. New York. HarperCollins Publishers, Inc. 1997.

Ford, Debbie. *Courage: Overcoming Fear and Igniting Self-Confidence*. New York. Harper One, 2012.

Ford, Debbie. *The Dark Side of the Light Chasers*. New York. Penguin Group, Inc, 1998.

Ford, Debbie. *The Secret of the Shadow*. New York. HarperCollins Publishers, Inc, 2002.

Forward, Susan. *Toxic Parents*. New York. Bantam Books, a division of Random House, Inc, 1989.

George, Marlene. *Your Life is Now!* Victoria. Trafford Publishing, 2004.

Glasser, Howard, and Easley, Jennifer. *Transforming the Difficult Child*. Tucson, Arizona. Center for the Difficult Child Publications, 1998.

Gordon, Mary. *Roots of Empathy*. Toronto. Thomas Allen Publishers, 2005.

Gottfried, Bob. *Shortcut to Spirituality*. North York. Deeper Dimension Publishing, 2004.

Gottman, John. *Raising an Emotionally Intelligent Child*. New York. Simon & Schuster, 1997.

Gray, Alice. *Inspiration for a Mother's Heart*. Sisters, Oregon. Multnomah Publishers, Inc, 2002.

Hay, Louise. *You Can Heal Your Life*. Carlsbad, CA. Hay House, Inc, 1999.

Hendrix, Harville, and Hunt, Helen. *Giving the Love that Heals*. New York. Pocket Books, a division of Simon & Schuster Inc, 1997.

Jawer, Michael, and Micozzi, Marc. *The Spiritual Anatomy of Emotion*. Rochester. Park Street Press, 2009.

Jenner, Paul. *Transform Your Life with NLP*. London. Hodder Education, 2010.

Kabat-Zinn, Myla, and Kabat-Zinn, Jon. *Everyday Blessings*. New York. Hyperion, 1997.

Kurcinka, Mary Sheedy. *Raising Your Spirited Child*. New York. HarperCollins Publishers, 1991.

Lesser, Elizabeth. *Broken Open*. New York. Random House, Inc, 2005.

Lincoln, Michael J. (fka Narayan-Singh Khalsa). *Messages from the Body*. Vancouver. Lynne R Henderson Publications, 2006.

McGraw, Phil. *Family First*. New York. Simon & Schuster Inc, 2004.

McKay, Matthew, and Fanning, Patrick. *Self-Esteem*. Third Edition. Oakland, CA. New Harbinger Publications, Inc, 2000.

McLaren, Karla. *The Language of Emotions*. Boulder, CO. True Inc, 2010.

Millman, Dan. *The Four Purposes of Life*. Novato, CA. HJ Kramer and New World Library, 2011.

Moorjani, Anita. *Dying to be Me*. Carlsbad, CA. Hay House Inc, 2012.

Myss, Caroline. *Anatomy of the Spirit*. New York. Three Rivers Press, 1996.

Myss, Caroline. *Why People Don't Heal and How They Can*. New York. Three Rivers Press, 1997.

Northrup, Christiane. *Women's Bodies, Women's Wisdom*. New York. Bantam Books, 1998.

Orliff, Judith. *Emotional Freedom*. New York. Random House, 2009.

Pipher, Mary. *Reviving Ophelia*. New York. Random House, 1994.

Preston, Kathy. *Expect a Miracle*. New York. St. Martin's Press, 2003.

Ruiz, Don Miguel. *The Four Agreements*. San Rafael, CA. Amber-Allen Publishing, Inc, 1997.

Schafer, Alyson. *Honey, I Wrecked the Kids*. Mississauga. John Wiley & Sons Canada, Ltd, 2009.

Shah, Neil. *Neurolinguistic Programming—A Practical Guide*. London. Icon Books Ltd, 2011.

Siegel, Bernie. *Peace, Love and Healing*. New York. HarperCollins Publishers, Inc, 1989.

Siegel, Daniel, and Hartzell, Mary. *Parenting from the Inside Out*. New York. Penguin, 2003.

Singer, Michael A. *The Untethered Soul*. Oakland, CA. New Harbinger Publications, Inc, 2007.

Spezzano, Chuck. *The Love Pack*. London. Collins & Brown Limited, 2002.

Truman, Karol. *Feelings Buried Alive Never Die ...* St.George, Utah. Olympus Distributing, 1991, 2003.

Vanzant, Iyanla. *In the Meantime*. New York. Simon & Schuster, 1998.

Virtue, Doreen. *Constant Craving*. New York. Hay House, Inc., 1995.

Virtue, Doreen. *The Lightworker's Way*. Carlsbad, CA. Hay House, Inc, 1997.

Williamson, Marianne. *The Age of Miracles*. California. Hay House, Inc, 2008.

Williamson, Marianne. *Enchanted Love*. New York. Simon & Schuster, 1999.

Williamson, Marianne. *Everyday Grace*. New York. Penguin Putnam Inc, 2002.

Williamson, Marianne. *The Law of Divine Compensation* . New York. HarperCollins, 2012.

Williamson, Marianne. *A Return to Love*. New York. HarperCollins Publishers, 1992.

Williamson, Marianne. *A Woman's Worth*. New York. Random House, Inc, 1993.

Zukav, Gary. *The Seat of the Soul*. New York. Simon & Schuster Inc, 1989.

Zukav, Gary, and Francis, Linda. *The Heart of the Soul*. New York. Fireside, 2001.

Teaching Manuals

Susan Howson, Kid's Coaching Connection Manual, Mississauga, ON, 2010

Magazines

Kase, Lori Miller. "Discipline for Your Little Ones." *Parents Magazine*. Oct 1999.

Lampert, Leslie. "10 Discipline Lessons to Live By." *Parents Magazine*. Jan 2000.

Lampert, Leslie. "Lessons to Live By." *Parents Magazine*. Jan 2000.

O'Mara, Peggy. "Reclaiming a New Archetype." *Mothering Magazine*. Nov-Dec 2006.

Pitman, Teresa. "To Tell the Truth." *Parents Magazine*. May 2005.

Stark, Marg. "Don't Bite Me." *Parents Magazine* . March 2000.

Pathways to Family Wellness. Issue 36, Winter 2012.

Pathways to Family Wellness, Issue 37, Spring 2013

Other

Hicks, Esther, and Hicks, Jerry. Getting Into the Vortex [CD]. Carlsbad, CA. Hay House, Inc, 2010.

The First Years Last Forever—I am Your Child. Printed and distributed in Canada by Canadian Institute of Child Health. www.iamyourchild.org.

Nolte, Dorothy Law. "Children Learn What They Live" [poem]. 1972.

Shane, Shaun. "Tongues Made of Glass" [poem, online]. Posted 7 October 2011. Accessed 12 April 2014 from http://www.poemhunter.com/poem/04-tongues-made-of-glass/.

About the Author

Meredith Deasley is passionate about making a difference in the lives of children and their parents. Her work is read in over 120 countries and 2,400 cities.

After obtaining a bachelor's degree in Sociology from the University of Western Ontario and working in the corporate world for ten years, Meredith began raising two daughters. Her journey with them led her to become who she is today—The Resourceful Mother. Meredith is a registered holistic nutritionist (RHN) and registered nutritional consulting practitioner (RNCP) specializing in pediatric nutrition since 1999. She teaches at the Canadian School of Natural Nutrition, and her book is the pediatric textbook at the Edison Institute of Nutrition. She is also a Kids Life Coach after graduating from the Kids Coaching Connection program, endorsed by the International Coach Federation. She conducts numerous seminars for parents and counsels them on an individual basis, teaching them how to nourish the bodies and souls of their children. She meets with individuals from age two to adulthood, helping them to see their inner beauty and lead the lives they want to live.

Meredith has lived in Aurora for over twenty years. All but five of those years have been with her daughters, Taylor and Paige. Meredith would *love* to receive your feedback or assist you in carrying out your parenting journey through the lens of your heart. You can reach her at www.theresourcefulmother.com.